with FAITH & GOODWILL

CANADIAN AMERICAN BUSINESS COUNCIL

with

FAITH & GOODWILL

CHRONICLING THE CANADA-U.S. FRIENDSHIP

SECOND EDITION

Edited by Maryscott Greenwood,
Arthur Milnes, and Scott Reid

Copyright © Canadian American Business Council, 2017, 2022

All rights reserved. No part of this publication may be reproduced, stored in a retrieval system, or transmitted in any form or by any means, electronic, mechanical, photocopying, recording, or otherwise (except for brief passages for purpose of review) without the prior permission of Dundurn Press. Permission to photocopy should be requested from Access Copyright.

Library and Archives Canada Cataloguing in Publication
Title: With faith and goodwill : chronicling the Canada-U.S. friendship / edited by
Maryscott Greenwood, Arthur Milnes, and Scott Reid.
Names: Greenwood, Maryscott, editor. | Milnes, Arthur, 1966- editor. | Reid, Scott, 1964- editor. |
Canadian American Business Council, issuing body.
Description: Second edition. | "Canadian American Business Council"--Cover. | Includes index.
Identifiers: Canadiana (print) 20210317981 | Canadiana (ebook) 20210318007 | ISBN 9781459749986 (hardcover) |
ISBN 9781459750142 (PDF) | ISBN 9781459750159 (EPUB)
Subjects: LCSH: Canada—Foreign relations—United States. | LCSH: United States—
Foreign relations— Canada. | LCGFT: Speeches.
Classification: LCC FC249 .W58 2022 | DDC 327.71073—dc23

Dundurn Press acknowledges the support of the Canada Council for the Arts and the Ontario Arts Council for its publishing program. The press also acknowledges the financial support of the Government of Ontario, through the Ontario Book Publishing Tax Credit and Ontario Creates, and the Government of Canada.

Care has been taken to trace the ownership of copyright material used in this book. The editors and the publisher welcome any information enabling them to rectify any references or credits in subsequent editions.

The publisher is not responsible for websites or their content unless they are owned by the publisher.

Printed and bound in Canada.

Dundurn Press
1382 Queen Street East
Toronto, Ontario, Canada M4L 1C9
dundurn.com, @dundurnpress

Washington
1800 Massachusetts Avenue NW,
Second Floor,
Washington, DC 20036

Ottawa
222 Queen Street,
Suite 1201
Ottawa, ON K1P 5V9

cabc.co cabc_co cabc.co

She clasps the American hand with her faith and goodwill.
That long frontier from the Atlantic to the Pacific Oceans,
guarded only by neighbourly respect and honourable obligations,
is an example to every country and a pattern for the future of the world.

— Sir Winston Churchill
Canada Club, London, United Kingdom
April 20, 1939

CONTENTS

List of Speeches	xi
Foreword by Kirsten Hillman, Ambassador of Canada to the United States	xv
Preface by Maryscott Greenwood	xvii
Introduction by Arthur Milnes	xix
FRIENDSHIP	**3**
Hopeful Renewal	6
President Barack Obama (2016)	6
Prime Minister Justin Trudeau (2016)	10
A Friend in Need	15
President Jimmy Carter (1980)	15
President Jimmy Carter (2011)	17
Early Days	18
Prime Minister Wilfrid Laurier (1899)	18
Vice President Charles Fairbanks (1908)	24
Prime Minister Robert Borden (1912)	28
William Lyon Mackenzie King (1913)	30
President Warren G. Harding (1923)	34
Bosom Buddies	42
Brian Mulroney (2004)	43
President George H.W. Bush (1999)	46
Joe Clark	47
President Bill Clinton (2002)	52
Prime Minister Justin Trudeau (2016)	53
Brian Mulroney (2018)	55

FRICTIONS	61
The Times They Are A-Changing	64
Prime Minister Lester B. Pearson (1965)	64
President Richard Nixon (1972)	67
Economic Tensions	76
Prime Minister Paul Martin (2005)	76
President Barack Obama (2015)	81
Personal Touch	86
President Donald J. Trump (2018)	87
AT WAR	91
Allied Against the Axis Powers	94
President Franklin D. Roosevelt (1943)	95
The Cold War Era	100
President Harry S. Truman (1947)	101
President Dwight D. Eisenhower (1953)	108
A New World Order	118
Prime Minister Jean Chrétien (2001)	118
President George W. Bush (2004)	120
Standing Together Against Tyranny	121
Prime Minister Stephen J. Harper (2007)	121
Prime Minister Stephen J. Harper (2011)	125
AT WORK	129
Building Bridges — and Highways and Seaways and …	132
Prime Minister William Lyon Mackenzie King (1927)	132
Vice President Charles Dawes (1927)	137
President Dwight D. Eisenhower (1959)	139
Free Trade: Taking the Leap of Faith	142
President Ronald Reagan (1987)	143
Prime Minister Brian Mulroney (1988)	148
President George H.W. Bush (1991)	153
President George H.W. Bush (1992)	156
The Quebec Question	158
President Bill Clinton (1999)	158
"A Permanent Reality"	163
Senator John F. Kennedy (1957)	163
One Canada	174
Prime Minister Pierre Elliott Trudeau (1977)	174
New Challenges, New Approaches	177
Speaker of the U.S. House of Representatives Nancy Pelosi (2019)	179

AT PLAY — HOLIDAYING IN EACH OTHER'S NATION 185

    President Theodore Roosevelt (1916) 188
    President William Howard Taft (1926) 192
    Sir Robert Borden (1934) 194
    Sir Robert Borden (1936) 194

  Home Away from Home 195
    President Franklin D. Roosevelt (1933) 195
    President Richard Nixon (1972) 198
    President George H.W. Bush (1997) 199

TOASTS AND TRIBUTES 205

    Prime Minister Wilfrid Laurier (1898) 207

  Tributes at a Time of Loss 208
    Ambassador Lester B. Pearson (1945) 208
    Prime Minister Lester B. Pearson (1963) 210
    NDP Leader Tommy Douglas (1963) 212
    President Richard Nixon (1972) 213
    President Gerald R. Ford (2001) 214

  Memories and Reflections 216
    Brian Mulroney (2007) 216
    President Bill Clinton (1995) 218
    First Lady Hillary Rodham Clinton (1999) 222
    President George W. Bush (2008) 225
    Prime Minister Stephen Harper (2009) 226
    President Barack Obama (2009) 228
    President Donald J. Trump (2017) 230

  A New Old Friend 233
    President Joe Biden and Prime Minister Justin Trudeau (2021) 234
    President Joe Biden and Prime Minister Justin Trudeau (2021) 235
    Prime Minister Justin Trudeau (2021) 235

  Entre Nous 237
    Vice President Kamala Harris (2020) 237
    Vice President Kamala Harris and Prime Minister Justin Trudeau (2021) 239

  Aligned and Allied: The Two Michaels 240

Timeline of Prime Ministers and Presidents, 1865–2022 242
Conclusion by Scott Reid 245
Afterword by The Hon. Kelly Craft 247
Acknowledgements from Arthur Milnes 249
Acknowledgements from Maryscott Greenwood 250
About the Editors 254
Image Credits 257
Index 259

LIST OF SPEECHES

CANADA

Prime Minister Wilfrid Laurier
On Abraham Lincoln, House of Commons, Ottawa, Ontario (May 26, 1898) | 207
Studebaker Hall, Chicago, Illinois (October 9, 1899) | 18

Prime Minister Robert Borden
Washington, D.C. (April 27, 1912) | 28
Atlantic City, New Jersey (March–April 1934) | 194
Holiday in the South (April 4, 1936) | 194

Prime Minister William Lyon Mackenzie King
New York City (December 10, 1913) | 30
Opening of the Peace Bridge, Buffalo, New York (August 7, 1927) | 132

NDP Leader Tommy Douglas
On the Death of President Kennedy, House of Commons,
Ottawa, Ontario (November 22, 1963) | 212

Prime Minister Lester B. Pearson
On the Death of President Franklin Roosevelt, Washington, D.C. (April 1945) | 208
On the Death of President Kennedy, House of Commons,
Ottawa, Ontario (November 22, 1963) | 210
Convocation Address, Temple University, Philadelphia, Pennsylvania (April 2, 1965) | 64

Prime Minister Pierre Elliott Trudeau
Address to a Joint Session of the United States Congress,
Washington, D.C. (February 22, 1977) | 174

Prime Minister Joe Clark
On Jimmy Carter: "A Pretty Good Canadian" | 47

Prime Minister Brian Mulroney
Address to the U.S. Congress, Washington, D.C. (April 27, 1988) | 148
Tribute at President Reagan's State Funeral, Washington, D.C. (June 11, 2004) | 43
On Ronald Reagan, George H.W. Bush, and Bill Clinton (2007) | 216
Eulogy for the Late President George H.W. Bush, State Funeral,
Washington, D.C. (December 5, 2018) | 55

Prime Minister Jean Chrétien
National Day of Mourning, Parliament Hill, Ottawa, Ontario (September 14, 2001) | 118

Prime Minister Paul Martin
Economic Club of New York, New York (October 6, 2005) | 76

Prime Minister Stephen J. Harper
Speech to Canadian Soldiers, Kandahar, Afghanistan (May 23, 2007) | 121
Joint Press Conference, Ottawa, Ontario (February 19, 2009) | 226
Joint Declaration on the Border with President Barack Obama,
Washington, D.C. (February 4, 2011) | 125

Prime Minister Justin Trudeau
State Dinner at the White House, Washington, D.C. (March 10, 2016) | 10
Toast to Vice President Joe Biden, Ottawa, Ontario (December 8, 2016) | 53
Joint Statement on a Roadmap for a Renewed U.S.-Canada Partnership
(February 23, 2021) | 235

UNITED STATES OF AMERICA

President Theodore Roosevelt
Excerpt from *A Book-Lover's Holidays in the Open* (1916) | 188

Vice President Charles Fairbanks
Quebec Tercentenary Celebration, Quebec City (July 23, 1908) | 24

President William Howard Taft
"Mr. Taft's Murray Bay" [Quebec] (September 4, 1926) | 192

President Warren G. Harding
Stanley Park, Vancouver, British Columbia (July 16, 1923) | 34

Vice President Charles Dawes
A Day at the Peace Bridge (August 7, 1927) | 137

President Franklin D. Roosevelt
Informal Remarks Delivered at Campobello Island, New Brunswick (June 29, 1933) | 195
Address to a Joint Session of Parliament, Ottawa, Ontario (August 25, 1943) | 95

President Harry S. Truman
Address to a Joint Session of Parliament, Ottawa, Ontario (June 11, 1947) | 101

President Dwight D. Eisenhower
Address to a Joint Session of Parliament, Ottawa, Ontario (November 14, 1953) | 108
Opening of the St. Lawrence Seaway (June 26, 1959) | 139

President John F. Kennedy
Convocation Address, University of New Brunswick,
Fredericton, New Brunswick (October 8, 1957) | 163

President Richard Nixon
Presidential Toast, Ottawa, Ontario (April 13, 1972) | 198
Address to a Joint Session of Parliament, Ottawa, Ontario (April 14, 1972) | 67
On the Death of Lester B. Pearson (December 28, 1972) | 213

President Gerald R. Ford
On Pierre Trudeau (September 4, 2001) | 214

President Jimmy Carter
On the Return of Six Americans from Iran (January 31, 1980) | 15
Recalling the "Canadian Caper," Plains, Georgia (April 30, 2011) | 17

President Ronald Reagan
Address to a Joint Session of Parliament, Ottawa, Ontario (April 6, 1987) | 143

President George H.W. Bush
At the Air Quality Agreement Signing Ceremony, Ottawa, Ontario (March 13, 1991) | 153
At the Initialling Ceremony for NAFTA, San Antonio, Texas (October 7, 1992) | 156
"The Thrill of Fishing in Arctic Canada," Fort Simpson,
Northwest Territories (August 31, 1997) | 199
On Brian Mulroney, Montreal, Quebec (June 1999) | 46

President Bill Clinton
Toast Delivered at the Canadian Museum of Civilization,
Hull, Quebec (February 23, 1995) | 218
Address to the Forum of Federations Conference,
Mont-Tremblant, Quebec (October 8, 1999) | 158
On Jean Chrétien's Retirement, Syracuse, New York (August 30, 2002) | 52

President George W. Bush
Toast Delivered at Gatineau, Quebec (November 30, 2004) | 120
On Prime Minister Stephen Harper, Lima, Peru (November 22, 2008) | 225

Secretary of State Hillary Rodham Clinton
Remarks at the Ninth Conference of the Spouses of Heads of State
and Government of the Americas, Ottawa, Ontario (September 30, 1999) | 222

President Barack Obama
Joint Press Conference, Ottawa, Ontario (February 19, 2009) | 228
Statement on the Keystone Pipeline Proposal, Washington, D.C. (November 6, 2015) | 81
State Dinner at the White House, Washington, D.C. (March 10, 2016) | 6

President Donald J. Trump
Joint Press Conference, Washington, D.C. (February 13, 2017) | 230
Tweets About Prime Minister Justin Trudeau (June 9, 2018) | 87

Speaker of the House Nancy Pelosi
Floor Speech of Transformed USMCA, Washington, D.C. (December 18, 2019) | 179

Vice President Kamala Harris
Election Victory Speech, Wilmington, Delaware (November 7, 2020) | 237
White House Press Release of Vice President's Telephone Call to Prime Minister Justin
Trudeau, Washington, D.C. (February 1, 2021) | 239

President Joe Biden
White House Press Release of Telephone Call to Prime Minister Justin Trudeau,
Washington, D.C. (January 22, 2021) | 234
Joint Statement on a Roadmap for a Renewed U.S.-Canada Partnership
(February 23, 2021) | 235

FOREWORD

The first edition of *With Faith & Goodwill* was published in 2017 to commemorate Canada's 150th anniversary. During the period between the first and second editions, I was honoured to be asked by Prime Minister Justin Trudeau to serve as Canada's twenty-fourth ambassador to the United States, becoming the first woman to occupy this important position. As I have travelled across the United States, I have had the privilege of witnessing the remarkable breadth and depth of the Canada-U.S. relationship. I have experienced first-hand how this partnership, which has been led by the prime ministers and presidents presented in this book, derives its strength and resilience from the millions of connections that occur between Americans and Canadians every single day.

The years between the first and second editions of *With Faith & Goodwill* have been intense, filled with tremendous progress as well as significant challenges for both our countries. In many ways, it was the relationships between our people that helped us navigate our difficulties and achieve our successes. Our businesses, small and large, our unions, many of which are binational, and our regional and local political leaders and communities were vital to the highly successful renegotiation of NAFTA, the most significant trade agreement in the world. Our experts and climate leaders are working together to address climate change and its effects on our communities and shared environment.

Most notably, we worked together to confront the immense challenges posed by Covid-19, from our businesses that quickly retooled to manufacture and supply personal protective equipment, to our people on both sides of the border, to our universities that worked together on research to combat the virus and protect our citizens. We saw border professionals draw on their deep relationships to manage a massive reduction in the traffic across our shared border — the longest international one in the world — while ensuring that our vital supply chains and commercial traffic

Ambassador Kirsten Hillman participates in a Canadian American Business Council Roundtable in Washington, D.C., in 2019.

continued efficiently. From my perspective, a light in the darkness imposed by the pandemic was witnessing first-hand how our two countries drew on our extraordinary connections to protect our citizens and our economies and ensure that we are prepared for the future.

These connections can also be seen in the countless other examples of how Canadians and Americans live, work, and partner together every single day. Our academics, artists, Indigenous communities, farmers, students, law enforcement officers, military personnel, neighbours, families, and so many others have created the strongest fabric made of shared values, goals, and dreams. Our countries' shared commitment to democracy, human rights, and the rule of law is inextricably woven into this fabric, underpinning our efforts to build inclusive, equitable societies that afford our citizens, in all their diversity, the opportunity to prosper. The path toward these ambitious goals will not always be an easy one, but it is one we walk together. The fabric of the enduring Canada-U.S. relationship will hold us together as we embrace the opportunities and face the challenges ahead. It will support the weight of honest disagreements, safe in the knowledge that, as *With Faith & Goodwill* so beautifully illustrates, Canada and the United States are blessed with an extraordinary relationship, and our histories, our futures, are forever intertwined.

I hope that you enjoy this wonderful collection that captures the warmth and complexity of this unique international friendship in a series of remarkable images and illuminating speeches.

KIRSTEN HILLMAN
Ambassador of Canada to the United States

PREFACE

This is the second edition of *With Faith & Goodwill*. The original volume was published in 2017 to celebrate Canada's sesquicentennial. The book was presented to numerous elected officials and luminaries of the U.S.-Canada bilateral relationship. Then we took the book on tour to spur discussions about our nations' great friendship with many of the principals whose speeches and photographs are featured in it. A roundtable was held with President George W. Bush and Prime Minister Stephen Harper at the Bush Library in Dallas. At that event, Mrs. Laura Bush asked me for another copy, as they were travelling to Kennebunkport, Maine, the next day and she wanted to share it with her in-laws, George H.W. Bush, the 41st president, and First Lady Barbara Bush.

We then travelled to Atlanta's Carter Presidential Center where we hosted a lovely and candid dialogue with President Jimmy Carter and Prime Minister Joe Clark who reminisced about

Former Prime Minister Jean Chrétien, former President Bill Clinton, and former U.S. Ambassador to Canada Gordon Giffin in Montreal for the launch of the first edition of *With Faith & Goodwill*.

CABC CEO Maryscott Greenwood, former First Lady Laura Bush, former President George W. Bush, and former Prime Minister Stephen Harper in Dallas for the launch of the first edition of *With Faith & Goodwill*.

their time together during the Iran Hostage Crisis, which came to define Canada-U.S. friendship for an era. The next stop was Montreal where we hosted a huge gathering at the Palais des congrès to hear Prime Minister Jean Chrétien reminisce with his good friend President Bill Clinton, in a conversation moderated by former U.S. Ambassador Gordon Giffin.

During the final event of the book tour that year, which was held at the iconic Indigo bookstore in Toronto's Manulife Centre and hosted by Heather Reisman, Prime Minister Paul Martin shared stories with his director of communications (and co-editor of this book), Scott Reid. All in all, it was a great way to remind Canadians and Americans of the special nature of our bilateral relations at a time when the partnership was about to be tested.

We worked on the first edition through 2016. The U.S. presidential election was underway, and we delayed publication until we knew the outcome. After Donald Trump, the forty-fifth president, had his first bilateral meeting with Prime Minister Justin Trudeau, we launched the book. And that's where the first edition ended. In the years that followed, the United States and Canada, together with Mexico, modernized the most comprehensive trade agreement on earth, despite the tweets and rhetoric coming out of the Oval Office. And then, with the presidential election in 2020 and the onset of a global pandemic, yet another new era in the Canada-U.S. relationship began. President Joe Biden had his first bilateral meeting with Prime Minister Justin Trudeau, and their governments launched a blueprint for Canada-U.S relations. It was clear to us then that *With Faith & Goodwill* should be updated and given a new subtitle: *Chronicling the Canada-U.S. Friendship*.

We are delighted that the first edition, inspired by the 1976 book *Between Friends/Entre Amis*, which Canada presented to the United States on that country's American Revolution bicentennial, is now worthy of a second edition. We remain devoted to our fundamental mission to raise awareness about the importance of the ties that bind our two nations. We hope that generations of Canadians and Americans will peruse the pages that follow and reflect on what has truly become a model for friendship and collaboration for the world.

MARYSCOTT GREENWOOD
CEO, Canadian American Business Council (CABC)

INTRODUCTION

WHEN YOU CONSIDER THAT AMERICA'S PRESIDENTS AND Canada's prime ministers have met bilaterally well over one hundred times between 1867 and 2022, it is no wonder that speechwriters and researchers in the Prime Minister's Office in Ottawa and Washington's White House often rely on standard themes and phrases. Our political leaders in their public remarks often make reference to the undefended border — and how Canadians and Americans are much like family.

For some reason, however, the uniqueness of the relationship's greatest rhetorical line and moment is rarely referred to. I speak, of course, about our joint high-noon moment. And when I say "high noon," I mean it.

A very special day took place eighty-six years before Canadian Confederation — and a generation before the events of 1812–1814 — that isn't discussed much these days. It was March 1, 1781, at 12:00 p.m. when a special ceremony was held in the youthful American Congress. United States leaders gathered to celebrate the fact that Maryland had become the thirteenth state to ratify America's famed Articles of Confederation.

Included in those Articles of Confederation was a section that truly demonstrated what a special place Canada and Canadians held in the American mind:

> Canada acceding to this confederation, and joining in the measures of the United States, shall be admitted into, and entitled to all the advantages of this union; but no other colony shall be admitted into the same unless such admission be agreed to by nine states.

Pierre Trudeau is one of the few prime ministers who has ever mentioned the unique status Canadians were granted during the earliest days of the Great Republic. It was in his famous speech at Washington's National Press Club in 1969 when, at the dawn of Richard Nixon's presidency, he famously compared being neighbours to living next to an elephant. After that memorable remark, Trudeau concluded his thoughts on America's invitation from 1781 with this: "In any event," he said matter-of-factly, "we did not join, and history has recorded our differences."

Decades later, at the White House, Trudeau's son Justin, now prime minister of Canada,

WITH FAITH & GOODWILL

quite effectively summed up the differences in how the United States and Canada evolved. "We're actually closer than friends," Justin Trudeau said in March 2016. "We're more like siblings, really. We have shared parentage, but we took different paths in our later years. We became the stay-at-home type — and you grew to be a little more rebellious."

French and British Colonial Masters

Our two countries did indeed start out on similar paths. Born of European colonialism — and both with a record of treatment of the Indigenous populations that brings credit to neither country — we began very much the same. The problem for our French and British colonial masters lay in the character of those they sent to colonize and populate our joint part of North America. The men and women who arrived here were a rugged and independent lot. They had to be.

We have to have some sympathy for the British at Whitehall and Downing Street who had to reign over such an unruly bunch from afar after the question of whether France or Britain would be in charge over here was settled. What seemed obvious from London, England, was far from clear in the streets of Boston, the island of Manhattan, the snows of Quebec City, or Halifax and Kingston.

So, as Prime Minister Justin Trudeau said, we both began to grow up and stretch our legs. Americans left home first. At Lexington and Concord and eventually Yorktown, the first Americans discovered that the British Empire was far from invincible. Not every American colonist agreed, however. These "Tories" or United Empire Loyalists weren't yet as ready to leave the family nest. They began to flood into Canada and they profoundly shaped the new country developing up north. With America an accomplished fact, an uneasy peace — more like a stalemate — settled along the border. Busy solidifying and expanding their new country and society, Americans didn't really pay much attention to activities to the north in what would someday be Canada. Taking Canada, after all, as Thomas Jefferson announced days after the start of the War of 1812, would be a "mere matter of marching." Besides, most American leaders probably thought the residents of British North America, who lacked for the most part even the very basics of truly responsible government, would soon come to their senses and join in the great democratic experience unfolding to the south.

[OPPOSITE]
Vice President Joe Biden and Prime Minister Justin Trudeau walk to the First Ministers' Meeting held in Ottawa on December 9, 2016.

The War of 1812

But British North Americans, including the French Canadians, did not join their newly independent southern neighbours. They started to develop their own version of a rugged New World independence.

And we saw that burst forth in 1812. Here is not the place to debate who truly "won" the war, but we can now see that something crucial happened during those years. In Canada, three splintered groups, those of British, French, and Indigenous heritage, united as one. At the end of the hostilities, British North American colonies remained and cooler heads prevailed. And Canada and America were stuck with each other.

During the 200th anniversary celebrations of the War of 1812, U.S. Ambassador to Canada David Jacobson remarked while at an appearance in Kingston, Ontario, that he had kept quiet the first hundred or so times he heard during his introductions how Canada had won that war. "Finally," he told the audience, "I said, 'Okay, you won. Do you want a rematch?'" Ambassador Jacobson's Canadian audience roared with good-natured laughter and gave him a heartfelt round of applause.

Sir Isaac Brock, felled by a bullet at the War of 1812's Battle of Queenston Heights.

INTRODUCTION

Armed Rebellions

As the two countries continued to evolve, with Canada heading toward its own Confederation in 1867, things were far from quiet in what would become the new Dominion of Canada. As people sought greater democratic freedom and truly responsible government, armed rebellions broke out in both Upper Canada and Lower Canada in 1837. The rebellion in Lower Canada, in particular, was violent, with pitched battles that pitted Quebec's *Patriotes* against British troops and militia. In Toronto, the rebels met at a tavern and marched down Yonge Street with pitchforks and muskets to take on the British, then melted away after the first volley or two. In response to the crisis in their remaining North American possessions, the British sent the great Liberal, Lord Durham, to study the unrest. He reported back that Upper and Lower Canada were basically failed states. He determined that the solution was to force Upper and Lower Canada to unite and become the United Province of Canada. With that accomplished, the march toward Confederation began.

Meanwhile, the United States was beginning its own march toward confronting slavery. This would take decades and end in a long and bloody civil war that Canadians like Sir John A. Macdonald and Thomas D'Arcy McGee watched with great fear. Hearing of the battles at such places as Gettysburg and Shiloh, these future Fathers of Confederation witnessed first-hand the dangers of failure if they didn't act.

Abraham Lincoln was one of Sir Wilfrid Laurier's personal heroes.

Abraham Lincoln and Slavery

In 1909, years after Generals Grant and Lee met at a Virginia courthouse to begin forging a very hard-fought and difficult peace between the North and South, Canadian leader Sir Wilfrid Laurier described to a Montreal audience how Americans, and Abraham Lincoln in particular, had faced history and confronted slavery.

Canada's Sir Wilfrid Laurier often quoted Abraham Lincoln in his speeches.

Abraham Lincoln is one of the greatest men in history. He had an intuitive and instructive discernment in political problems and, with all, he had a most tender heart and the most humane soul. When he was a young man he had gone down the Mississippi as far as New Orleans on a business errand and he had seen with his eyes something of the cruelty, shame and degradation of slavery, and it is said that he remarked to a friend, "If ever I have an opportunity, I shall hit slavery hard." He was elected President of the United States, he was installed in office, and you might have thought he could have hit slavery hard; but he could not do it because public opinion would not permit him to do it. The Civil War broke out; it was to go on for four long years; the Northern States were invaded by the Southern armies, and even then Abraham Lincoln could not carry out his own instinct. He had to submit to contumely, and to insults, and to taunts from ardent abolitionists, but he stood the infliction and did not move until he thought the time had come....

At first the Northern people, who were averse to slavery, out of the respect they had for the views of their fellow countrymen in the South, had refused to interfere with it; but, when they found their country invaded, the Union jeopardized, then they were prepared to go to the bottom and to deal with slavery, and Abraham Lincoln, the keenest judge of the fluctuation of public opinion that ever lived, saw the time was ripe. He advised the Republican Convention, which met in 1864, to adopt a plank in favour of the total abolition of slavery. His advice was accepted, the plank was adopted, and in November following the principle was ratified by the people, and, in March 1865, the curse and the shame of slavery was forever blotted out from the fair name of the American Republic.

During this same Montreal address, Laurier recited President Lincoln's immortal Second Inaugural Address word for word.

INTRODUCTION

Laurier's Canadian predecessors, the future Fathers of Confederation, kept their watchful eyes on America as the Civil War continued. For while officially neutral, Britain made it clear where her sympathies lay — with the South. This was truly revealed for all when colonial authorities turned a blind eye to the Confederate raiders who sacked St. Alban's, Vermont, after travelling south from Montreal. And as the war came to an end, Canada's founding fathers had good reason to fear what might happen if Grant's armies turned their attention north.

Sir John A. Macdonald, the Old Chieftain.

A New Nation Is Born

Canada came into being on July 1, 1867. While there were great celebrations in Ottawa and throughout Quebec, Ontario, Nova Scotia (as well as black flags flying to protest Confederation), and New Brunswick, President Andrew Johnson, Lincoln's successor as president, ignored Canada's big day. But another American did not: Jefferson Davis, who until 1865 had served as the first and only president of the American Confederacy. After his release from prison, he lived for a time in Quebec, where he was very popular. He spoke to a crowd of cheering Canadians from his train in Lennoxville, Quebec, only a few days after Canadian Confederation. Reportedly, he said:

> I thank you most kindly for this hearty British reception, which I take as a manifestation of your sympathy and goodwill for one in misfortune. I hope that you will hold fast to their British principles, and that you may ever strive to cultivate close and affectionate connection with the mother country. Gentlemen, again, I thank you.

With the union of the British North American colonies into a single Dominion on America's doorstep, the stage was set for the continuing story of perhaps the most fascinating bilateral relationship between leaders the world has ever known. Many of these leaders have been friends, such as Franklin Roosevelt and Mackenzie King, or George H.W. Bush and Brian Mulroney. Some have been unfriendly, such as John Diefenbaker and John Kennedy,

WITH FAITH & GOODWILL

and many operated in between, such as Wilfrid Laurier and Theodore Roosevelt, or Lyndon Johnson and Lester Pearson.

Their joint stories were and often are played out where you'd expect it — at the White House, on Parliament Hill, at international summits, in Camp David, or at state dinners. But in between, our leaders, like so many American and Canadian citizens, share some unique and fascinating links with each other's country. A young Lester Pearson, for example, spent part of his youth living in Chicago. He described this city of his youth in his memoirs, *Mike*, published by the University of Toronto Press:

> Chicago was the stockyard, slums, vice, crime, and graft; but Chicago was also the university, the opera, the symphony orchestra, the world's finest

[BELOW]
President Lyndon Johnson and Prime Minister Lester B. Pearson during an official state visit to Washington, D.C., in 1964. Theirs was a complex, sometimes difficult journey.

WITH FAITH & GOODWILL

[PREVIOUS PAGE]
The good relationship between William Lyon Mackenzie King and Franklin Delano Roosevelt was one of the high points of Canadian-American relations in the modern era.

[BELOW]
President George H.W. Bush invited Prime Minister Brian Mulroney to spend the final weekend of his presidency with him at Camp David.

collection of French modern paintings, and a most imaginative plan for city development. It was throbbing with energy and full of excitement. It was the new industrial frontier with all the vigour and crudity of a pioneering community.

Prime Minister Pierre Trudeau, as recounted by John Kenneth Galbraith, was more succinct in describing his love of an American city: "Better a weekend in New York," he quipped, "than a week in Montreal."

One of America's presidents, William Howard Taft, spent many decades holidaying each year at what is now La Malbaie, Quebec. Back then it was known as Murray Bay, and Taft was often asked where it was. "Murray Bay is a state of mind," he'd reply, adding, "as intoxicating as champagne, but without the headache of the morning after." And even in the darkest days of an economic depression, Franklin Roosevelt returned to his beloved Canadian island, Campobello, for rest and relaxation. Roosevelt's elder cousin Theodore (father of the Bull

INTRODUCTION

Moose Party) even once set off on a Canadian hunting trip, only to find himself attacked by a Canadian bull moose!

Each Canadian prime minister and U.S. president, in words and actions, has added a new chapter to the Canadian-American relationship since 1867. When two neighbours' domestic and foreign affairs are so closely entwined, it could hardly be otherwise. And every president and prime minister has left a personal stamp on the two countries' relationship, whether at work in Washington or Ottawa, on holiday, or on state visits. Their joint story has been recorded in their successes in managing this most this most enduring friendship between peoples — and in their words and images, presented in this book.

ARTHUR MILNES

Prime Minister Kim Campbell and President Bill Clinton held private talks at the Tokyo G7 Summit in July 1993.

FRIENDSHIP

IN THE WORLD OF CANADA-U.S. RELATIONS, A SPEECH BY A PRESIDENT TO THE Canadian Parliament, or one by a Canadian prime minister to the U.S. Congress is, to use sporting analogies, the World Series or Stanley Cup final of bilateral relations. It simply can't be topped.

In 1995, shortly after President Bill Clinton spoke to Canada's Parliament, quick-thinking and historically minded staff at the American embassy in Ottawa produced the book *United States Presidential Addresses to the Canadian Parliament: 1943–1995*. In his foreword, then American Ambassador to Canada James Blanchard noted the following about these special addresses:

> Presidential speeches in the House of Commons have always been a special moment in U.S.-Canadian history. Each speech powerfully captures the mood of the times. Each represents an important portrait of this, the most unique bilateral relationship in history.

When President Bill Clinton spoke to Canada's MPs and senators, it fell to Prime Minister Jean Chrétien to introduce his counterpart. In introducing Clinton, the wily man from Shawinigan reminded Canada's distinguished visitor that a speech to Canada's Parliament could also bring good political luck to a president who, as with Chrétien himself, was still in his first term. As the man from Hope, Arkansas, listened intently, the prime minister observed that presidents such as Eisenhower, Reagan, and Nixon had all addressed Canada's Parliament and were later returned to second terms at the White House. To laughter, Chrétien noted that other

[PREVIOUS PAGE]
President Barack Obama and Prime Minister Justin Trudeau walk toward the Oval Office following a joint press conference in the Rose Garden of the White House, March 10, 2016.

presidents like Ford, Carter, and George H.W. Bush had not addressed Parliament and had not received second terms.

It was a great line and very much appreciated by Clinton, who was down in the polls then. "I have never believed in the iron laws of history as much as I do now," the president told Parliament.

The fact that later presidents like George W. Bush and Barack Obama were elected to second terms after *not* addressing Canada's Parliament shows that this "law" of history can now be forgotten.

Ambassador Blanchard was right in what he said, though. A presidential visit to Parliament Hill that lacks an address to Parliament may still be important and exciting, but it remains a bit of a letdown. So when, in June 2016, President Barack Obama finally took his turn behind a podium in Canada's House of Commons to proclaim "the world needs more Canada," the now-veteran president was met with a wave of enthusiasm.

What many observers forget, however, is that a presidential speech to Parliament actually is a relatively recent custom. Franklin Roosevelt in August 1943 was the first to address Canadian MPs and senators. And it wasn't until 1977 that a Canadian prime minister, Pierre Trudeau, was honoured by an invitation to speak to Congress in Washington. Fans

Here's to a successful visit. U.S. Ambassador James Blanchard (second from right) and Canadian Ambassador Raymond Chrétien join their bosses in celebrating a successful meeting between Prime Minister Jean Chrétien and President Bill Clinton.

FRIENDSHIP

I have never believed
in the iron laws of history
as much as I do now.
— President Bill Clinton

of Canada's connection to the British monarchy will note with pride that Governor General Vincent Massey, the Queen's representative in Canada, beat Trudeau to Congress by many years. He spoke there in 1954.

No matter the occasion, however, the persistent and perhaps even defining characteristic of the relationship between the two countries is their friendship. This is not the whole of the partnership, certainly, but it is the foundation. Unsurprisingly, then, some presidents and prime ministers have discovered over the decades that the need to work together closely on bilateral, continental, and global matters can produce a bond that becomes personal. Professional responsibilities can produce — and often have produced — friends in truly high places.

President Clinton's address to a joint session of Parliament in 1995 is fondly remembered by many.

HOPEFUL RENEWAL

A SENSE BOTH OF NEW BEGINNINGS AND OF PRIDE IN THE PAST HUNG IN the air at the White House in March 2016. President Barack Obama, in the final months of his presidency, hosted a Canadian prime minister at a state dinner.

In his toast celebrating the new prime minister, President Obama reminded the audience that Prime Minister Pierre Trudeau had played host to President Richard Nixon and his wife, Pat, in the 1970s. On that occasion, Obama recalled, Nixon had made a good-humoured prediction.

President Barack Obama

State Dinner at the White House, Washington, D.C.
March 10, 2016

FORTY-FOUR YEARS AGO, PRESIDENT NIXON MADE A VISIT TO OTTAWA. AND HE WAS hosted by Prime Minister Pierre Trudeau. At a private dinner, there was a toast. "Tonight, we'll dispense with the formalities," President Nixon said. "I'd like to propose a toast to the future Prime Minister of Canada — Justin Trudeau." He was four months at the time.

Tonight, we want our Canadians friends to feel at home…. This visit has been a celebration of the values that we share. We, as people, are committed to the principles of equality and opportunity — the idea that if you work hard and play by the rules, you can make it if you try, no matter what the circumstances of your birth, in both of our countries….

This visit reminds us of what we love about Canada. It's the solidarity shown by so many Canadians after 9/11 when they welcomed stranded American travellers into their homes. It's the courage of your service members, standing with us in Afghanistan and now in Iraq. It's the compassion of the Canadian people welcoming refugees — and the prime minister himself, who told those refugees, "You're safe at home now."

[OPPOSITE]

A Trudeau returns. President Barack Obama, First Lady Michelle Obama, Prime Minister Justin Trudeau, and Madame Sophie Grégoire-Trudeau wave from the Blue Room Balcony of the White House, March 10, 2016.

FRIENDSHIP

I'd like to propose a toast to the future Prime Minister of Canada — Justin Trudeau.

— President Richard Nixon

Justin, we also see Canada's spirit in your mother's brave advocacy for mental health care — and I want to give a special welcome to Margaret Trudeau tonight. And we see Canada's spirit in Sophie — a champion of women and girls, because our daughters deserve the same opportunities that anybody's sons do.

And this spirit reminds us of why we're all here — why we serve. Justin, Sophie, your children are still young. They are adorable and they still let you hug them. When we first spoke on the phone after your election, we talked not only as president and prime minister, but also as fathers. When I was first elected to this office, Malia was ten and Sasha was just seven. And they grow up too fast. This fall, Malia heads off to college. And I'm starting to choke up ... But there is a point to this, though, and that is that we're not here for power. We're not here for fame or fortune. We're here for our kids. We're here for everybody's kids — to give our sons and our daughters a better world. To pass to them a world that's a little safer and a little more equal

Margaret Trudeau introduces a three-month-old Justin Trudeau to Pat Nixon during President Nixon's visit to Ottawa in April 1972.

FRIENDSHIP

and a little more just, a little more prosperous so that a young person growing up in Chicago or Montreal or on the other side of the world has every opportunity to make of their life what they will, no matter who they are or what they look like, or how they pray or who they love.

Justin, I believe there are no better words to guide us in this work than those you once used to describe what your father taught you and your siblings — to believe in yourself. To stand up for ourselves. To know ourselves and to accept responsibility for ourselves. To show a genuine and deep respect for each other and for every human being.

And so I would like to propose a toast — to the great alliance between the United States and Canada; to our friends, Justin and Sophie; to the friendship between Americans and Canadians and the spirit that binds us together — a genuine and deep and abiding respect for each and every human being.

[Cheers. A toast is offered.]

Prime Minister Justin Trudeau was not the first member of his family to be honoured with a White House state dinner. Here is his father, Pierre, at a Carter White House state dinner — the first hosted by the Carter White House — in 1977.

Prime Minister Justin Trudeau

State Dinner at the White House,
Washington, D.C.
March 10, 2016

———

IN THINKING ABOUT WHAT I WANTED TO SAY THIS EVENING, I CAME ACROSS A QUOTE from President Truman, who shared these words with the Canadian Parliament nearly seventy years ago. He said that Canada's relationship with the United States did not develop spontaneously. It did not come about merely through the happy circumstance of geography, but was "compounded of one part proximity, and nine parts goodwill and common sense."

It is that enduring goodwill and common sense that I believe defines our relationship to this day. It's what makes our constructive partnership possible. It's what allows us to respectfully

> Canada's relationship with the United States was "compounded of one part proximity, and nine parts goodwill and common sense."
> — PRIME MINISTER JUSTIN TRUDEAU, QUOTING PRESIDENT HARRY S. TRUMAN

disagree and remain friends and allies on the few occasions we do. For example, I would argue that it's better to be the leader of a country that consistently wins Olympic gold medals in hockey. President Obama would likely disagree. And yet, you still invited us over for dinner. Because that's what friends do.

Because, now that I think of it, we're actually closer than friends. We're more like siblings, really. We have shared parentage, but we took different paths in our later years. We became the stay-at-home type — and you grew to be a little more rebellious. I think the reason that goodwill and common sense comes so easily is because we are Canadians and Americans alike, guided by the same core values. Values like co-operation and respect. Co-operation because it keeps us safe and prosperous. And respect because it's the surest path to both safeguarding the world we share and honouring the diverse people with whom we share it.

[OPPOSITE]
President Barack Obama with Prime Minister Justin Trudeau in the Oval Office, March 10, 2016.

FRIENDSHIP

When it comes to security, for example, we agree that our countries are stronger and the world is safer when we work together. For more than half a century, we've joined forces to protect our continent. And we've been the closest of allies overseas for even longer, fighting together on the beaches of France, standing shoulder to shoulder with our European partners in NATO, and now confronting violent extremism in the Middle East.

> Our children and grandchildren will judge us not by the words we said, but by the actions we took — or failed to take.
>
> — Prime Minister Justin Trudeau

In every instance, we realize that our concerns were better addressed together than alone, and together we have realized the longest, most peaceful, and most mutually beneficial relationship of any two countries since the birth of the nation state. It's a relationship that doesn't just serve its own interests — it serves the entire world. Canadians and Americans also value economic interdependence, because we know that it brings greater prosperity for all of us....

Together, Canada and the United States negotiated trade agreements that have expanded opportunities for our businesses, created millions of good, well-paying jobs for our workers, and made products more affordable for more Canadian and American families. We must never take that partnership for granted, and I can promise you that my government never will.

But nor should we forget that our responsibilities extend beyond our ruling borders and across generations, which means getting rid of that outdated notion that a healthy environment and a strong economy stand in opposition to one another. And it means that when we come to issues like climate change, we need to acknowledge that we are all in this together. Our children and grandchildren will judge us not by the words we said, but by the actions we took — or failed to take.

If we truly wish to leave them a better world than the one we inherited from our own parents — and I know, Mr. President, that you and the First Lady want this as strongly as Sophie and I do — we cannot deny the science. We cannot pretend that climate change is still up for debate.

Thank you, Mr. President, for your leadership — your global leadership on the pressing issue of the environment and climate change.

FRIENDSHIP

And finally, we believe — Canadians and Americans — in the fundamental truth that diversity can be a source of strength. That we are thriving and prosperous countries not in spite of our differences but because of them.

We know that if we seek to be even greater, we must do greater things — be more compassionate, be more accepting, be more open to those who dress differently or eat different foods, or speak different languages. Our identities as Canadians and Americans are enriched by these differences, not threatened by them.

On our own, we make progress. But together, our two countries make history. Duty-bound, loyal, and forever linked, whatever the future holds, we will face it together. Neighbours, partners, allies, and friends. This is our experience and our example to the world.

Barack, thank you for all that you have done these past seven years to preserve this most important relationship. May the special connection between our two countries continue to flourish in the years to come, and may my grey hair come in at a much slower rate than yours has.

And with that, on behalf of thirty-six million Canadians, I propose a toast to the president, to the first lady, and to the people of the United States of America.

> Duty-bound, loyal, and forever linked, whatever the future holds, we will face it together. Neighbours, partners, allies, and friends. This is our experience and our example to the world.
>
> — Prime Minister Justin Trudeau

WITH FAITH & GOODWILL

FRIENDSHIP

A FRIEND IN NEED

O F THE MANY EXPRESSIONS OF FRIENDSHIP BETWEEN THE TWO COUNtries, there is no greater example than that of the so-called Canadian Caper. Later dramatized in the Oscar-winning film *Argo*, this 1979 event saw Canada's embassy and the ambassador's residence in Iran transformed into a secret hideout for American officials after regime change had led to the hostage-taking of fifty-two other Americans in a 444-day ordeal.

At risk to their own lives, Canadian officials sheltered their American colleagues for months and smuggled them out of Iran to safety. It was a bold, dangerous ploy that places in sharp relief the lengths to which true friends will go to help one another in a moment of need. In the aftermath of the diplomats' escape, President Jimmy Carter spoke to Prime Minister Joe Clark to express his nation's gratitude. Years later he recalled the event in emotional terms while speaking to a Canadian audience.

President Jimmy Carter

*On the Return of Six Americans from Iran —
Telephone Discussion with Prime Minister Joe Clark
January 31, 1980*

Mr. Prime Minister, good morning to you.

[The prime minister responds.]

I called — as you know, we've had a series of communications back and forth privately, sometimes almost in verbal code, on the telephone and otherwise — but I wanted to call, now that our six Americans are back in this country and safe, publicly and on behalf of all the American people, Joe, to thank you and Ambassador Taylor and the Canadian government and people for

[OPPOSITE]

The Canadian Caper. President Jimmy Carter thanks Prime Minister Joe Clark on January 31, 1980, after Canada's role in keeping six Americans safe in revolutionary Iran is revealed.

> *I wanted to call, now that our six Americans are back in this country and safe, to thank you … [for your] personal and political courage.*
> — President Jimmy Carter

a tremendous exhibition of friendship and support and, I think, personal and political courage. You've probably seen the outpouring of appreciation that has come from the American people on their own volition. And it's typical of the way we all feel. I might point out that the congressional parliamentarians tell me that the action taken by our Congress yesterday toward the Canadian government is the first time in the history of our nation that the Congress has ever expressed its thanks personally to another government for an act of friendship and heroism. And I just wanted to relay that historical note to you as well.

[The prime minister responds.]

Well, I thank you. I don't believe that the revelation of their departure will be damaging to the well-being of our other hostages. You're nice and very perceptive to express that concern. I think it was a remarkable demonstration of mutual trust that the fact of the existence of those Americans was kept confidential so long, and the fact that it was not revealed publicly until after they'd already left, is very good. But Joe, good luck to you. And I hope that you'll not only send a copy of my letter to Ambassador Taylor but also publicly express to the people of Canada my deep appreciation, both to you, to Ambassador Taylor, to all of the embassy officials, and indeed to your whole country. We are deeply grateful for this, a new demonstration of the closeness that is very beneficial to us.

[The prime minister responds.]

FRIENDSHIP

President Jimmy Carter

Recalling the "Canadian Caper"
Book Launch for Jimmy and Rosalynn Carter: A Canadian Tribute
Plains, Georgia
April 30, 2011

———

When I was president of the United States — all the way through 1980 — very few events occurred in my White House experience that were positively emotional and gratifying. But I would say that obviously one of the high points of my life was when the so-called Canadian Caper occurred. Canada made the decision to do all it could to help protect six of my hostages who were hiding in Iran. Those six hostages went into the Canadian Embassy [in Tehran] and were protected for a long time. Eventually, at the right moment, I agreed and the Canadian prime minister [Joe Clark] agreed, that they should be evacuated from Iran pretending not to be related to the United States at all. They pretended to be Canadians and they

> Your own government right up to the prime minister —
> ## put themselves in political and sometimes physical danger
> to rescue six of my American friends.
>
> — President Jimmy Carter

got out safely. I think you all will remember, those of you who are old enough, how the closeness of this event affected every citizen in the Northern hemisphere when, without having to do so, the entire Canadian embassy staff — and your own government right up to the prime minister — put themselves in political and sometimes physical danger to rescue six of my *[choking back tears]* American friends.

EARLY DAYS

Long before the first official state dinner and when Canada was still struggling to establish itself as a somewhat autonomous dominion, leaders from the two nations were already crossing the border and building bridges — sometimes literally. Prime ministers like Wilfrid Laurier and William Lyon Mackenzie King knew the United States well. Presidents and their Cabinet members travelled to Canada often. Some even had homes in the land to their north. These personal interests helped to knit together strategic and national ones to follow.

Both as Opposition leader and later as prime minister, Laurier appeared before American audiences to air differences between the two countries and smooth out relations. The second speech, delivered in Chicago, uses an astonishing rhetorical legerdemain to argue the Canadian position on the Alaska boundary dispute: he points out the path of conciliation to the Americans by pretending momentarily to have forgotten himself and to be speaking as the U.S. and not the Canadian representative!

Elsewhere in these speeches, Laurier, in the parlance of the time, naturally appeals to the kinship between the American and Canadian peoples as one of "race" and "blood" — words that leave us cold today, but a century and more ago were meant to soothe.

[OPPOSITE]

Navigating Canadian-American relations was not always easy. Sir Wilfrid Laurier, the seventh prime minister of Canada, sometimes had tough words for his American neighbours on his trips south.

Prime Minister Wilfrid Laurier

Studebaker Hall, Chicago, Illinois
October 9, 1899

———

I must say that I feel that though the relations between Canada and the United States are good, though they are brotherly, though they are satisfactory, in my judgment they are not as good, as brotherly, as satisfactory as they ought to be.

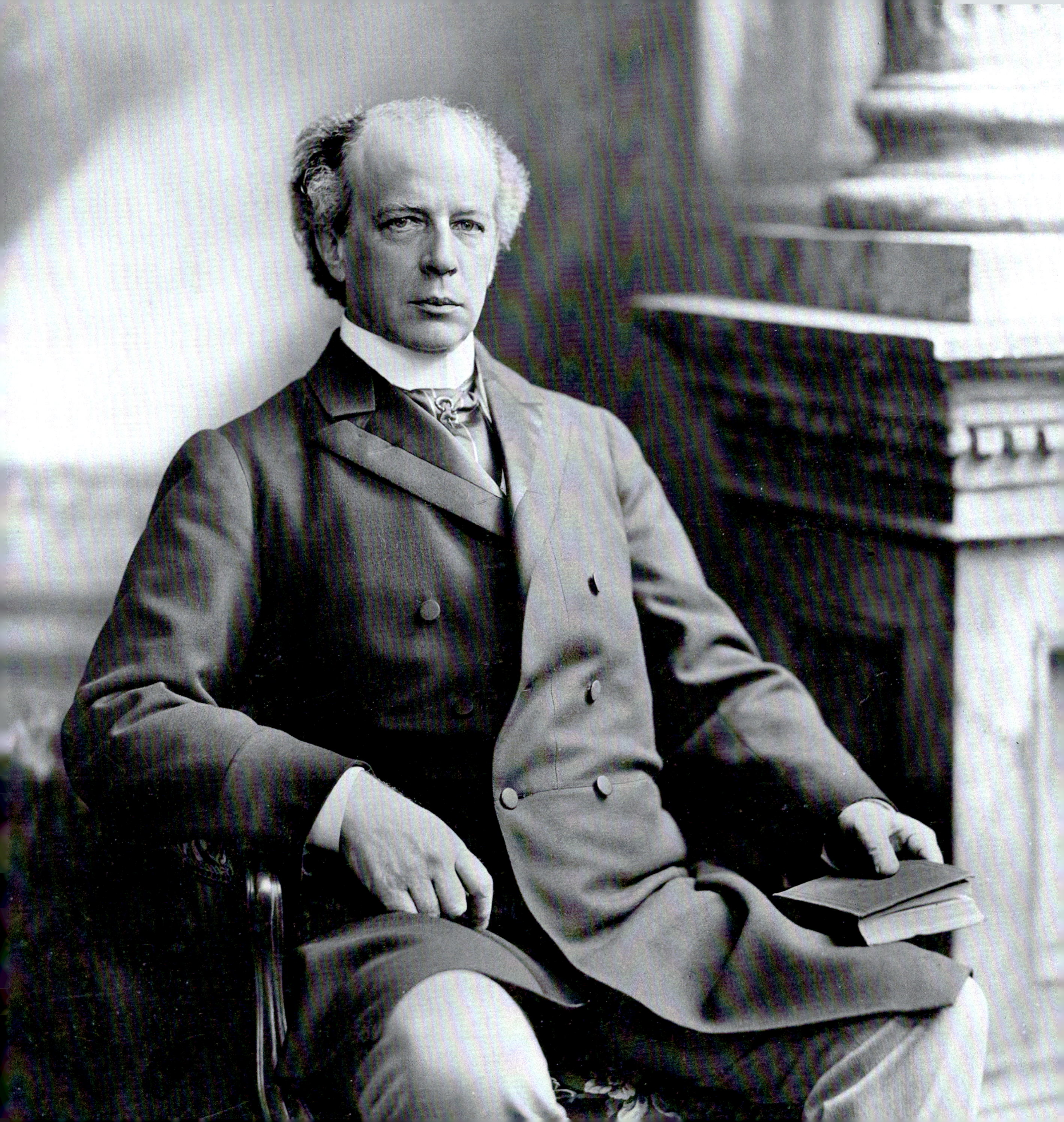

We are of the same stock. We spring from the same races on one side of the line as on the other. We speak the same language. We have the same literature, and for more than a thousand years we have had a common history.

Let me recall to you the lines which, in the darkest days of the Civil War, the Puritan poet of America [John Greenleaf Whittier] issued to England:

> Oh, Englishmen! Oh, Englishmen!
> In hope and creed,
> In blood and tongue, are brothers,
> We all are heirs of Runnymede.

Brothers we are, in the language of your own poet. May I not say that while our relations are not always as brotherly as they should have been, may I not ask, Mr. President, on the part of Canada and on the part of the United States, if we are sometimes too prone to stand by the full conceptions of our rights, and exact all our rights to the last pound of flesh? May I not ask if there have not been too often between us petty quarrels, which happily do not wound the heart of the nation?

Sir, I am proud to say in the presence of the chief executive of the United States that it is the belief of the Canadian government that we should make a supreme effort to better our relations and make the government of President McKinley and the present government of Canada, with the assent of Great Britain, so to work together as to remove all causes of dissension between us. Shall I speak my mind? *[Cries of "Yes!"]* We met a stumbling block in the question of the Alaskan frontier. Well, let me say here and now the commission would not settle that question, and referred it to their particular governments, and they are now dealing with it. May I be permitted to say here and now that we do not desire one inch of your land?

But if I state, however, that we want to hold our own land, will not that be an American sentiment, I want to know? However, though that would be a British sentiment or Canadian, I am here to say, above all, my fellow countrymen, that we do not want to stand upon the extreme limits of our rights. We are ready to give and to take. We can afford to be just; we can afford to be generous, because we are strong. We have a population of seventy-seven million. I beg pardon, I am mistaken, it is the reverse of that. But pardon my mistake; although it is the reverse, I am sure the sentiment is the same.

But though we may have many little bickerings of that kind, I speak my whole mind, and I believe I speak the mind of all you gentlemen when I say that, after all, when we go down to the bottom of our hearts we will find that there is between us a true, genuine affection.

There are no two nations today on the face of the globe so united as Great Britain and the United States of America. The secretary of state told us some few months ago that there was no treaty of alliance between Great Britain and the United States of America. It is very true there

[OPPOSITE]
President William McKinley was in the audience for Prime Minister Wilfrid Laurier's famous Chicago speech.

FRIENDSHIP

is between the United States of America and Great Britain today no treaty of alliance which the pen can write and which the pen can unmake, but there is between Great Britain and the United States of America a unity of blood which is thicker than water, and I appeal to recent history when I say that whenever one nation has to face an emergency — a greater emergency than usual — forthwith the sympathies of the other nation go to her sister.

Sir, an incident took place in the month of June last which showed to me at all events conclusively that there is between us a very deep and sincere affection. I may be pardoned if I recall that instance, because I have to speak of myself.

In the month of June last I spoke on the floor of the House of Commons of Canada on the question of Alaska, and I enunciated the very obvious truism that international problems can be settled in one of two ways only: either by arbitration or war. And although I proceeded to say immediately that war between Great Britain and the United States would be criminal and would not be thought of for a moment, still the very word "war" created quite an excitement in this country.

> May I be permitted to say here and now that we do not desire one inch of your land?
> — Prime Minister Wilfrid Laurier

With that causeless excitement, though I was indirectly the cause of it, I do not at this moment find any fault, because it convinced me, to an absolute certainty, that between your country and my country the relations have reached a degree of dignity and respect and affection that even the word "war" is never to be mentioned in a British assembly or in an American assembly. The word is not to be pronounced, not even to be predicated. It is not to be pronounced at all. The very idea is abhorrent to us.

There was a civil war in the last century. There was a civil war between England and her American colonies, and their relations were severed. If they were severed, American citizens, as you know they were, through no fault of your fathers, the fault was altogether the fault of the British government of that day. If the British government of that day had treated the American colonies as the British government for the last twenty or fifty years has treated its colonies; if Great Britain had given you then the same degree of liberty which it gives to Canada, my country; if it had given you, as it has given us, legislative independence absolute,

FRIENDSHIP

the result would have been different — the course of victory, the course of history, would have been different.

But what has been done cannot be undone. You cannot expect that the union which has been severed shall ever be restored; but can we not expect, can we not hope that if the unity cannot be restored under the law, at least there can be a union of hearts? Can we not hope that the banners of England and the banners of the United States shall never, never again meet in

> But can we not expect, can we not hope that if the unity cannot be restored under the law, at least there can be a union of hearts?
> — Prime Minister Wilfrid Laurier

conflict, except in those conflicts provided by the arts of peace, such as we see today in the harbour of New York, in the contest between the *Shamrock* and the *Columbia* for the supremacy of naval architecture and naval prowess?

Can we not hope that if ever the banners of England and the banners of the United States are again to meet on the battlefield, they shall meet entwined together in the defence of the oppressed, for the enfranchisement of the downtrodden, and for the advancement of liberty, progress, and civilization?

Vice President Charles Fairbanks

Quebec Tercentenary Celebration
Quebec City
July 23, 1908

The eyes of the Western world are upon this historic city. The celebration of the tercentenary of Champlain's founding of Quebec is altogether admirable both in the comprehensiveness of its conception and in the excellence of its execution, and is an event which awakens interest not only in the Dominion of Canada but in the United States also.

From this point as a base, intrepid explorers blazed the pathway of civilization through trackless forests and explored lakes and rivers in territory which is now within the jurisdiction of the United States. Names associated with the early history of Quebec are landmarks in our geography and are indelibly impressed upon our civilization.

Three hundred years is but a brief period in the history of Quebec and all of Anglo-Saxon America. Here has been written an interesting story. Here have been witnessed the victories and

[THIS PAGE]
President Theodore Roosevelt and Vice President Charles Fairbanks, July 16, 1904. Fairbanks made history when he visited Quebec City to celebrate its 300th anniversary.

[OPPOSITE]
Then Senator Fairbanks and party at Summit of White Pass, on the border between the Alaska Territory and British Columbia, June 28, 1899. As a senator and later a vice president under Theodore Roosevelt, Fairbanks was involved in the Alaska boundary dispute.

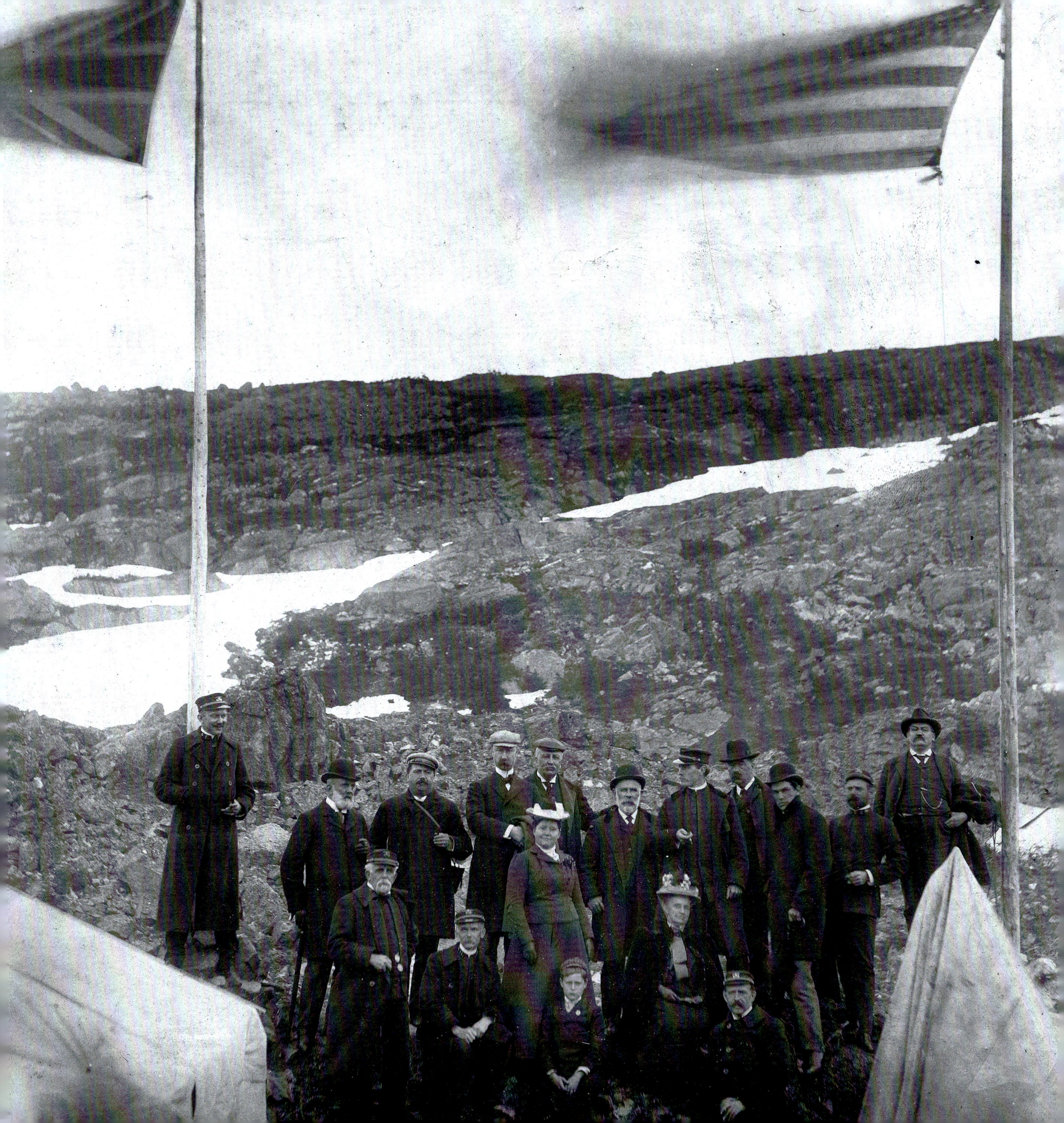

defeats of war and the blessed triumph of peace. The battleships of great nations rest yonder upon the bosom of the St. Lawrence. The representatives of these powers assembled here are recalling past differences, but only to emphasize the present prevalence of a spirit of genuine friendship between them.

It is with unusual pleasure I bring you greetings from the president [Theodore Roosevelt] and the people of the United States, who rejoice with you in the progress you have made in manifold ways, which make for the strength and honour of a great people. We are not indifferent to your welfare, nor are you indifferent to ours. The blood of a common ancestry is in our

> Names associated with the early history of Quebec are **landmarks in our geography** and are indelibly impressed upon our civilization.
>
> — Vice President Charles Fairbanks

veins. We have much in common. We glory in many of the same traditions and we have the same jurisprudence. Our standards of civilization are alike. Here, side by side, owing to allegiance to different sovereignties, we are, in God's providence, to work out our destiny. We wish you that contentment which comes from the cultivation of the arts of peaceful industry under those political institutions which are the guaranty of justice and liberty among men. The United States and Canada have but fairly entered upon their career. Each has vast areas either sparsely settled or unoccupied, where many will make their homes in the future. Many millions will be added to our population and to yours. We have each made much advance in the scale of civilization and are gratified with the progress we have made. Back of us lays a brief but honourable history and before us stretch illimitable opportunities. We confidently believe that we are each destined to play a large and worthy part in the progress of the human race upon the Western continent. We have no rivalries except in the ways of peace. We neither covet the other's territory. We rest upon a common frontier more than five thousand miles in length. It is crossed and re-crossed by instrumentalities of commerce which tended to strengthen our neighbourly ties.

There are no fortifications upon our frontier and no battleships upon the waters which divide us, and we believe and fervently hope that there will never be need of any defensive preparation between us.

As we behold this majestic celebration in which the representatives of different nations participate and witness the manifestations of a genuine fraternal spirit among them, we are impressed with the thought that there is no nation that should resort to war. May we not, on

FRIENDSHIP

this theatre of past conflicts, surrounded now by the impressive monuments of peace, venture to hope that the widespread movement which seeks to insure the maintenance of peace among the nations of the world without invoking the sword, may grow in strength and at no distant day become incorporated as a part of the fixed policy of nations.

To advocate measures for the maintenance of international tranquillity, to endeavour to substitute reason for force, is not evidence of any decay in the courage or manhood of nations, but it is the proclamation of the great truth that modern civilization is not a failure if it does not

> # We have no rivalries except in the ways of peace.
> ### We neither covet the other's territory.
> ### We rest upon a common frontier more than five thousand miles in length.
> ### It is crossed and re-crossed by instrumentalities of commerce which tended to
> # strengthen our neighbourly ties.
> — Vice President Charles Fairbanks

substitute for force the serene and all-powerful chamber of reason and deliberation. There is such a thing as righteousness among nations.... Let nations, by every honourable means which enlightened statesmanship may suggest, avoid an appeal to that court where might alone turns the balance. We have no need to fear that the relations between the United States and Great Britain will ever again be disturbed. We have faith to believe that our flags, which grace this historic occasion and which mingle together and salute each other upon the Plains of Abraham, will never confront each other in conflict upon either land or sea.

Prime Minister Robert Borden

Washington, D.C.
April 27, 1912

———

Robert Borden defeated Laurier in a general election in 1911 that turned on the repudiation of Laurier's favoured policy of reciprocity — in other words, free trade. Here the new prime minister assures his U.S. audience that the anti-American rhetoric deployed in the campaign will have no effect on the friendship between the two nations.

. . .

During the [Canadian] general election, which was waged on the issue of reciprocity, the question was very thoroughly discussed from all angles. The echo of that discussion had not died down. When the negotiations on the treaty were completed [between the Taft and Laurier administrations in 1911], it was agreed that it should be subject to the action of the legislatures of both countries. Canada saw fit to turn it down. The fight against it was fair and open and it was the people of Canada who decided what attitude their nation would take. This action should leave no bitterness on either side, and I feel sure there is no bitterness. We felt that for us to accept the pact would amount to reversing Canada's policy of the last quarter-century. We had held out offers of reciprocity, the kind we thought was fair to us, for a number of years, and the United States did not feel prepared to accept it. Therefore there should be no hard feeling on this side of the line because Canada in its turn saw fit to refuse an unfair offer from

> The fight against it was fair and open and it was the **people of Canada who decided what attitude their nation would take.**
> — Prime Minister Robert Borden

FRIENDSHIP

> We had held out offers of reciprocity, **the kind we thought was fair to us,** for a number of years, and the United States **did not feel prepared to accept it.**
>
> — PRIME MINISTER ROBERT BORDEN

the United States. We all want international peace, and the example set by Great Britain and the United States in settling amicably more than sixteen questions concerning Canada by peaceful means should encourage us greatly. We must be careful to keep a stand while settling disputes which will keep war at a minimum. We must be careful also lest our zeal leads us into agreements which we will not be willing to keep to the end.

It is significant that there are more than four thousand miles of boundary between the United States and Canada, and that the boundary is not even policed, and that on the Great Lakes there is no armament that amounts to anything. It shows how closely the two peoples feel toward each other. There is every reason why the two countries should have the closest relations. We have the same industrial problems to face, and in many ways conditions are the same. We are both seeking to pass laws to insure every man equal opportunity to earn a living. [And in conclusion,] both are great and growing nations.

"No truck or trade with the Yankees!" Sir Robert Laird Borden, the eighth prime minister of Canada, in office from 1911 to 1920, came to office after fighting a campaign against free trade with the United States.

William Lyon Mackenzie King

New York City
December 10, 1913

———

Defeated in the 1911 election, William Lyon Mackenzie King, a Harvard graduate and former Canadian minister of labour, found himself in high demand as an expert in the field of industrial relations. He spent part of the war years working in the United States with the Rockefeller family.

. . .

The one great continent of America sustains us both. While the separation which marks the beginning of American history is likely to be enduring, in historical record it is marked by a moment of time. While the boundary which assigns us the respective portions of the continent we share is apparent to all the world, the line which designates it is so fine as to be invisible. Time and geography speak of a common ancestry and a common abode. To be unmindful of this is as great an omission as to forget all that makes us distinctive peoples. It is not the breath of the New World nor its wide expanses which makes the Americans and ourselves lovers of liberty; that love of liberty comes in the blood, through centuries of Old World struggles. It was not the soil of America that made the United States a federation of free states and Canada a self-governing dominion. It was the spirit that inspired Hampden, Pym, and Pitt, the spirit which was found in the men who wrested the great charter from John, and the Petition of Right from Charles. A new continent may afford new scenes of action, but the genius of a people is interwoven in the mysteries of a race.

In this relationship of a common race to a continent held in common lie the perils and possibilities of our joint trusteeship. Here we may each help the other to realize the dangers and advantages of our common inheritance. A material foundation is essential to all development and growth. In sharing as we do the hidden wealth and vast resources of a continent, material prosperity would seem to be amply assured. Seeing some of the consequences of that development, as yet scarcely begun, the thought suggests itself — are we to surrender ourselves, through greed of possession and power, to the vulgar conception that material gains are a supreme concern? Or are we, in the working out of our respective destinies, to conceive ideas and fashion ideals which shall be of lasting benefit to mankind? That, it seems to me, is the supreme question for Canada and the United States, and one which, because of our similarities in temperament and the vastness of our possessions, is the same for both.

In this New World, with the wealth which makes possible higher forms of development, are we to emulate the lust of nations which have exhausted their resources or which have concerned themselves with expansion only for the sake of power? It were better a thousand times for civilization and mankind that this continent should have remained unknown and unexplored, a wilderness for the savage and his prey, than that it should become, as under a mere materialism it is certain to become, a place of bondage for millions of sensitive hearts.

Is it not true that in the very prosperity which both Canada and the United States enjoy, lies the danger of forgetting that it is only in the social, moral, and intellectual well-being of its citizenship that the real strength and greatness of a people is to be found? Labour is essential to development. Labour to noble ends brings freedom. But labour which alone administers to greed is servitude. Dollars and mileage, acres and bushels, tons and rates, stocks and bonds are necessary indices of present day organized industrial and commercial life. We should never forget that these are but indices of a material foundation which should be made to serve the higher ends of existence. Even in the noblest of utterances, the patriotic, emphasis is all too frequently put upon extent of territory rather than upon national character. The size and strength of armies and navies are continually stressed, as if instruments for the destruction of human life were of more concern than life itself. While it would be unwise to ignore what may be necessary to a nation's expansion and security, it is still more serious to forget that the arts of peace constitute the permanent and enduring side of a nation's progress, and that human life and the realization of its highest possibilities should ever be the supreme concern of men of nations.... It is at this point I would seek to emphasize the opportunity shared by the two peoples on this continent in the shaping of world ideals. Compared with the Greek city state, what opportunities of expression are to be found in the mighty and complex life of continents as we are privileged to know it today! Compared with Israel and her tribes, what obligations are ours in the multitudes that have come to our shores from all portions of the globe, to say nothing of

Dr. King, I presume? Mackenzie King knew America well, even earning his doctorate from Harvard and serving as valedictorian for his class.

the millions of the Orient to whom also we have obligations, albeit seemingly more remote! It is a Japanese saying that the ordinary man thinks only in terms of today, that the higher man thinks in years, but that the really great man thinks in generations. To the Greek and the Hebrew conception of public duty, we may be obliged, if we are adequately to discharge our national obligations, to add this further idea, borrowed from a remote Oriental philosophy. As we of Canada and the United States have shared in the past a common background, and drawn inspiration from a common source, so as we look into the future and consider its problems, a vision too vast for one people meets our gaze. The horizon ever widens as the centuries unroll. To the New World vaster obligations and opportunities are being presented than were ever known to the old. Geography, which keeps us side by side, has placed us midway between other continents of this world, and the problems arising for each of us out of the new contacts will be much the same. We do well, as nations sprung from one great family, to make our friendships fast and sure. In the fashioning of world ideals, British and American endeavour must go hand in hand. Already something toward this end has been attained.

> The ordinary man thinks only in terms of today …
> the higher man thinks in years …
> ## the really great man thinks in generations.
> — Prime Minister William Lyon Mackenzie King

[OPPOSITE]
Good friends. Governor General of Canada Lord Tweedsmuir (John Buchan), Prime Minister Mackenzie King, President Franklin Roosevelt, and his son James Roosevelt.

Our common race, inheriting a common continent, has given to mankind a world ideal which is expressed in the unprotected frontier of four thousand miles, which separates the United States of America from the part of the British Empire from which we come. This world ideal will be heralded far and wide when, in little more than the compass of another year, a century of unbroken peace will be rounded out between the British and American peoples. It is difficult to realize that one hundred years ago we were at war. In the success which, in the interval, has attended upon conferences and arbitration, we see in the settlement of our boundary disputes the triumph of reason over force. If, to international peace, we on this continent can add industrial peace, in the furtherance of which beginnings have already been made, so then men's minds may be liberated and men's energies freed to give to the problems of humanity the consideration they deserve, to what joint service for mankind may we not yet be called!

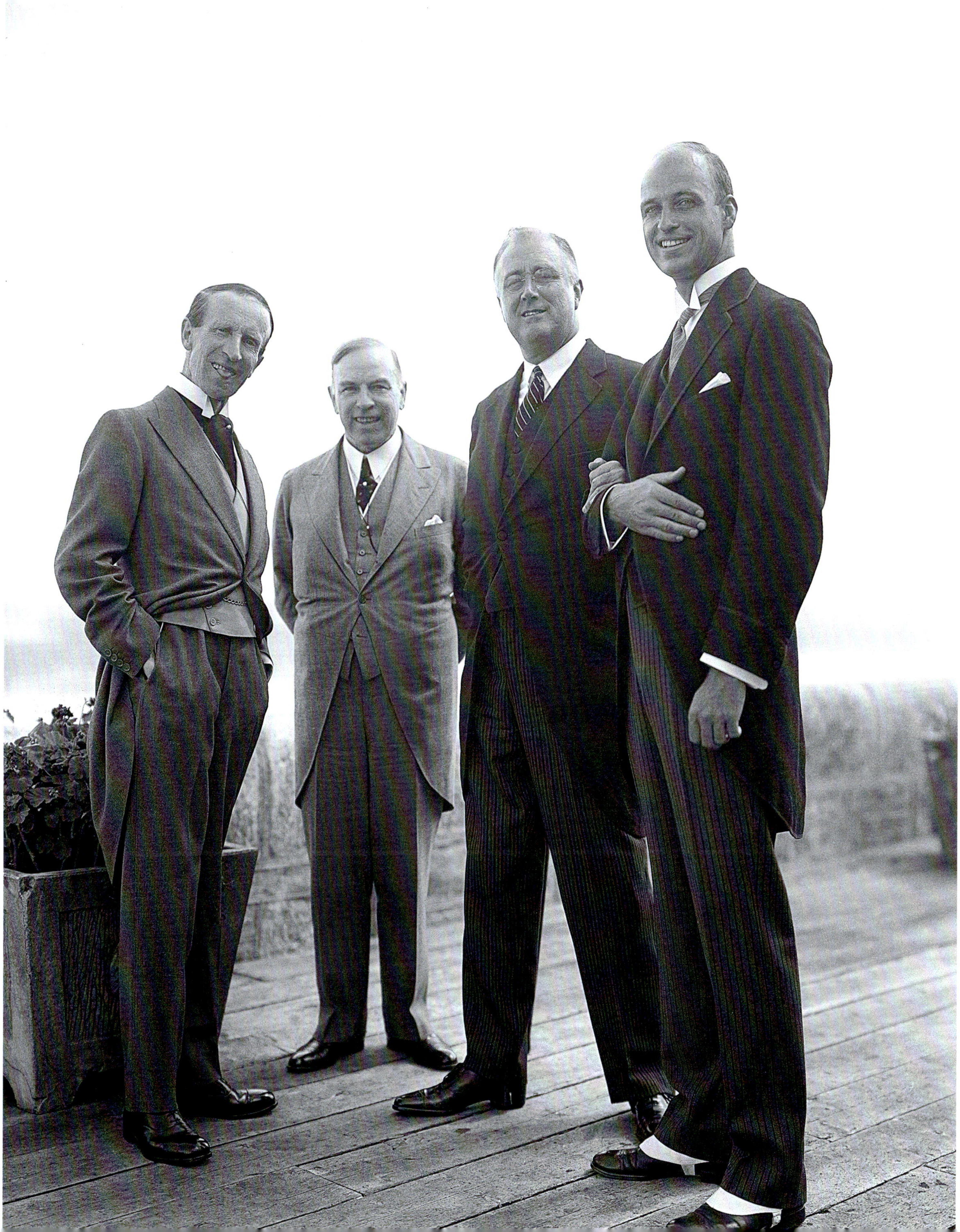

President Warren G. Harding

Stanley Park, Vancouver, British Columbia
July 16, 1923

———

I may as well confess to you at the outset a certain perplexity as to how I should address you. The truth of the matter is that this is the first time I have ever spoken as president in any country other than my own. Indeed, so far as I can recall, I am, with the single exception of my immediate predecessor [Woodrow Wilson], the first president in office even to set foot on politically foreign soil.

True, there is no definite inhibition upon one doing so, such as prevents any but a natural born citizen from becoming president, but an early prepossession soon developed into a tradition, and for more than a hundred years, held the effect of unwritten law. I am not prepared to say that the custom was not desirable, perhaps even needful, in the early days, when time was the chief requisite of travel. Assuredly too, at the present, the chief magistrate of a great republic ought not to cultivate the habit or make a hobby of wandering over all the continents of the Earth.

But exceptions are required to prove rules. And Canada is an exception, a most notable exception, from every viewpoint of the United States. You are not only our neighbour, but a very good neighbour, and we rejoice in your advancement and admire your independence, no less sincerely than we value your friendship.

I need not depict the points of similarity that make this attitude of the one toward the other irresistible. We think the same thoughts, live the same lives, and cherish the same aspirations of service to each other in times of need. Thousands of your brave lads perished in gallant and generous action for the preservation of our Union. Many of our young men followed Canadian colours to the battlefields of France before we entered the war and left their proportion of killed to share the graves of your intrepid sons.

This statement is brought very intimately home to me, for one of the brave lads in my own newspaper office felt the call of service to the colours of the sons of Canada. He went to the front, and gave his life with our boys for the preservation of the American and Canadian concept of civilization....

I may not address you, to be sure, as "fellow citizens," as I am accustomed to designate assemblages at home, but I may and do, with respect and pride, salute you as "fellow men," in mutual striving for common good. What an object lesson of peace is shown today by our two countries to all the world! No grim-faced fortifications mark our frontiers, no huge battleships patrol our dividing waters, no stealthy spies lurk in our tranquil border hamlets. Only a scrap of paper, recording hardly more than a simple understanding, safeguards lives and properties on the Great

[OPPOSITE]

A presidential first. President Warren Harding, shown here with Florence Harding, departs the USS Henderson *during their visit to Vancouver, July 26, 1923. On that date, Harding became the first president to officially visit Canada.*

FRIENDSHIP

Lakes, and only humble mileposts mark the inviolable boundary line for thousands of miles through farm and forest.

Our protection is in our fraternity, our armour is our faith; the tie that binds more firmly year by year is ever-increasing acquaintance and comradeship through interchange of citizens; and the compact is not of perishable parchment, but of fair and honourable dealing which, God grant, shall continue for all time.

> No grim-faced fortifications mark our frontiers, no huge battleships patrol our dividing waters, no stealthy spies lurk in our tranquil border hamlets.
> — President Warren G. Harding

An interesting and significant symptom of our growing mutuality appears in the fact that the voluntary interchange of residents to which I have referred is wholly free from restrictions. Our national and industrial exigencies have made it necessary for us, greatly to our regret, to fix limits to immigration from foreign countries.

But there is no quota for Canada. We gladly welcome all of your sturdy, steady stock who care to come, as a strengthening ingredient and influence. We nonetheless bid Godspeed and happy days to the thousands of our own folk, who are swarming constantly over your land and participating in its remarkable development. Wherever in either of our countries any inhabitant of the one or the other can best serve the interests of himself and his family is the place for him to be.

A further evidence of our increasing interdependence appears in the shifting of capital. Since the armistice, I am informed, approximately $2.5 billion has found its way from the United States into Canada for investment. That is a huge sum of money, and I have no doubt it is employed safely for us and helpfully for you. Most gratifying to you, moreover, should be the circumstance that one-half of that great sum has gone for purchase of your state and municipal bonds, a tribute, indeed, to the scrupulous maintenance of your credit, to a degree equalled only by your mother country across the sea and your sister country across the hardly visible border.

These are simple facts, which quickly resolve into history for guidance of mankind in the seeking of human happiness. "History, history!" ejaculated Lord Overton to his old friend, Lindsay, himself a historian, "what is the use of history? It only keeps people apart by reviving recollections of enmity."

[OPPOSITE]
What's a presidential visit without the Mounties? President Harding with Canadian dignitaries and members of the Royal Canadian Mounted Police in Vancouver.

FRIENDSHIP

President Bill Clinton also found time to golf in Canada, but President Warren Harding was the first to do that.

President Harding's parade procession to Stanley Park at the corner of Granville Street and Dunsmuir Street, on July 26, 1923.

FRIENDSHIP

As we look forth today upon the nations of Europe, with their armed camps of nearly a million more men in 1923 than in 1913, we cannot deny the grain of truth in this observation. But not so here! A hundred years of tranquil relationships, throughout vicissitudes which elsewhere would have evoked armed conflict rather than arbitration, affords truly, declared James Bryce, the finest example ever seen in history of an undefended frontier, whose very absence of armaments itself helped to prevent hostile demonstrations; thus proving beyond question that "peace can always be kept, whatever be the grounds of controversy, between peoples that wish to keep it."

It is public will, not public force, which makes for enduring peace.

— PRESIDENT WARREN G. HARDING

There is a great and highly pertinent truth, my friends, in that simple assertion. It is public will, not public force, which makes for enduring peace. And is it not a gratifying circumstance that it has fallen to the lot of us North Americans, living amicably for more than a century, under different flags, to present the most striking example yet produced of that basic fact? If only European countries would heed the lesson conveyed by Canada and the United States, they would strike at the root of their own continuing disagreements and, in their own prosperity, forget to inveigh constantly at ours. Not that we would reproach them for resentment or envy, which after all is but a manifestation of human nature. Rather should we sympathize with their seeming inability to break the shackles of age-long methods, and rejoice in our own relative freedom from the stultifying effect of Old World customs and practices? Our natural advantages are manifold and obvious.

We are not palsied by the habits of a thousand years. We live in the power and glory of youth. Others derive justifiable satisfaction from contemplation of their resplendent pasts. We have relatively only our present to regard, and that with eager eyes fixed chiefly and confidently upon our future. Therein lies our best estate. We profit both mentally and materially from the fact that we have no "departed greatness" to recover, no "lost provinces" to regain, no new territory to covet, no ancient grudges to gnaw eternally at the heart of our national consciousness. Not only are we happily exempt from these handicaps of vengeance and prejudice, but we are animated correspondingly and most helpfully by our better knowledge, derived from longer experience, of the blessings of liberty. These advantages we may not appreciate to the full at all times, but we know that we possess them, and the day is far distant when, if ever, we shall fail to cherish and defend them against any conceivable assault from without or from within our borders.

I find that, quite unconsciously, I am speaking of our two countries almost in the singular, when perhaps I should be more painstaking to keep them where they belong, in the plural. But I feel no need to apologize. You understand as well as I that I speak in no political sense. The ancient bugaboo of the United States scheming to annex Canada disappeared from all our minds years and years ago. Heaven knows we have all we can manage now, and room enough to spare for another hundred million, before approaching the intensive stage of existence of many European states.

> The ancient bugaboo of the United States scheming to annex Canada disappeared from all our minds years and years ago.
>
> — President Warren G. Harding

And if I might be so bold as to offer a word of advice to you, it would be this: Do not encourage any enterprise looking to Canada's annexation of the United States. You are one of the most capable governing peoples in the world, but I entreat you, for your own sakes, to think twice before undertaking management of the territory that lies between the Great Lakes and the Rio Grande.

No, let us go our own gaits along parallel roads, you helping us and we helping you. So long as each country maintains its independence, and both recognize their interdependence, those paths cannot fail to be highways of progress and prosperity. Nationality continues to be a supreme factor in modern existence; make no mistake about that; but the day for the Chinese wall, enclosing a hermit nation, has passed forever. Even though space itself were not in process of annihilation by airplane, submarine, wireless, and broadcasting, our very propinquity enjoins that most effective co-operation which comes only from clasping of hands in true faith and good fellowship.

It is precisely in that spirit, men and women of Canada, that I have stopped on my way home from a visit to our pioneers in Alaska to make a passing call upon my very good neighbour of the fascinating Iroquois name, "Kanada," glorious in her youth and strength and beauty, on behalf of my own beloved country. I stretch forth both my arms in the most cordial fraternal greeting, with gratefulness for your splendid welcome in my heart, and from my lips the whispered prayer of our famed Rip Van Winkle: "May you all live long and prosper!"

[OPPOSITE]
Thousands gathered in Stanley Park to greet President Harding.

FRIENDSHIP

BOSOM BUDDIES

PRESIDENTS AND PRIME MINISTERS SEE A LOT OF EACH OTHER. From annual summits such as the G7, G20, APEC, and others, to frequent bilateral meetings set up as needed and telephone conversations that happen more often than people sometimes imagine, these neighbours get plenty of time to mix company.

It's hardly surprising then that, upon occasion, the friendship between the countries rises to genuine and even close-knit camaraderie on a personal level. Brian Mulroney and Ronald Reagan sang "When Irish Eyes Are Smiling" together in Quebec City, and that bond passed on into a lifelong friendship between Mulroney and the Bush family. In fact, Mulroney holds the unique designation of eulogizing not one but two American presidents, having spoken at the funerals of both Ronald Reagan and George H.W. Bush, as well as the service for First Lady Nancy Reagan. Other relationships also took off. But the so-called bromance between Justin Trudeau and Barack Obama set a new watermark as the world celebrated their telegenic friendship during the final years of the Democratic president's second mandate.

He possessed a rare and prized gift called leadership, that ineffable and magical quality that sets some men and women apart so that millions will follow them …

— Prime Minister Brian Mulroney

FRIENDSHIP

Brian Mulroney

Tribute at President Reagan's State Funeral
Washington, D.C.
June 11, 2004

———

Presidents and prime ministers everywhere, I suspect, sometimes wonder how history will deal with them. Some even evince a touch of the insecurity of Thomas D'Arcy McGee, an Irish immigrant to Canada who became a father of our Confederation. In one of his poems, McGee, thinking of his birthplace, wrote poignantly,

> Am I remembered in Erin?
> I charge you, speak me true!
> Has my name a sound, a meaning,
> In the scenes my boyhood knew?

Former Soviet President Mikhail Gorbachev, former British Prime Minister Margaret Thatcher, and former Canadian Prime Minister Brian Mulroney take part in funeral services for former President Ronald Reagan at the National Cathedral in Washington, June 11, 2004.

WITH FAITH & GOODWILL

Ronald Reagan will not have to worry about Erin because they remember him well and affectionately there. Indeed they do. From Erin to Estonia, from Maryland to Madagascar, from Montreal to Monterey, Ronald Reagan does not enter history tentatively. He does so with certainty and panache. At home and on the world stage, his were not the pallid etchings of a timorous politician. They were the bold strokes of a confident and accomplished leader.

Some in the West, during the early 1980s, believed communism and democracy were equally valid and viable. This was the school of moral equivalence. In contrast, Ronald Reagan saw Soviet communism as a menace to be confronted in the genuine belief that its squalid underpinnings would fall swiftly to the gathering winds of freedom, provided, as he said, that NATO and the industrialized democracies stood firm and united. They did. And we know now who was right.

Ronald Reagan was a president who inspired his nation and transformed the world. He possessed a rare and prized gift called leadership, that ineffable and magical quality that sets some men and women apart so that millions will follow them as they conjure up grand visions and invite their countrymen to dream big and exciting dreams.

I always thought that President Reagan's understanding of the nobility of the presidency coincided with that American dream. One day, in Brussels, President Mitterrand, in referring

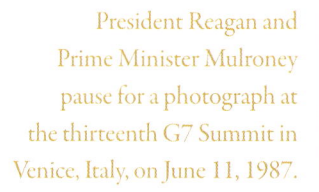

President Reagan and Prime Minister Mulroney pause for a photograph at the thirteenth G7 Summit in Venice, Italy, on June 11, 1987.

FRIENDSHIP

to President Reagan, said, "*Il a vraiment la notion de l'état*"; rough translation: "He really has a sense of the state about him."

The translation does not fully capture the profundity of the observation. What President Mitterrand meant is that there is a vast difference between the job of president and the role of president.

Ronald Reagan fulfilled both with elegance and ease, embodying himself that unusual alchemy of history and tradition and achievement and inspirational conduct and national pride that defined the special role the president of the United States of America must assume at all times at home and around the world.

La notion de l'état; no one understood it better than Ronald Reagan. And no one could more eloquently summon his nation to high purpose or bring forth the majesty of the presidency and make it glow better than the man who referred to his own nation as a city on the hill.

May our common future and that of our great nations be guided by wise men and women who will remember always the golden achievements of the Reagan era and the success that can be theirs if the values of freedom and democracy are preserved, unsullied and undiminished, until the unfolding decades can remember little else.

And no one could more eloquently summon his nation to high purpose
or bring forth the majesty of the presidency ...

— Prime Minister Brian Mulroney

I have been truly blessed to have been a friend of Ronald Reagan. I am grateful that our paths crossed and that our lives touched. I shall always remember him with the deepest admiration and affection. And I will always feel honoured by the journey that we travelled together in search of better and more peaceful tomorrows for all God's children everywhere.

And so in the presence of his beloved and indispensable Nancy, his children, his family, his friends, and all of the American people that he so deeply revered, I say *au revoir* today to a gifted leader and historic president and a gracious human being.

And I do so with a line from Yeats, who wrote, "Think where man's glory most begins and ends, / And say 'my glory was I had such friends.'"

President George H.W. Bush

On Brian Mulroney
Montreal, Quebec
June 1999

———

BRIAN MULRONEY, WITH WHOM I FIRST WORKED WITH AS VICE PRESIDENT, AFTER I became president, and as our relationship grew, I always appreciated his wise counsel, his constructive criticism — he could be very frank with the criticism, constructive criticism — and he'd offer these things up. We'd talk very frankly about U.S.-Canada issues, and also on issues of global import, I learned from him, a learned a lot from your prime minister. While I expect Brian paid a political price for being perceived as being too close to us, maybe to me, I can tell you however close our working relationship was, that Prime Minister Mulroney always had Canada's interest at the forefront of whatever discussion, never yielding on principle as to what was best for his country.

The Mulroney-Bush friendship continued until Bush's death in 2018. Here they are at the Bush family estate, Kennebunkport, Maine, 1990.

FRIENDSHIP

Joe Clark

On Jimmy Carter: "A Pretty Good Canadian"

———

My first encounter with President Jimmy Carter was indirect, but prophetic. I was leader of Her Majesty's Loyal Opposition in the Canadian Parliament, and was in Chicago in 1976, in the aftermath of Watergate, to meet Americans interested in Canada, and address the Chicago Council on Foreign Relations. One of the hosts of my visit was a leading figure in the Democratic Party of Illinois, who told me he would have to miss my speech because of a prior commitment to meet "my candidate for the Democratic nomination for the presidency, Governor Carter."

> In his Habitat for Humanity initiatives, Jimmy Carter doesn't just arrange for houses to be built, he helps actually build them.
> — Prime Minister Joe Clark

The Canadian: "I can certainly understand that priority, and I'm interested in Governor Carter. Could you tell me about him?"
The Democrat: "I've never met him."
The Canadian: "Why are you, a prominent Democrat, supporting a candidate you've never met?"
The Democrat: "Governor Carter is not implicated."

That was because Jimmy Carter had not been part of the Washington of Watergate — the scandals and distrusts of that period in American politics did not splash over to the governor of Georgia. Indeed, his style and temperament and reputation seemed to represent a clear departure from — almost a repudiation of — the politics of that era. Jimmy Carter was not part of that Washington milieu. He was an "outsider" in a system of "insiders." Many commentators believe that caused, or complicated, some of his challenges as president, and I'll leave that argument to Americans, and to historians.

WITH FAITH & GOODWILL

FRIENDSHIP

What is more striking is that virtually every observer agrees that those qualities as an outsider contributed significantly to his later, stellar success as the most significant former president in American history. His roots are unquestionably deep in his country — both in the "ideal" of America as a society of freedom and equality and opportunity, but embedded also in the practical attributes of American accomplishment — ambition, ability, faith, luck — and "can do" optimism, the profound belief that obstacles can be overcome.

But he strikes a higher chord than mere ambition and accomplishment — a chord of purpose, empathy, and obligation. Typically, in his Habitat for Humanity initiatives, Jimmy Carter doesn't just arrange for houses to be built, he helps actually build them. So the "outsider" status which may have hindered him in dealing with the power bases in his own superpower have made him sympathetic to, and influential among, people, countries, and groups who were themselves suspicious of, or were considered marginal by, those very power bases.

Jimmy Carter's interest in human rights and development was not simply an aspect of his presidency — it was at the core of his personality, and was seen to be genuine enough to be trustworthy.

Now, what does that have to do with Canada, and the relations between his presidency and our country? I see two impacts. One is systemic: However important our mutual trade, however broad and deep our human relations, however compelling our North American geography, Canada is not a major preoccupation of the "power bases" of the United States

[OPPOSITE]
Former Prime Minister Joe Clark, National Public Radio host Rickey Bevington, and former President Jimmy Carter shake hands in Atlanta, Georgia, at the 2017 launch for the first edition of *With Faith & Goodwill*.

[THIS PAGE]
Former U.S. President Jimmy Carter and Cuban President Fidel Castro leave Pierre Trudeau's funeral in Montreal on October 3, 2000. Their Montreal meeting led to Carter's historic visit to Cuba.

of America. That is true of American business, American workers, America's culture industries, and, in the case in question, certainly America's government and politics. In terms of actual "face time" — actual detailed attention by the leaders at the heart of any U.S. administration — we rank well below California, or New York, or Texas — or Cuba, or Russia, or Mexico, or China. That may not be a ranking by importance, but it is a ranking by attention.

Of course, in a real crisis, virtually any Canadian government can get the quick attention of Washington — but quick is different from sympathetic. And usually, on issues which are genuinely serious to Canada, our complex and multiple connections can make our voices heard — again, heard is different from heeded. We might be rich, and reasonable, and right next door, but we are rarely top-of-mind. That's why Canadian governments have to work so hard at ensuring our vital interests are understood in Washington.

In Jimmy Carter, we had two advantages. One was that he had actually worked here, with Canadians as partners, during a crucial and early period of his development and in an

Pierre Trudeau and Jimmy Carter, seen here with their wives Margaret Trudeau (right) and Rosalynn Carter (left) at the White House in 1977, remained friends the rest of Trudeau's life.

FRIENDSHIP

area of vital interest to him when he was later president. In the late fall of 1953, when he was only twenty-nine years old, Jimmy Carter was stationed with the U.S. Navy in upper New York State. When Canada's reactor at Chalk River, Ontario, went into crisis in December of that year, we sought assistance from our American neighbours. Lt. Jimmy Carter led a team that worked hand-in-hand with Canadians in cleaning up that damaged reactor. It was the very dawn of the nuclear age. President Carter's later biographer and colleague, Dr. Peter Bourne, has written about the profound impact these weeks in Canada had on Jimmy Carter.

Beyond that, he was interested in Canadian health care. Committed to providing a more comprehensive system of health care for his country, Jimmy Carter had examined our system and found much to admire in it. As much as any American president understands Canada, President Carter did. That was reflected in his working relationship with both Pierre Trudeau and myself, and, of course, was reflected in some of the testing last days of his presidency.

> In terms of what Jimmy Carter says and does in the world, **he's a pretty good Canadian.**
> — Prime Minister Joe Clark

Jimmy Carter was president in one of those unusual periods when the United States genuinely needed help, in extricating six American hostages from Iran, and Canada provided that help, quickly, effectively, in conditions of high risk, and without bargaining or posturing. The drama of how that happened — the courage and ingenuity of Ken and Pat Taylor and their colleagues in Tehran and Ottawa, the leadership of Flora MacDonald, the decisiveness of our Cabinet, the tensions in Parliament — are a separate story, but one result was that Canada was firmly and positively fixed in the minds of the American administration and public.

Canada's other advantage with Jimmy Carter was in the way he saw the world, which was broadly similar to the international goals which most Canadians supported, for at least sixty years after the end of World War II. That consonance of view was true generally during his presidency, but became even clearer in his conduct and priorities as a ground-breaking former president. His Carter Center could have been merely another important library, cataloguing and reflecting upon a presidency in turbulent times. He and Rosalynn Carter instead transformed it into an unprecedented international "bully pulpit," able to both enunciate high principles and then pursue them concretely. They are a beacon of the international values which most Canadians like to think we represent. In terms of what Jimmy Carter says and does in the world, he's a pretty good Canadian.

President Bill Clinton

On Jean Chrétien's Retirement
Syracuse, New York
Interview with Canadian Journalist Arthur Milnes
August 30, 2002

I THINK THAT HIS RECORD WILL ONLY GROW BRIGHTER IN THE YEARS AHEAD. I think the more time people have to reflect on the remarkable job he did, the more Canadians will appreciate him. I think, first of all, he was a great prime minister. He was great for the Canadian economy. He was great for Canada's leadership in the world on a whole host of issues. He was a real force for peace. He stood against ethnic cleansing. He stood against terrorism. Of course he [also] had tremendous political success and served a long time.

President Clinton on one of several golf outings with Prime Minister Chrétien, along with (from the left) Clinton's stepfather, Richard Kelley, Raymond Chrétien, and (on the far right) James Blanchard, April 1996. Both leaders have never revealed their golfing scores, labelling them "state secrets."

FRIENDSHIP

Prime Minister Justin Trudeau

Toast to Vice President Joe Biden
Ottawa, Ontario
December 8, 2016

———

IT IS AN EXTRAORDINARY PLEASURE TO BE HERE TONIGHT TO CELEBRATE AND MARK this extraordinary deep friendship between Canada and the United States, and host a state dinner for Vice President Joe Biden.

You know, about six months ago, President Obama graciously hosted a state dinner in Washington for us Canadians, but he sent Joe out of town that night and he missed it, so we're ever polite as Canadians, happy to be hosting Joe here tonight for his very own state dinner. Although, I have to say, there'll be no Ryan Reynolds or Blake Lively here tonight for you, Joe. I'm the only eye candy you get to sit with tonight.

But we've turned out our best tonight, not just in this room but outside of this room as we've put on our very best winter wonderland show for you. The first snowfall of the year in Ottawa is always wonderful, Joe, because the snow is fresh and clean and it hasn't yet turned into that grey sludge or cement we deal with for the rest of the ... winter.

But I ... it got me thinking. I went home tonight after work to help the kids with their homework and get them ready for bed, and then I decided to go for a run to clear my head, and as I ran

In Ottawa for the First Ministers' Meeting on December 9, 2016, Vice President Joe Biden shows with a big hug the warm friendship he and Prime Minister Justin Trudeau have for each other.

Prime Minister Justin Trudeau chats with Vice President Joe Biden in Ottawa on December 9, 2016.

through the snow, I got to thinking about the cycle of seasons, about how we Canadians thrive through whatever the conditions. And it got me thinking obviously about tonight and this extraordinary friendship between Canada and the United States. One that thrives through all the cycles of political seasons, whether it's warm sunshine or heavy snow, whether it's paddling in a canoe over a glassy lake or lifting the elbows in the corners in a hockey game, we do very well in all conditions, and this friendship endures through whatever situations we encounter.

It's a special friendship. One that is unique on the world stage. As all good friends, we agree on a great many things and disagree on a few others, but always remain united in our hope for a stronger North America, and mostly, a better world for our kids and our grandkids. We are the closest of friends, steadfast partners, and unwavering allies.

Our relationship is bigger than trade and security. Canada and the U.S. share common core values like equality of opportunity, and the fundamental belief that if you work hard, you will succeed. I believe in these values and I know Joe does, too. His life's work in politics reflects that.

As most people in this room know, Joe has dedicated the past four decades of his life to public service since his election to the U.S. Senate in 1973. And the first time I met Joe a number of months ago he told me stories of my dad and how they had gotten along famously well back in the 1970s when he was a young senator and my father was doing what he was doing up here. And I know that my dad and Joe had some great talks about public service and political life in the 1970s, and I know all of us would've loved to have been a fly on the wall in those conversations.

Because Joe has fought all his life for causes he believes in. Things like combatting sexual assault, domestic violence, and gun violence. It's fitting for Joe to visit us right now at the tail end of the 16 Days of Activism Against Gender-Based Violence campaign. This has long been an important cause for him and we thank him for his continued leadership on the world stage on this issue.

And Joe's commitment and the United States' commitment to helping the middle class grow and prosper is one that we certainly share.

So, Joe, it's a pleasure to have you with us in Ottawa for a few days. Tomorrow will be a great opportunity for you to hear from provincial, territory, and Indigenous leaders, many of whom are here with us tonight — thank you for being here — for you to hear about climate change, about clean growth, and about the far-reaching impact and importance of this Canada-U.S. friendship. A tried and tested partnership, Canada and the U.S. will forever remain friends and allies as we tackle the world's greatest challenges together.

Thank you for your leadership, Joe, and thank you for your, and for your country's, enduring friendship. Thank you, my friend.

FRIENDSHIP

Brian Mulroney

Eulogy for the Late President George H.W. Bush
State Funeral, Washington, D.C.
December 5, 2018

———

Do you remember where you were the summer you left your teenage years behind and turned twenty? I was working as a labourer in my hometown in northern Quebec trying to make enough money to get back into law school. It was a tough job, but I was safe and secure and had the added benefit of my mother's home cooking every night.

On September 2, 1944, twenty-year-old Lieutenant George Bush was preparing to attack Japanese war installations in the Pacific. He was part of a courageous generation of young Americans who led the charge against overwhelming odds in the historic and bloody battle for supremacy in the Pacific against the colossal military might of Imperial Japan. That's what George Bush did the summer he turned twenty.

Many men of differing talents and skills have served as president, and many more will do so as the decades unfold, bringing new strength and glory to these United States of America. And fifty or one hundred years from now, as historians review the accomplishments and the context of all who have served as president, I believe it will be said that in the life of this country, the United States ... I believe it will be said that no occupant of the Oval Office was more courageous, more principled, and more honourable than George Herbert Walker Bush.

George Bush was a man of high accomplishment, but he also had a delightful sense of humour and was a lot of fun. At his first NATO meeting in Brussels, as the new American president, he

> I believe it will be said that no occupant of the Oval Office was **more courageous, more principled,** and more **honourable** than **George Herbert Walker Bush.**
>
> — Prime Minister Brian Mulroney

President Donald Trump, First Lady Melania Trump, former President Barack Obama and Michelle Obama, former President Bill Clinton and Hillary Rodham Clinton, and former President Jimmy Carter listen intently to Mulroney.

sat opposite me, actually, that day.... After [other leaders] had spoken, it was the turn of the prime minister of Iceland who ... went on and on and on and on, ending only when the secretary general of NATO firmly decreed a coffee break. George put down his pen, walked over to me, and said, "Brian, I've just learned the fundamental principle of international affairs." I said, "What's that, George?" He said, "The smaller the country, the longer the speech."

In the second year of the Bush presidency ... the Soviet Union imploded. This was, in my judgment, the most epical event, political event, of the twentieth century. An ominous situation that could have become extremely menacing to world security was instead deftly challenged by the leadership of President Bush ... providing the Russian people with the opportunity to build an embryonic democracy in a country that had been ruled by czars and tyrants over a thousand years. And then, as the Berlin Wall collapsed ... leaving dictators and dogma in the trash can of history, no challenge assumed greater importance for Western solidarity than the unification of Germany within an unswerving NATO. But all fears in Western Europe and unrelenting hostility by the military establishment in the Soviet Union

FRIENDSHIP

and the Warsaw Pact rendered this initiative among the most complex and sensitive ever undertaken. One serious misstep and this entire process could have been compromised perhaps irretrievably....

Much has been written about the First Gulf War. Simply put, the coalition of twenty-nine disparate nations assembled under the aegis of the United Nations ... and led by the United States, will rank with the most spectacular and successful international initiatives ever undertaken in modern history, designed to punish an aggressor, defend the cause of freedom, and ensure order in a region that had seen too much of the opposite for far too long. This was President Bush's initiative from beginning to end.

President Bush was also responsible for the North American Free Trade Agreement ... which created the largest and richest free trade area in the history of the world [and his] decision to go forward with strong environmental legislation, including the Clean Air Act, that resulted in the acid raid accord with Canada is a splendid gift to future generations of Americans and Canadians to savour in the air they breathe and the water they drink and the forests they enjoy and the lakes, rivers, and streams they cherish. There's a word for this. It's called leadership. Leadership.

And let me tell you, that when George Bush was the president of the United States of America, every single head of government in the world knew that they were dealing with a gentleman, a genuine leader, one who was distinguished, resolute, and brave.

Former Prime Minister Brian Mulroney was perhaps former President George H.W. Bush's closest friend among world leaders. Here, he delivers the late president's eulogy.

FRICTIONS

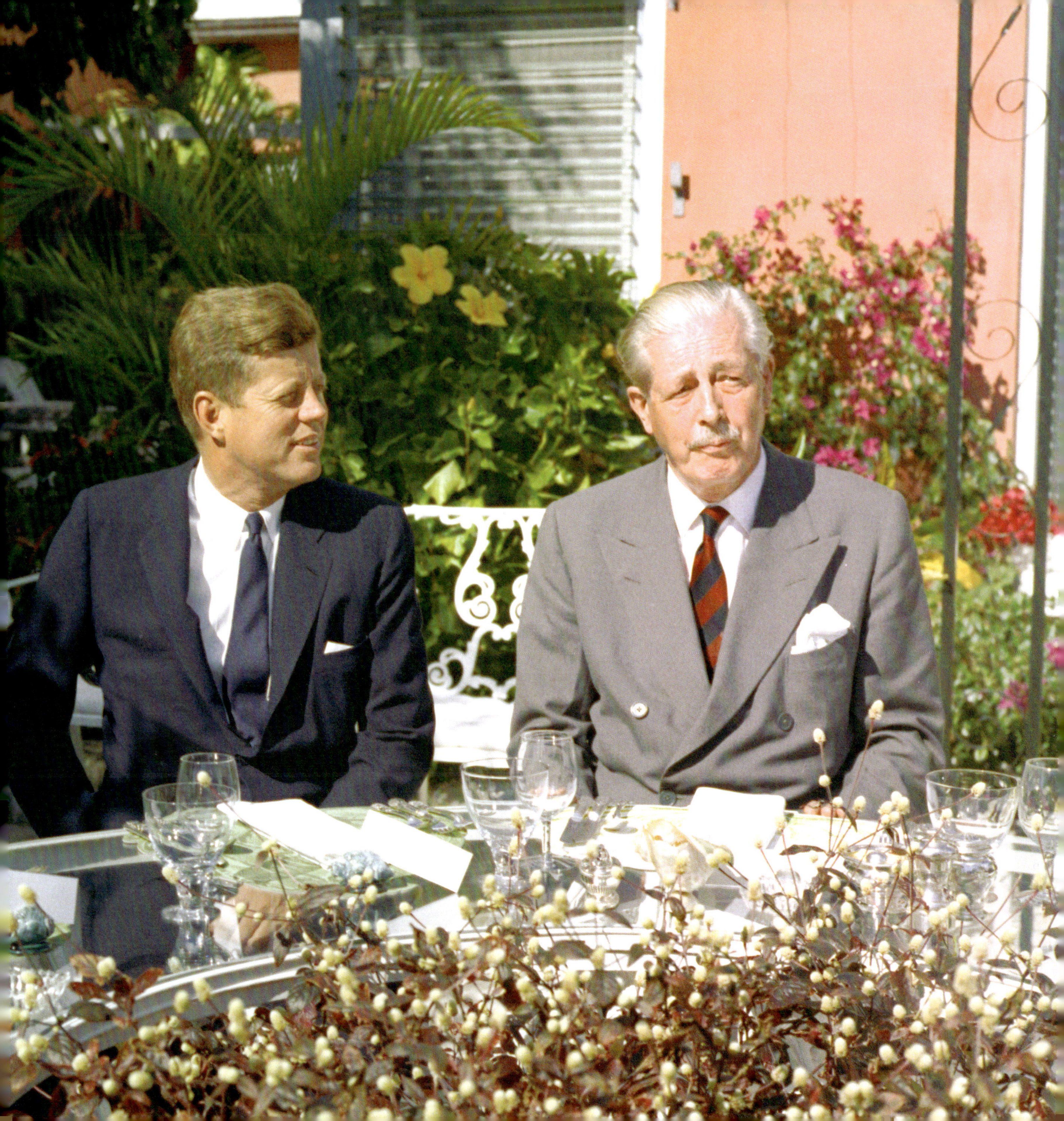

THE SKIPPER OF THE U.S. NAVY'S *PT-109* COULD CUSS LIKE A SAILOR. And when it came to his relationship with John Diefenbaker, John Kennedy did a lot of that. Diefenbaker once even accused Kennedy of writing "S.O.B." on a memo the president inadvertently left behind in the Prime Minister's Office after one of the pair's stormy meetings. Kennedy denied he'd ever do something that stupid on an official memo. He told his friend, journalist Ben Bradlee, "At that time, I didn't think Diefenbaker was a son of a bitch. I thought he was a prick."

On another occasion, after the alleged "S.O.B." incident, Diefenbaker invited himself to a meeting in the Caribbean taking place between Kennedy and the British prime minister, Harold Macmillan. After threatening not to attend the lunch hastily scheduled to include Diefenbaker, Kennedy relented. Don't think, however, that the hero of *PT-109* enjoyed the experience. "There we sat," he later said, "like three whores at a christening."

There probably hasn't been another bilateral hatred as deep as the one between Diefenbaker and JFK in our long joint history. And Diefenbaker gave as good as he got. (He had kinder thoughts for Jimmy Carter, though. In his last speech to the House of Commons, shortly before his death in 1979, Diefenbaker called for President Carter to receive the Nobel Peace Prize for brokering the Camp David Peace Accord between Israel and Egypt.)

Just as personal relations among next-door neighbours are sometimes strained, so, too, has an apparently too-close association with the neighbours not always been seen as a good thing.

Just ask President Chester A. Arthur. Born in northern Vermont near the Canadian border, Arthur was subjected to a nasty dose of negative campaigning when he was tapped to be James

[PREVIOUS PAGE]
"Like three whores at a christening" was how JFK described being forced to break bread with John Diefenbaker in Nassau, Bahamas, in December 1962. The United Kingdom's Harold Macmillan was also no fan of Dief but didn't leave as delicious a description of the trio's lunch as Kennedy did.

WITH FAITH & GOODWILL

In 1962, to the anger of President John F. Kennedy in particular, Prime Minister John Diefenbaker invited himself to a luncheon in the Caribbean with JFK and Harold Macmillan, Britain's prime minister. JFK barely hid his negative feelings toward Diefenbaker on that day.

Canada's seventeenth prime minister, John Napier Turner, led the opposition to the free trade agreement reached by President Ronald Reagan and Prime Minister Brian Mulroney. Turner's entire 1988 election campaign was built around resisting the deal. He took his concerns directly to Reagan during a private meeting in Ottawa with the visiting president in April 1987.

FRICTIONS

Garfield's running mate in 1880. His opponents started a whispering campaign that quickly went public. Arthur was accused of being Canadian-born and therefore ineligible to serve. The "birther" phenomenon was alive well before the Obama era.

Canadian journalist Lawrence Martin, a student of the relations between presidents and prime ministers, reminds us in his book *The Presidents and the Prime Ministers* of some of the less-than-flattering views early Canadian leaders had of their American counterparts. "These Yankee politicians are the lowest race of thieves in existence," observed future prime minister Sir John Thompson from Washington in the late nineteenth century. "Nothing will come of our mission but the board bills." Thanks again to Lawrence Martin, we are aware of Sir John A. Macdonald's private views during one early negotiation. "I think the Americans are bargaining like costermongers," Macdonald wrote.

> These Yankee politicians are **the lowest race of thieves in existence.**
> — Prime Minister Sir John Thompson

Former U.S. ambassador to Canada Gordon Giffin used the term "Goldilocks conundrum" to describe the balancing act prime ministers have to perform in their dealings with presidents. This means a prime minister can neither get too close nor be too distant from the occupant of the White House. The Canadian, Giffin continued, must get it "just right." And if this wasn't hard enough, Giffin points out that the definition of just right varies greatly by region in Canada.

In the future we can expect that no leader on either side of the border will ever get it just right and satisfy all, but we can be sure of one thing: Canadians and Americans will be watching keenly as they try.

THE TIMES THEY ARE A-CHANGING

The 1960s and 1970s saw times of wrenching change and upheaval on both sides of the border. Cold War tensions were at their height. Vietnam added still more tension with millions of American youth joining the counter-culture revolution and many more heading north to live in Canada as draft dodgers. Civil rights marches, FLQ bombings and, of course, Watergate created a period of nearly constant change that altered the relationship between citizens and their leaders.

It is hardly surprising, therefore, that this same period saw some of the more obvious frictions between Canada and the United States. Differences of policy were compounded by significant differences of personality. Jack Kennedy ushered in Camelot while John Diefenbaker struggled to keep his own Cabinet together. LBJ's Texas-sized power politics contrasted with the diplomatic gentility of Lester B. Pearson. Pearson, however, dropped his diplomatic mask when he walked into the United States and publicly questioned Johnson's handling of the Vietnam War. This led to a stormy meeting between the two leaders at Camp David and accusations that LBJ grabbed Pearson and lifted him off his feet in anger. And Richard Nixon and Pierre Trudeau were, at least by virtue of outward appearances, as different as two leaders could possibly be.

Prime Minister Lester B. Pearson

Convocation Address, Temple University
Philadelphia, Pennsylvania
April 2, 1965

In this tragic conflict [the Vietnam War], the United States intervened to help South Vietnam defend itself against aggression and at the request of the government of the country that was under attack. Its motives were honourable; neither mean nor imperialistic.

FRICTIONS

The Johnson treatment. Prime Minister Pearson and Maryon Pearson, President Johnson and Lady Bird Johnson, Secretary Dean Rusk, Texas Governor John Connally, and others during an informal visit to LBJ's ranch in Stonewall, Texas, on January 15, 1965.

Lost friendship. The relations between LBJ and Pearson never fully recovered from Pearson's very undiplomatic address on Vietnam in the United States.

Its sacrifices have been great and they were not made to advance any selfish American interest. United States civilians doing peaceful work had been wantonly murdered.

The dilemma is acute and seems intractable. On the one hand, no nation — and particularly no newly independent nation — could ever feel secure if capitulation in Vietnam led to the sanctification of aggression through subversion and spurious "wars of national liberation."

On the other hand, the progressive application of military sanctions can encourage stubborn resistance, rather than a willingness to negotiate. Continued and stepped-up intensification of hostilities in Vietnam could lead to uncontrollable escalation.

> **Continued and stepped-up intensification of hostilities in Vietnam could lead to uncontrollable escalation.**
>
> — Prime Minister Lester B. Pearson

What are the conditions for such a settlement? First, a cease-fire. Aggressive action by North Vietnam to bring about a Communist "liberation" (which means Communist rule) of the South must end. Only then can there be negotiation.

There are many factors which I am not in a position to weigh. But there does appear to be at least a possibility that a suspension of such air strikes against North Vietnam, at the right time, might provide the Hanoi authorities with an opportunity, if they wish to take it, to inject some flexibility into their policy without appearing to do so as the direct result of military pressure.

If such a suspension took place for a limited time, then the rate of incidents in South Vietnam would provide a fairly accurate way of measuring its usefulness and the desirability of continuing it. I am not, of course, proposing any compromise on points of principle, nor any weakening of resistance to aggression by South Vietnam; indeed, resistance may require increased military strength to be used against the armed and attacking communists. I merely suggest that a measured and announced pause in one field of military action at the right time might facilitate the development of diplomatic resources which cannot easily be applied to the problem under the existing circumstances.

President Richard Nixon

Address to a Joint Session of Parliament
Ottawa, Ontario
April 14, 1972

———

Ever since Canadians learned via the infamous Watergate tapes that Richard Nixon once called Pierre Trudeau an "asshole," a myth has taken hold that the two leaders had a relationship that was anything but productive for Canada and the United States. The truth is much more complicated. While neither would have likely chosen the other as a friend, it is also true that both men were highly professional and knew their jobs well. President Nixon's address to Canada's Parliament is a case in point. Trudeau and his officials had direct input into the president's address that day, and the speech, even today, stands as a hallmark of civility and reason regarding the bilateral relationship. And when Nixon was at his lowest during the Watergate scandal, Trudeau even picked up the phone and called his colleague in Washington to offer him personal support. Appearances, as the Trudeau-Nixon relationship demonstrates, are definitely not always what they seem.

• • •

I am grateful for this chance to return to Canada, for the opportunity of signing here a historic agreement to restore and protect forever the quality of the Great Lakes we share together. That agreement testifies to the continuing vitality of our unique relationship, which has been described so eloquently by the prime minister. I wish to discuss that relationship today in a way that has not always been customary when leaders of our two countries have met.

Through the years, our speeches on such occasions have often centred on the decades of unbroken friendship that we have enjoyed, and on our four thousand miles of unfortified boundary. In focusing on our peaceful borders and our peaceful history, they have tended to gloss over the fact that there are real problems between us. They have tended to create the false impression that our countries are essentially alike.

It is time for Canadians and Americans to move beyond the sentimental rhetoric of the past. It is time for us to recognize that we have very separate identities; that we have significant differences; and that nobody's interests are furthered when these realities are obscured.

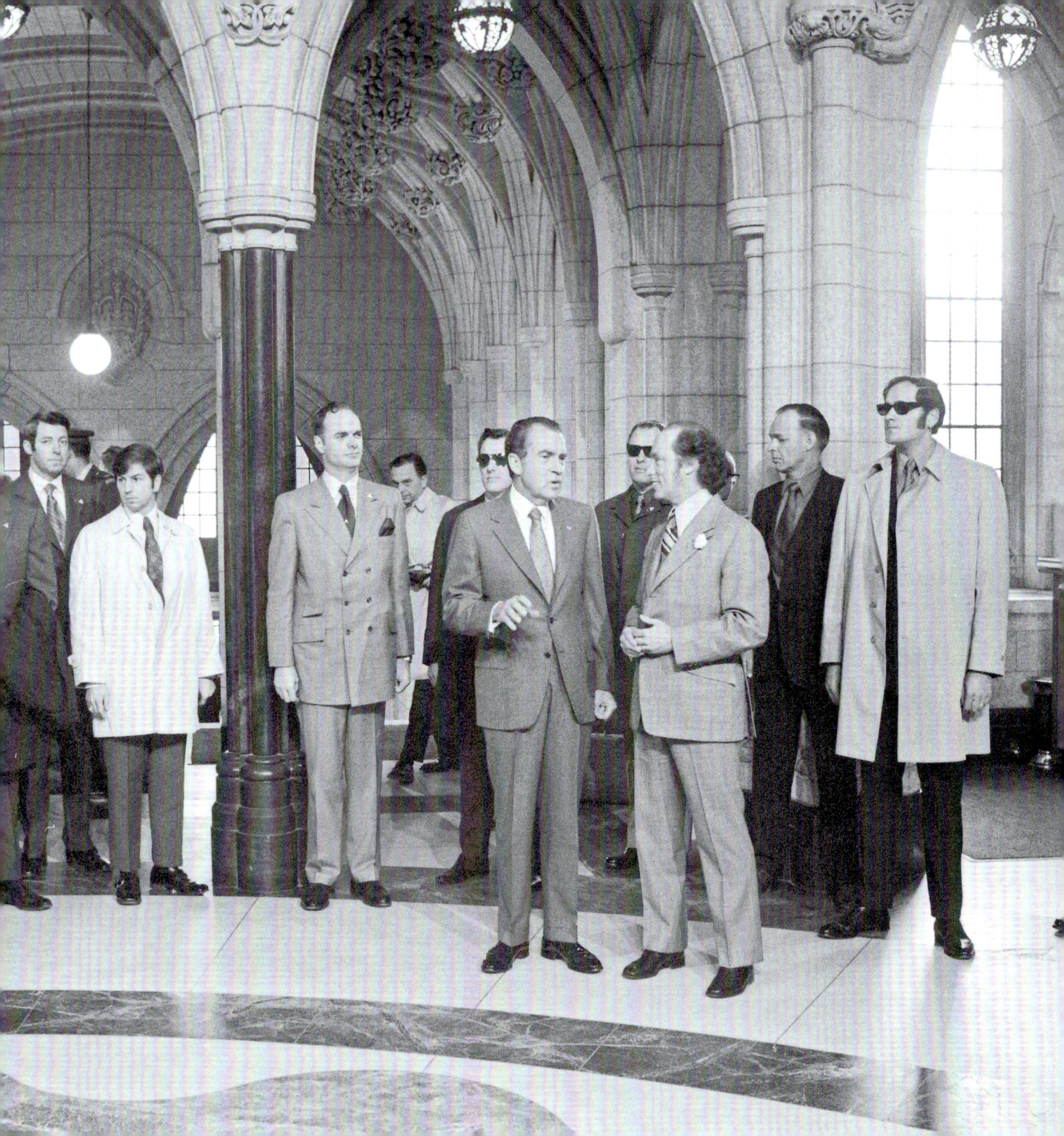

Our peaceful borders and our peaceful history are important symbols, to be sure. What they symbolize, however, is the spirit of respect and restraint which allows us to co-operate, despite our differences, in ways which help us both.

American policy toward Canada is rooted in that spirit. Our policy toward Canada reflects the new approach we are taking in all of our foreign relations — an approach which has been called the Nixon Doctrine. That doctrine rests on the premise that mature partners must have autonomous, independent policies. Each nation must define the nature of its own interests. Each nation must decide the requirements of its own security. Each nation must determine the path of its own progress.

> It is time for Canadians and Americans to move beyond the sentimental rhetoric of the past.
> — President Richard Nixon

What we seek is a policy which enables us to share international responsibilities in a spirit of international partnership. We believe that the spirit of partnership is strongest when partners are self-reliant. For among nations — as within nations — the soundest unity is that which respects diversity and the strongest cohesion is that which rejects coercion.

Over the years, the people of Canada have come to understand these concepts particularly well. Within your own borders, you have been working to bring a wide variety of peoples and provinces and points of view into a great national union — a union which honours the integrity of its constituent elements.

It was Prime Minister Laurier who said of Canada's differing components: "I want the marble to remain the marble; I want the granite to remain the granite; I want the oak to remain the oak." This has been the Canadian way. As a result, Canadians have helped to teach the world, as Governor General Massey once said, that the "toleration of differences is the measure of civilization."

Today, more than ever before, we need to apply that understanding to the whole range of world affairs. And to begin with, we must apply it to our dealings with one another. We must realize that we are friends, not because there have been no problems between us, but because we have trusted one another enough to be candid about our problems — and because our candour has nourished our co-operation.

[OPPOSITE]
Very different men. President Richard Nixon and Prime Minister Pierre Trudeau in the rotunda of the Centre Block, Parliament Hill, April 1972.

Last December, your prime minister and I met in Washington, and he asked me if I thought that the United States would always want a surplus trade balance with Canada so that we could always export capital here. My answer then, and my answer now, is "no." As I said to him at that time, we in the United States saw this same problem from the other side before World War I. We then depended on European capital for our development, and we wanted to free ourselves from that dependence. And so we fully understand that Canada is in that same position today.

Canada is the largest trading partner of the United States. It is very important that that be noted in Japan, too. *[Laughter.]* Our economies have become highly interdependent. But the fact of our mutual interdependence and our mutual desire for independence need not be inconsistent traits. No self-respecting nation can or should accept the proposition that it should always be economically dependent upon any other nation. And so, let us recognize, once and for all, that

> We must realize that we are friends, **not because there have been no problems between us,** but because we have trusted one another enough to be candid about our problems …
> — President Richard Nixon

the only basis for a sound and healthy relationship between our two proud peoples is to find a pattern of economic interaction which is beneficial to both our countries — and which respects Canada's right to chart its own economic course.

We must also build a new spirit of partnership within the Western hemisphere that we share together. It has been said that Canada is bounded "on the north by gold, on the west by the East, on the east by history, and on the south by friends." We hope that will always be the case and we hope it will be the case not only with respect to the United States, your immediate neighbour to the south, but with respect to all your southern neighbours — and ours — who are bound by the great forces of geography and history which are distinctive to the New World.

But geography and history alone do not make a community. A true community must be a living entity in which the individuality of each member is a source of pride to all members, in which the unity of all is a source of strength to each. The great community of the Americas

[OPPOSITE]
President Nixon addressing Parliament, April 14, 1972.

FRICTIONS

WITH FAITH & GOODWILL

FRICTIONS

cannot be complete without the participation of Canada. That is why we have been encouraged by the recent decisions of Canada to upgrade its participation as an observer in the Organization of American States to ambassadorial status, and to apply for membership in the Inter-American Development Bank, for both of these institutions make the abstract concept of community within the Americas a living reality.

It is our responsibility to make this new world a better world
than the world we have known.
— PRESIDENT RICHARD NIXON

A sound concept of community is also important in another international arena that we share, the Atlantic Alliance. Just one month after my inauguration as president of the United States, I observed that a new spirit of co-operation within that Alliance was essential, as we began a new search for co-operation between East and West. The recent agreements concerning Berlin — the fact, for example, that thousands of families were reunited this Easter for the first time in many years — these are among the first fruits of a new era of East-West negotiation.

But as we seek better relations with our adversaries, it becomes all the more important to strengthen the alliances with our friends. We must never forget that the strength and the unity of the West has been an indispensable element in helping to bring about the new era of negotiation with the East. And that is why we began our round of summit talks last December by meeting with the prime minister of Canada, and then with the leaders of other close allies. That is why our East-West conversations will always be accompanied by full and genuine consultation within the Atlantic Alliance. That Alliance began as a way of pooling military resources. Today, it is a way of pooling our intellectual and our diplomatic resources as well. Like our federal approaches to nationhood, like our Canadian-American brotherhood, like our inter-American neighbourhood, the Atlantic Alliance has achieved a creative unity in which the individuality of its members is respected and advanced.

Let us turn now to the world as a whole — for this is where the challenge of building a true community will be most difficult and most important. We in Canada and the United States have always been proud to live in what is called the New World. Today, there is a new world coming for everyone who lives on this globe. It is our responsibility to make this new world a better world than the world we have known.

[OPPOSITE]
Nixon and Trudeau meeting in the Oval Office in 1971. It was later revealed via the Watergate Tapes that Nixon called Trudeau an "asshole."

Canadians and Americans have fought and died together in two world wars in this century. We live now in what has been called the post-war era. But mankind has known a long succession of post-war eras. And each one of them has turned out to be a pre-war era as well. The challenge we face today is to build a permanent post-war era — an era of lasting peace.

My visit to Ottawa comes midway between visits to Peking and to Moscow. In many respects, these journeys are very different. In the People's Republic of China, we opened a new dialogue after twenty-two years of virtually no communication. In the Soviet Union, there is an opportunity to bring a continuing dialogue to productive conclusions. But in their central aim, these journeys to Peking and Moscow are alike. Neither visit is directed against anyone — adversary or ally. Both are for the betterment of everyone — for the peace of all mankind. However, we must not allow the fact of summit meetings to create any unrealistic euphoria.

The responsibility for building peace rests with special weight upon the great powers. Whether the great powers fulfill that responsibility depends not on the atmospherics of their diplomacy, but on the realities of their behaviour. Great powers must not treat a period of *détente* as an interlude between periods of tension. Better relations among all nations require restraint by great nations, both in dealing with each other and in dealing with the rest of the world.

We can agree to limit arms. We can declare our peaceful purposes. But neither the limitation of arms nor the declaration of peaceful purposes will bring peace if, directly or indirectly, the aggressive use of existing weapons is encouraged. And great powers cannot avoid responsibility for the aggressive actions of those to whom they give the means for embarking on such actions. The great powers must use their influence to halt aggression — and not to encourage it. The structure of world peace cannot be built unless the great powers join together to build it, and its strength will grow only as all nations — of all political and social systems —come to accept its validity and sustain its vitality....

As we have prepared for both of these journeys, the experience of Canada has been most helpful. I am grateful to both the prime minister and to the opposition leader, Mr. [Robert L.] Stanfield, for sharing their insights with us as we embark on these endeavours.

As we continue toward our common quest for a better world order, let us apply the lessons we have learned so well on this continent:

- that we can walk our own road in our own way without moving further apart, that we can grow closer together without growing more alike;
- that peaceful competition can produce winners without producing losers, that success for some need not mean setbacks for others;
- that a rising tide will lift all our boats, that to go forward at all is to go forward together;
- that the enemy of peace is not independence but isolation, and that the way to peace is an open world.

FRICTIONS

And let us remember, too, these truths that we have found together:

- that variety can mean vitality;
- that diversity can be a force for progress; and
- that our ultimate destiny is indivisible.

When I spoke at the St. Lawrence Seaway ceremonies in 1969, I borrowed some words from the monument there which I had joined Queen Elizabeth in dedicating just ten years before. That monument, as its inscription puts it, "bears witness to the common purpose of two nations whose frontiers are the frontiers of friendship, whose ways are the ways of freedom, whose works are the works of peace."

For the ability of our two nations, Canada and the United States, to preserve the frontiers of friendship, to walk in the ways of freedom, and to pursue the works of peace provides example and encouragement to all …

— PRESIDENT RICHARD NIXON

The truth to which that inscription testifies is of profound importance to people everywhere in this world. For the ability of our two nations, Canada and the United States, to preserve the frontiers of friendship, to walk in the ways of freedom, and to pursue the works of peace provides example and encouragement to all who seek those same objectives, wherever they may live.

There is nothing more exciting than a time of new beginnings. A member of this body [Sir George Foster] caught that spirit when he spoke in Parliament about the beginnings of Canadian nationhood one hundred years ago. Listen to him: "Blood pulsed in our veins, new hopes fired our hearts, new horizons lifted and widened, new visions came to us in the night watches."

May that same sense of excitement inspire our two nations as we help lead the world to new beginnings today.

ECONOMIC TENSIONS

The increasing integration of the American and Canadian economies has generated a host of benefits for people in both countries. This has always been true, but globalizing forces and the maturation of NAFTA have given rise to particular complexity since the 1980s. Naturally, with such entwined interests there occasionally arise conflicts.

For Canadian leaders, the economic power of the United States makes it imperative to keep these conflicts well managed. But prime ministers are also elected leaders, and from time to time it proves necessary to show that the mouse is capable of roaring. And U.S. presidents know that the White House must always appear focused on putting its people first.

Prime Minister Paul Martin

Economic Club of New York
October 6, 2005

Representing nearly one-third of the world's gross domestic product, North America has become the largest trading bloc on the planet. And at last count, Canada was the number one export destination for thirty-nine of the fifty United States. Last year's trade between Canada and the state of New York alone was worth more than $30 billion. Canada is also the number one export market for states as far south as Georgia and Alabama. That is why so many U.S. governors pay close attention to our trade arrangements. NAFTA has enabled our two countries to integrate our economies with uncommon precision. Our north-south trade corridors are reliable and secure, and have created opportunities for growth in just about every region and every sector of our economies. In short, our partnership has presented us with enormous opportunities.

But, speaking frankly, it has also presented us with challenges. Over the years we have met these with open and constructive dialogue. This is how friends talk to each other. So as well

[OPPOSITE]
Prime Minister Martin delivering his remarks. Menu items included softwood lumber and Canadian beef.

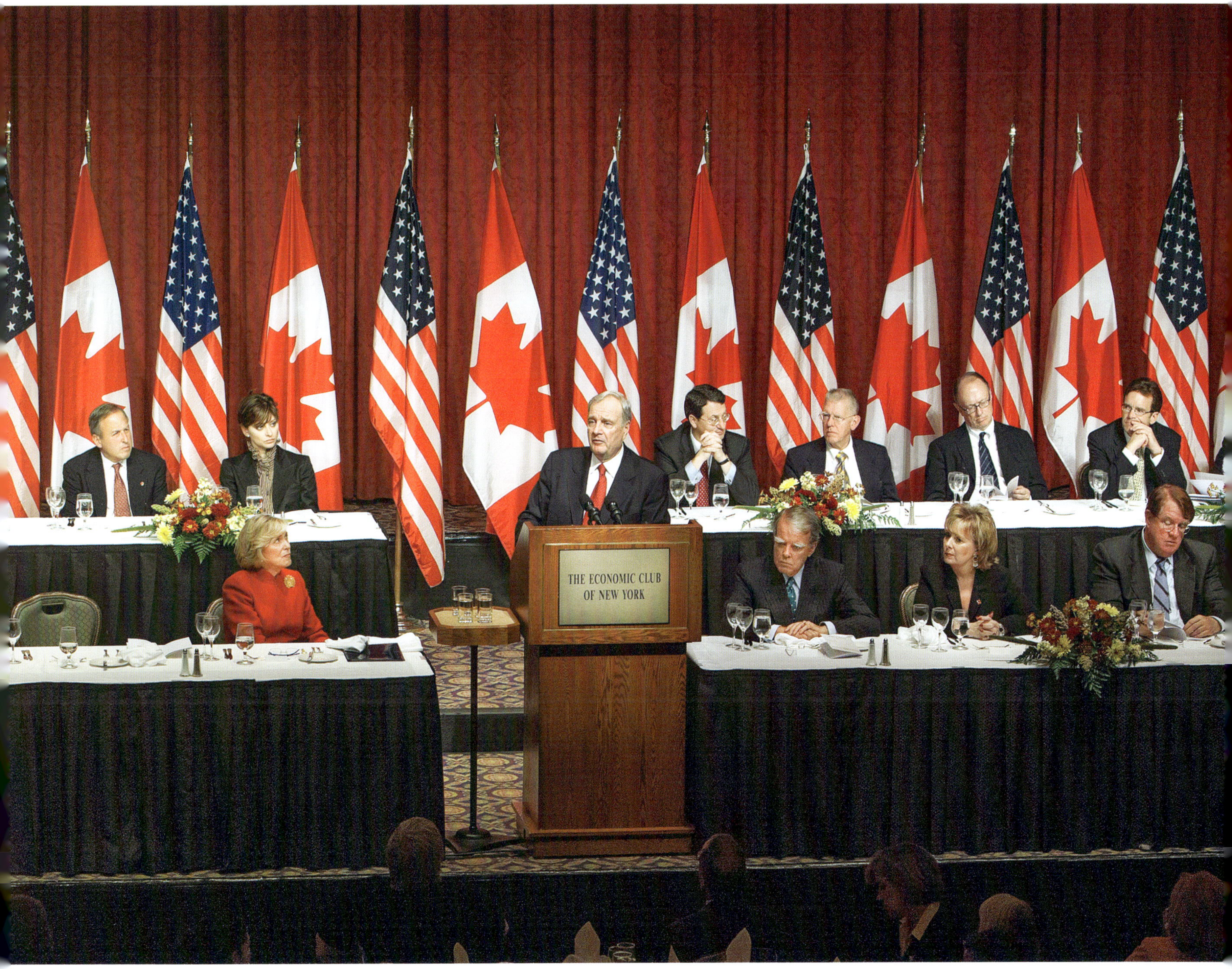
THE ECONOMIC CLUB
OF NEW YORK

as talking about the ways our partnership is working, I would like to highlight two concerns tonight. First, the softwood lumber dispute, what it symbolizes about NAFTA, and our respect for the dispute settlement mechanism we have in place to protect its integrity.

The softwood lumber issue is basically a disagreement between special interests in the U.S. and your national interest. Canada provides about one-third of your softwood lumber supply. We trade this commodity fairly and within the agreed rules of NAFTA. But in the last several years our firms have been charged a total of $5 billion in tariffs.

Forgive my sudden departure from the safe language of diplomacy, but this is nonsense.
More than that, it's a breach of faith.
Countries must live up to their agreements.
— Prime Minister Paul Martin

This, in spite of the fact that Canada has won panel decision after panel decision under NAFTA's process for the settlement of disputes. Recently, we won a unanimous decision which confirmed these findings — this, in NAFTA's "Final Court of Appeal," which included a majority of U.S. judges. The problem is, instead of honouring this decision, the United States has decided to ignore it.

Forgive my sudden departure from the safe language of diplomacy, but this is nonsense. More than that, it's a breach of faith. Countries must live up to their agreements. The duties must be refunded. Free trade must be fair trade.

In any business relationship, you're going to have differences of opinion, but you establish a mechanism to settle these differences, you accept the verdict, and move on. NAFTA established such a mechanism, and ignoring it hurts not just Canadians, but Americans.

Supporting the integrity of NAFTA is in your self-interest. According to numbers cited by the *Wall Street Journal*, removing the tariffs on Canadian lumber would lower the cost of each new American home by $1,000 on average, and make about 300,000 more moderate-income Americans eligible for mortgages. The *Journal* writes, and I quote: "This whole inane scheme may very well lead to a net reduction in employment in the U.S. because for every lumber and sawmill job there are about 25 Americans working in industries that depend on low-priced Canadian lumber." In short, these tariffs make your lumber companies happy — American consumers and workers, not so happy. When we ignore the rules, our economies suffer. I hope that is well understood — and by Congress in particular.

Let me give you another example: the border closures prompted by mad cow disease, or BSE. For many years, we have profited, both of us, from a highly integrated North American cattle market, extending from feed manufacturers to ranchers to processors. Now when BSE was first discovered in a Canadian cow, it was a Canadian problem; but long after scientific evidence demonstrated — unequivocally — that Canadian beef was safe, some very loud and persistent American ranchers succeeded in keeping the U.S. border closed. This is when the problem became a crisis, not just for Canadian ranchers but for a continental industry — and the president himself spoke out emphatically for the resumption of trade. I appreciated President Bush's leadership, and the situation has improved substantially since then.

But the effect of the lengthy closing has led to a restructuring in the Canadian industry, to the detriment of its U.S. counterpart. Why? Because whereas at one time Canadian beef was shipped for processing into the United States, our industry has adapted, ramping up its own processing capacity to compete with yours. Furthermore, rather than looking only to the U.S. market, we will be your direct competitors in China, Japan, and Korea. It's the law of unintended consequences at work.

At the Toronto book launch for the first edition of *With Faith & Goodwill* in 2017, former PMO Director of Communications Scott Reid (far right) reminisces with his former boss, Prime Minister Paul Martin, about the dinner they both attended at the Economic Club of New York in 2005, with Indigo Books owner Heather Reisman joining in.

Now, to get back to lumber. It's clear that the U.S. approach to softwood brings into question the integrity of NAFTA in general, and the efficacy of the dispute resolution mechanism in particular.

In the North American context, we have to recognize that NAFTA is a framework, not just for the trade of commodities, but for the trade of most all goods and services, investment and energy — and for this to operate smoothly we have to be able to rely on the dispute settlement mechanism.

Canada will continue to enforce its legal rights under NAFTA and before the U.S. courts. We will also take our case to the court of public opinion: in Congress, to the business community, and to the American consumer, as well as to the Administration.

But we shouldn't have to do this. There's already a mechanism in place — and we have a final decision. That decision should be accepted. That mechanism should be respected. If anything, it should be strengthened, to provide greater certainty and finality.

The integrity of this process is imperative. Indeed, the test of our commitment to NAFTA isn't taken in those many instances when we agree. It is taken in those few cases when we don't agree.

The second concern I want to discuss tonight addresses another dimension of our partnership — that of joint stewardship of the North American environment. In this context, the U.S. interest in drilling in the Arctic National Wildlife Refuge — ANWR — gives rise to great reservations on the part of Canada and Canadians.

Now, you may ask what business is it of the Canadian prime minister to question what the United States can do in its own territory. Fair enough. The answer is that Canada and the United States have a mutual obligation to the fragile ecosystem of the North. It must be protected and nurtured, not despoiled. Drilling in the ANWR puts both wildlife and the culture of the G'witchin people at risk. It's our mutual obligation to ensure they are not.

And it's not a new obligation. Some twenty years ago, we jointly agreed to protect the Porcupine River caribou herd, which each year migrates from the Yukon in Canada to the refuge's coastal plain. Now, we can argue the limits of that specific agreement but surely the underlying principle — that of shared stewardship — is one that we should recognize.

This is not to say we don't understand the impulse to ensure a secure supply of oil for American consumers. But even by optimistic estimates, there is only enough oil under the refuge to meet America's energy needs for two hundred days. If you're looking for a long-term solution, this isn't it. And in Canada's view, it simply is not worth the risk of permanent environmental damage.

Now, you may well say, "we need that oil." Our alternative sources around the world are too risky. But let's look at the reality. Our nation is already your number one supplier of imported energy: nearly all of the electricity, nearly 85 percent of the natural gas, and about 16 percent of the refined oil and crude that you import comes from Canada. Add to this the Alberta oil sands — with at least 175 billion barrels of recoverable supply, which represents more than two-thirds of Saudi Arabia's equivalent reserves — and our vast, unexploited hydroelectric resources, and there is no reason why, as joint stewards of the environment, we can't cover whatever potential output might have otherwise come from ANWR.

President Barack Obama

Statement on the Keystone Pipeline Proposal
Washington, D.C.
November 6, 2015

———

Good morning, everybody. Several years ago, the State Department began a review process for the proposed construction of a pipeline that would carry Canadian crude oil through our heartland to ports in the Gulf of Mexico and out into the world market.

This morning, Secretary Kerry informed me that, after extensive public outreach and consultation with other Cabinet agencies, the State Department has decided that the Keystone XL Pipeline would not serve the national interest of the United States. I agree with that decision.

This morning, I also had the opportunity to speak with Prime Minister Trudeau of Canada. And while he expressed his disappointment, given Canada's position on this issue, we both agreed that our close friendship on a whole range of issues, including energy and climate change, should provide the basis for even closer coordination between our countries going forward. And in the coming weeks, senior members of my team will be engaging with theirs in order to help deepen that co-operation.

> This pipeline would neither be a silver bullet for the economy, as was promised by some, nor the express lane to climate disaster proclaimed by others.
> — President Barack Obama

Now, for years, the Keystone Pipeline has occupied what I, frankly, consider an overinflated role in our political discourse. It became a symbol too often used as a campaign cudgel by both parties rather than a serious policy matter. And all of this obscured the fact that this pipeline would neither be a silver bullet for the economy, as was promised by some, nor the express lane to climate disaster proclaimed by others.

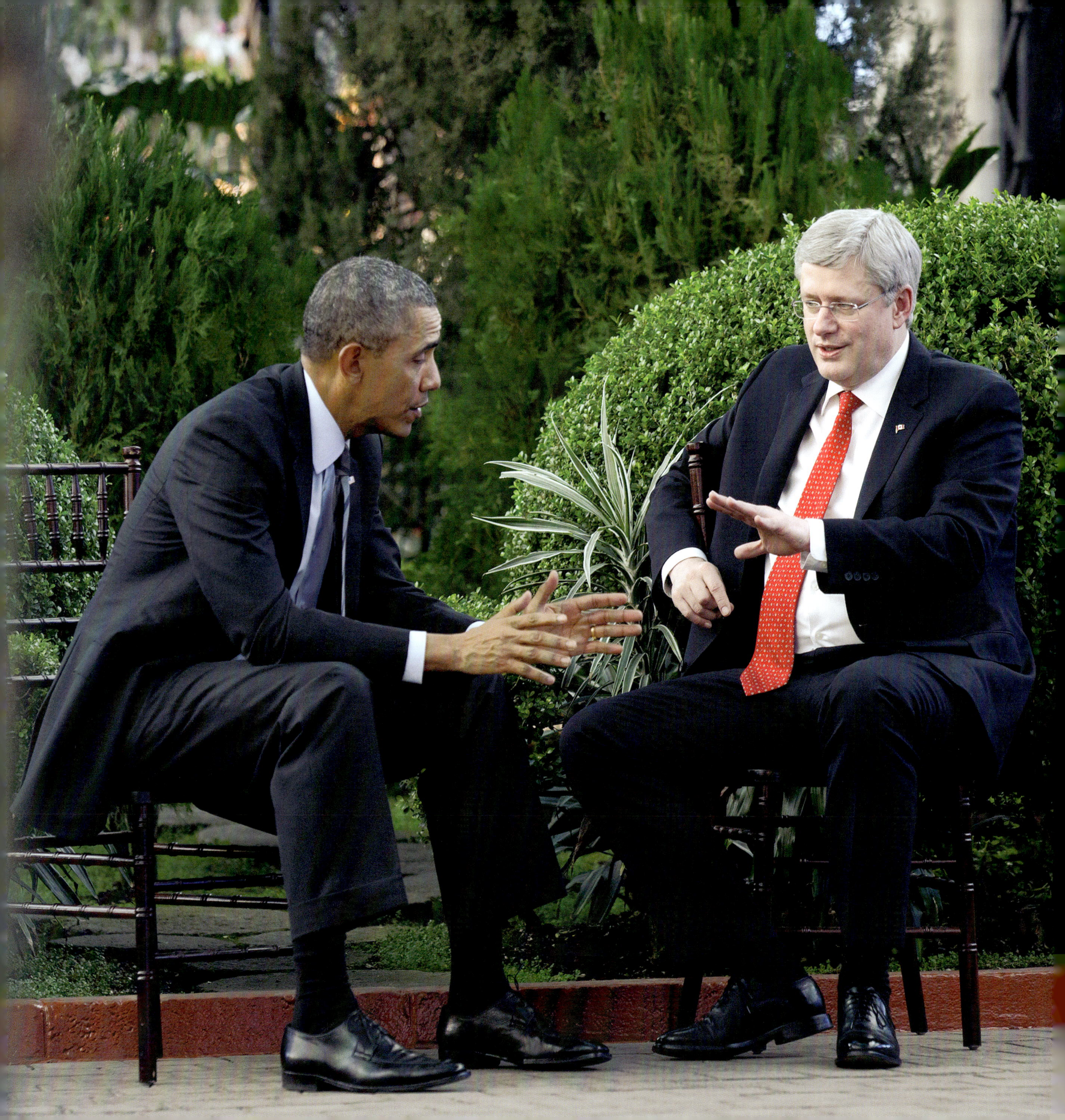

To illustrate this, let me briefly comment on some of the reasons why the State Department rejected this pipeline.

First: The pipeline would not make a meaningful long-term contribution to our economy. So if Congress is serious about wanting to create jobs, this was not the way to do it. If they want to do it, what we should be doing is passing a bipartisan infrastructure plan that, in the short term, could create more than thirty times as many jobs per year as the pipeline would, and in the long run would benefit our economy and our workers for decades to come.

Our businesses created 268,000 new jobs last month. They've created 13.5 million new jobs over the past sixty-eight straight months — the longest streak on record. The unemployment rate fell to 5 percent. This Congress should pass a serious infrastructure plan, and keep those jobs coming. That would make a difference. The pipeline would not have made a serious impact on those numbers and on the American people's prospects for the future.

Second: The pipeline would not lower gas prices for American consumers. In fact, gas prices have already been falling — steadily. The national average gas price is down about 77 cents over a year ago. It's down a dollar over two years ago. It's down $1.27 over three years ago. Today, in forty-one states, drivers can find at least one gas station selling gas for less than two bucks a gallon. So while our politics have been consumed by a debate over whether or not this pipeline would create jobs and lower gas prices, we've gone ahead and created jobs and lowered gas prices.

[OPPOSITE]
"Now, about that Keystone pipeline …" Prime Minister Stephen Harper talks with U.S. President Barack Obama during the North American Leaders' Summit in Toluca, Mexico, February 19, 2014.

[THIS PAGE]
"Did I mention the pipeline?" Prime Minister Stephen Harper with U.S. President Barack Obama during the North American Leaders' Summit in Toluca, Mexico, February 19, 2014.

Third: Shipping dirtier crude oil into our country would not increase America's energy security. What has increased America's energy security is our strategy over the past several years to reduce our reliance on dirty fossil fuels from unstable parts of the world. Three years ago, I set a goal to cut our oil imports in half by 2020. Between producing more oil here at home, and using less oil throughout our economy, we met that goal last year — five years early. In fact, for the first time in two decades, the United States of America now produces more oil than we buy from other countries.

Now, the truth is, the United States will continue to rely on oil and gas as we transition — as we must transition — to a clean energy economy. That transition will take some time. But it's also going more quickly than many anticipated. Think about it. Since I took office, we've doubled the distance our cars will go on a gallon of gas by 2025; tripled the power we generate from the wind; multiplied the power we generate from the sun twenty times over. Our biggest and most successful businesses are going all-in on clean energy. And thanks in part to the investments we've made, there are already parts of America where clean power from the wind or the sun is finally cheaper than dirtier, conventional power.

The point is the old rules said we couldn't promote economic growth and protect our environment at the same time. The old rules said we couldn't transition to clean energy without squeezing businesses and consumers. But this is America, and we have come up with new ways and new technologies to break down the old rules, so that today, homegrown American energy is booming, energy prices are falling, and over the past decade, even as our economy has continued to grow, America has cut our total carbon pollution more than any other country on Earth.

Today, the United States of America is leading on climate change with our investments in clean energy and energy efficiency. America is leading on climate change with new rules on power plants that will protect our air so that our kids can breathe. America is leading on climate change by working with other big emitters like China to encourage and announce new commitments to reduce harmful greenhouse gas emissions. In part because of that American leadership, more than 150 nations representing nearly 90 percent of global emissions have put forward plans to cut pollution.

America is now a global leader when it comes to taking serious action to fight climate change. And frankly, approving this project would have undercut that global leadership. And that's the biggest risk we face — not acting.

Today, we're continuing to lead by example. Because ultimately, if we're going to prevent large parts of this Earth from becoming not only inhospitable but uninhabitable in our lifetimes, we're going to have to keep some fossil fuels in the ground rather than burn them and release more dangerous pollution into the sky.

As long as I'm president of the United States, America is going to hold ourselves to the same high standards to which we hold the rest of the world. And three weeks from now, I look forward

FRICTIONS

to joining my fellow world leaders in Paris, where we've got to come together around an ambitious framework to protect the one planet that we've got while we still can.

If we want to prevent the worst effects of climate change before it's too late, the time to act is now. Not later. Not someday. Right here, right now. And I'm optimistic about what we can accomplish together. I'm optimistic because our own country proves, every day — one step at a time — that not only do we have the power to combat this threat, we can do it while creating new jobs, while growing our economy, while saving money, while helping consumers, and most of all, leaving our kids a cleaner, safer planet at the same time.

That's what our own ingenuity and action can do. That's what we can accomplish. And America is prepared to show the rest of the world the way forward.

Prime Minister Harper and President Obama share a private joke.

WITH FAITH & GOODWILL

PERSONAL TOUCH

Donald Trump's victory in the 2016 presidential election swept the politics of America First populism into the White House and across Canada-U.S. relations. Working with the new president would sometimes prove challenging for Prime Minister Justin Trudeau's government, which quickly realized that with the new president all politics were personal. Trump was alert to perceive slights and was not shy about harnessing the direct power of social media to express his views publicly. At no point was this more apparent than in the aftermath of the G7 meeting in Charlevoix, Quebec, in 2018. President Trump, displeased by the tone of Trudeau's closing remarks, reacted with hostility in what came to be known as the "Tweet Heard Around the World."

Diplomatic relations had moved into new and unfamiliar territory. Still, the tug of history and mutual interests kept the two governments operating closely. The Trudeau PMO worked hard to establish direct and personal ties with Trump's most senior advisers. It appointed David

German Chancellor Angela Merkel, alongside other world leaders, implores U.S. President Donald J. Trump to engage on key agenda items during the 2018 G7 meeting in Charlevoix, Quebec.

MacNaughton, a trusted Trudeau confidant, to the post of ambassador as an indication of priority. And the prime minister dedicated considerable personal energy to keeping relations with Trump on track through frequent phone calls and conversations. The relationship was tested at times, but significant results were achieved. The breakthrough renegotiation of NAFTA into the new USMCA stood as the centrepiece of those efforts, coming into effect on July 1, 2020.

Tweets of President Donald J. Trump

June 9, 2018

Donald J. Trump
@realDonaldTrump

Based on Justin's false statements at his news conference, and the fact that Canada is charging massive Tariffs to our U.S. Reps not to endorse the Communique as we look at Tariffs on automobiles flooding the U.S. Market!

7:03 PM · Jun 9, 2018

♡ 122K   💬 63.8K people are talking about this

Donald J. Trump
@realDonaldTrump

PM Justin Trudeau of Canada acted so meek and mild during our @G7 meetings only to give a news conference after I left saying that, "US Tariffs were kind of insulting" and he "will not be pushed around." Very dishonest & weak. Our Tariffs are in response to his of 270% on dairy!

7:04 PM · Jun 9, 2018

♡ 116K   💬 95.4K people are talking about this

AT WAR

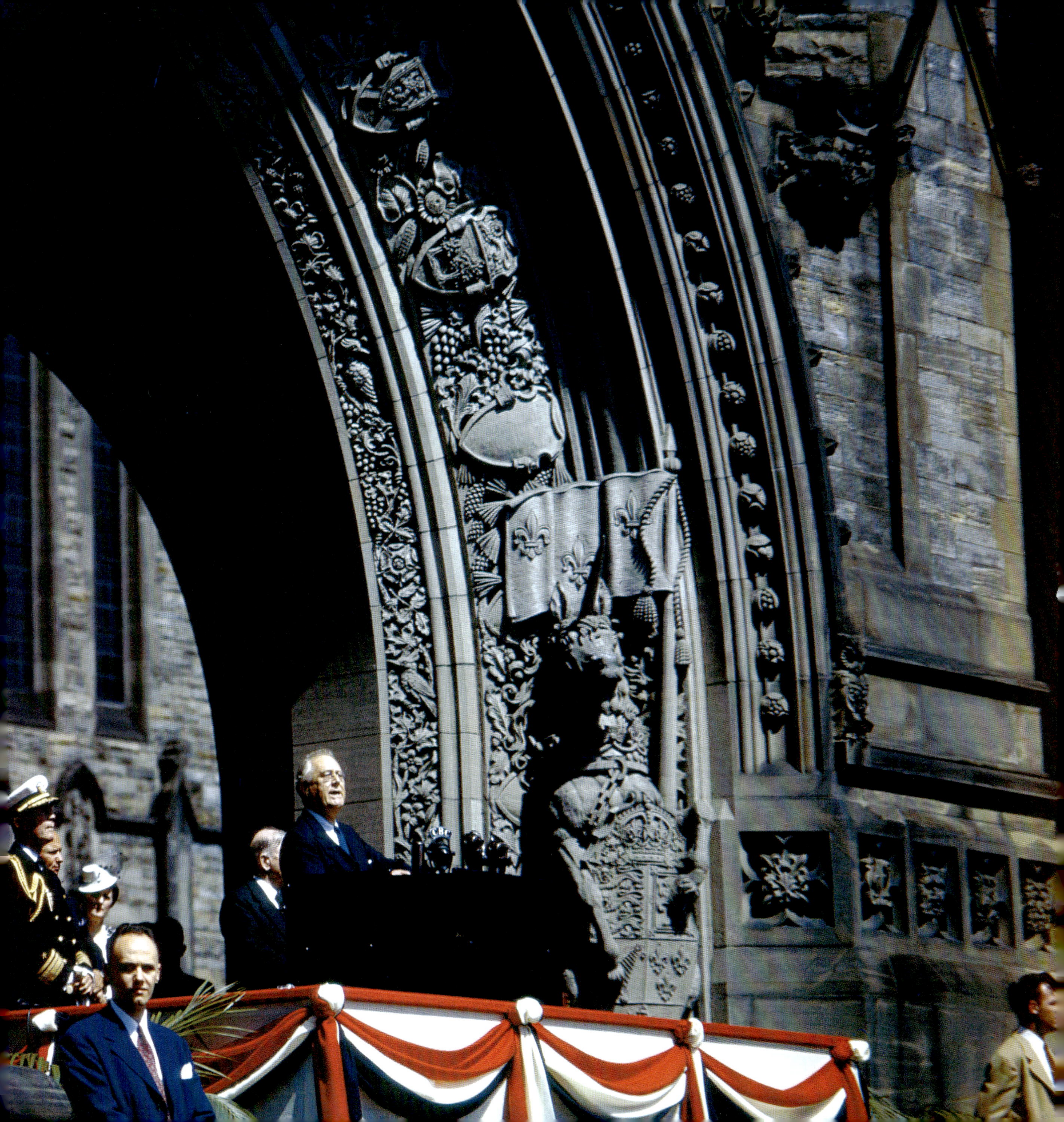

IN THE PERPETUAL EFFORT TO CAPTURE THE DIFFERENCES BETWEEN THE American and Canadian people — who, after all, have so much in common — one of the touchstones that observers frequently mention is the role of war in the cultural and historical life of each country. The United States, it is pointed out, was born of revolution, taking up arms to overthrow British rule and establish itself as an independent republic. By contrast, Canada remains a Commonwealth nation to this day and, in fact, the migration of anti-republican Loyalists from the United States into Upper Canada (known today as the province of Ontario) left a lasting resonance. These two distinct histories — one nation forged in revolution and the other opting to openly resist that course — are reflected in the words that the two countries use to define and describe themselves. America is the land of freedom where the right to bear arms persists as a tangible protection against the power of the state. Canada is the land that celebrates "peace, order, and good government" — no revolutionary zeal detectable in those words.

But when called upon, both nations have proven their measure during times of war. Indeed, because of Imperial ties, Canadians fought earlier and longer in both world wars of the twentieth century. For its part, a substantial isolationist impulse has sometimes kept the United States from early intervention in global military affairs.

The Cold War witnessed occasional tensions between Canada and the United States on military matters. A strong multilateral streak in Canada steered the two nations apart during the war in Vietnam. Not only did Canada not join in the exercise, the country became a home to thousands of draft-dodging youth. Many of them remained after the war, laying

[PREVIOUS PAGE]

Franklin Roosevelt speaking on Parliament Hill, 1943.

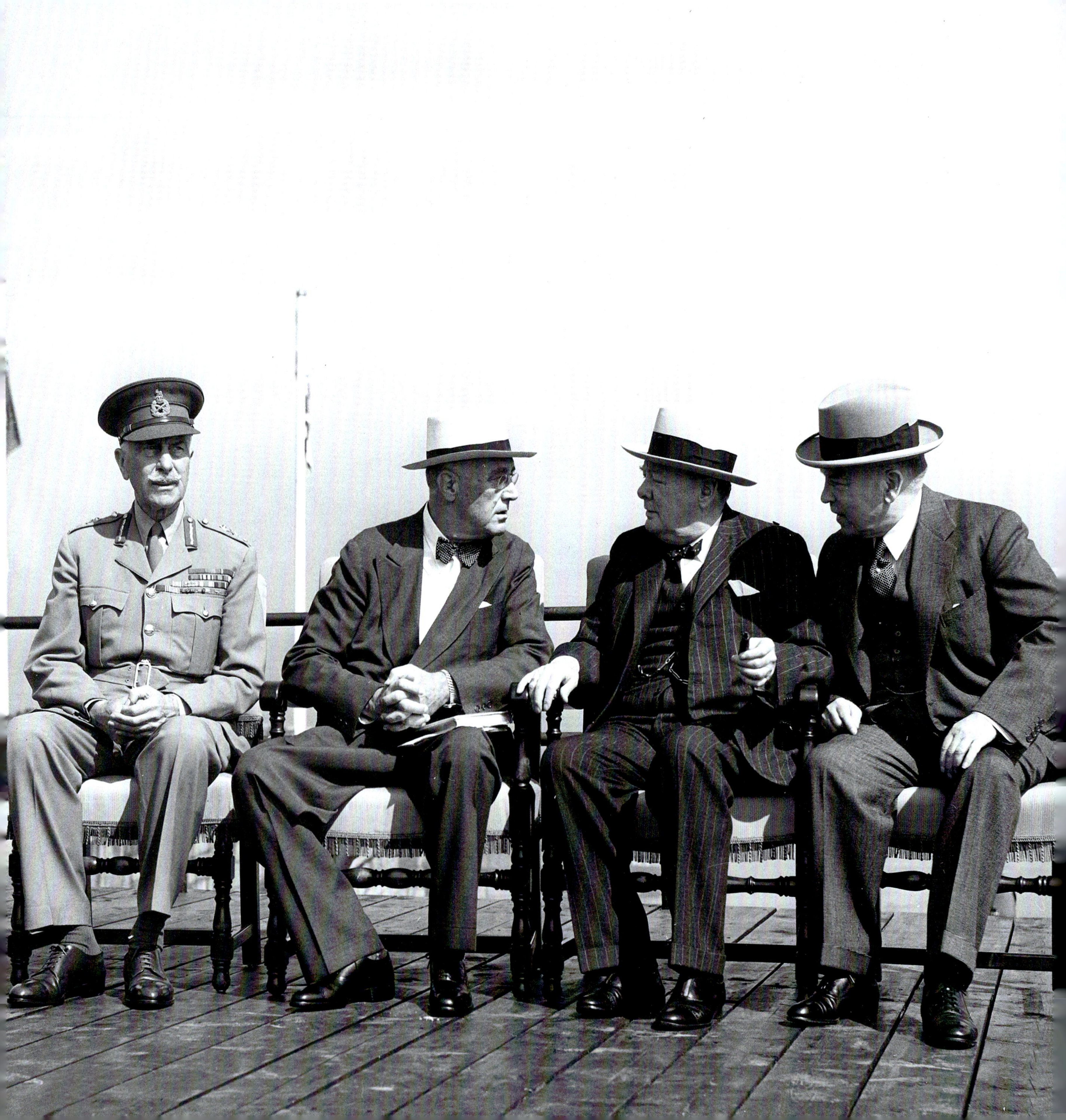

down roots, raising families and, in their own way, further entwining the bonds between the two countries.

Canadians celebrated along with the rest of the world as Ronald Reagan and George H.W. Bush helped to bring down the Berlin Wall, striking a symbolic end to the Cold War and marking the launch of a new post-Soviet era. When Desert Storm was assembled to push back against Saddam Hussein's aggression into Kuwait, Canada's multilateral commitment was on display once again as it joined the U.S.-led coalition of the willing. Ten years later, however, Canada took a pass on the more narrowly cast group of nations that pushed all the way into Iraq with the United States on a mission of regime change.

That difference of opinion was heavily muted by the combined effort in Afghanistan. The shock of 9/11 was felt across North America and, in tragedy, brought the two countries together in ways large and small. Elsewhere in this book some of the expressions of shared support that emerged from that day in New York are highlighted. But the clearest measure of the connection created was to be found in locations such as Kandahar and Kabul.

[OPPOSITE]
Total war. Lord Lothian, President Franklin Roosevelt, Prime Minister Winston Churchill, and Prime Minister Mackenzie King at the second Quebec Conference in September 1944.

[BELOW]
Prime Minister Brian Mulroney and U.S. Secretary of State James Baker in Mulroney's office in January 1991.

ALLIED AGAINST THE AXIS POWERS

Canada entered World War II in support of the British Empire and in response to Nazi Germany's aggression more than two years before Pearl Harbor would see the United States join the Allies. Despite a divided American public, it was apparent to Franklin Delano Roosevelt that war was an inevitability — and from the late 1930s on, he took steps both large and small to lend America's support. His constant correspondence during these years with Winston Churchill is well known. Sometimes overlooked is the equally unbroken communication he maintained with another prime minister, William Lyon Mackenzie King.

The eccentricities of King are well known to the public now, but any examination of the war years provides a thorough tutorial in the man's remarkable political skills as he nurtured, served,

Another presidential first. Prime Minister Mackenzie King welcoming President Franklin Roosevelt to Parliament Hill, 1943.

AT WAR

and shaped public opinion all at once. In this respect, his only real peer was FDR himself. That the two men — whose colleagues thought them to be almost unknowable on a truly personal level — would become such close confidants is both fitting and understandable. Their relationship echoed the deep ties that World War II would produce between the two nations.

President Franklin D. Roosevelt

Address to a Joint Session of Parliament
Ottawa, Ontario
August 25, 1943

———

It was exactly five years ago last Wednesday that I came to Canada to receive the high honour of a degree at Queen's University. On that occasion, one year before the invasion of Poland, three years before Pearl Harbor, I said that we in the Americas are no longer a faraway continent, to which the eddies of controversies beyond the seas could bring no interest or no harm. Instead, we in the Americas have become a consideration to every propaganda office and to every general staff beyond the seas. The vast amount of our resources, the vigour of our commerce, and the strength of our men have made us vital factors in world peace whether we choose it or not.

We did not choose this war — and that "we" includes each and every one of the United Nations. War was violently forced upon us by criminal aggressors who measure their standards of morality by the extent of the death and the destruction that they can inflict upon their neighbours.

Canadians and Americans have fought shoulder to shoulder —
as our men and our women and our children have worked together and played together in happier times of peace.

— President Franklin D. Roosevelt

In this war, Canadians and Americans have fought shoulder to shoulder — as our men and our women and our children have worked together and played together in happier times of peace. Today, in devout gratitude, we are celebrating a brilliant victory won by British and Canadian and American fighting men in Sicily.

Today, we rejoice also in another event for which we need not apologize. A year ago, Japan occupied several of the Aleutian Islands on our side of the ocean, and made a great "to do" about the invasion of the continent of North America. I regret to say that some Americans and some Canadians wished our governments to withdraw from the Atlantic and the Mediterranean campaigns and divert all our vast supplies and strength to the removal of the [Japanese] from a few rocky specks in the North Pacific.

Today, our wiser councils have maintained our efforts in the Atlantic area, the Mediterranean, the China Seas, and the Southwest Pacific, with ever-growing contributions; in the Northwest Pacific a relatively small campaign has been assisted by the [Japanese] themselves in the elimination of that last [Japanese soldier] from Attu and Kiska. We have been told that the [Japanese] never surrender; their headlong retreat satisfies us just as well.

[THIS PAGE]
President Franklin Roosevelt receiving an honorary degree from Queen's University in Kingston, Ontario, before an overflow crowd at George Richardson Memorial Stadium, August 18, 1938.

[OPPOSITE]
Canine diplomacy. First Lady Eleanor Roosevelt and Prime Minister William Lyon Mackenzie King with the Roosevelts' dog, Fala, during the second Quebec Conference in September 1944.

AT WAR

Great councils are being held here on the free and honoured soil of Canada — councils which look to the future conduct of this war and to the years of building a new progress for mankind. To these councils Canadians and Americans alike again welcome that wise and good and gallant gentleman, the prime minister of Great Britain.

Mr. King, my old friend, may I, through you, thank the people of Canada for their hospitality to all of us. Your course and mine have run so closely and affectionately during these many long years that this meeting adds another link to that chain. I have always felt at home in Canada, and you, I think, have always felt at home in the United States.

During the past few days in Quebec, the combined staffs have been sitting around a table — which is a good custom — talking things over, discussing ways and means, in the manner of friends, in the manner of partners, and may I even say in the manner of members of the same family. We have talked constructively of our common purposes in this war — of our determination to achieve victory in the shortest possible time, of our essential co-operation with our great and brave fighting allies. And we have arrived, harmoniously, at certain definite conclusions. Of course, I am not at liberty to disclose just what these conclusions are. But, in due time, we shall communicate the secret information of the Quebec Conference to Germany, Italy, and Japan. We shall communicate this information to our enemies in the only language their twisted minds seem capable of understanding.

Sometimes I wish that great master of intuition, the Nazi leader, could have been present in spirit at the Quebec Conference. I am thoroughly glad that he wasn't there in person. If he and his generals had known our plans, they would have realized that discretion is still the better part of valour and that surrender would pay them better now than later.

The evil characteristic that makes a Nazi is his utter inability to understand, and therefore to respect, the qualities or the rights of his fellow men. His only method of dealing with his neighbour is first to delude him with lies, then to attack him treacherously, then to beat him down and step on him, and then either to kill him or enslave him. And the same thing is true of the fanatical militarists of Japan. Because their own instincts and impulses are essentially inhuman, our enemies simply cannot comprehend how it is that decent, sensible, individual human beings manage to get along together and to live together as good neighbours.

That is why our enemies are doing their desperate best to misrepresent the purposes and the results of this Quebec Conference. They still seek to divide and conquer allies who refuse to be divided, just as cheerfully as they refuse to be conquered. We spend our energies and our resources and the very lives of our sons and daughters because a band of gangsters in the community of nations declines to recognize the fundamentals of decent, human conduct.

We have been forced to call out what we, in the United States, would call the sheriff's posse, to break up the gang in order that gangsterism may be eliminated in the community of nations. We are making sure — absolutely, irrevocably sure — that this time, the lesson is driven home to them once and for all. Yes, we are going to be rid of outlaws this time.

AT WAR

Every one of the United Nations believes that only a real and lasting peace can justify the sacrifices we are making, and our unanimity gives us confidence in seeking that goal. It is no secret that at Quebec, there was much talk of the post-war world. That discussion was doubtless duplicated simultaneously in dozens of nations and hundreds of cities and among millions of people.

There is a longing in the air. It is not a longing to go back to what they call "the good old days." I have distinct reservations as to how good "the good old days" were. I would rather believe that we can achieve new and better days. Absolute victory in this war will give greater opportunities to the world, because the winning of the war in itself is certainly proving to all of us up here that concerted action can accomplish things. Surely we can make strides toward a greater freedom from want than the world has yet enjoyed. Surely by unanimous action in driving out the outlaws and keeping them under heel forever, we can attain a freedom from fear of violence.

> I am everlastingly angry only at those who assert vociferously that the Four Freedoms and the Atlantic Charter are nonsense because they are unattainable.
>
> — PRESIDENT FRANKLIN D. ROOSEVELT

I am everlastingly angry only at those who assert vociferously that the Four Freedoms and the Atlantic Charter are nonsense because they are unattainable. If those people had lived a century and a half ago, they would have sneered and said that the Declaration of Independence was utter piffle. If they had lived nearly a thousand years ago, they would have laughed uproariously at the ideals of the Magna Carta. And if they had lived several thousand years ago, they would have derided Moses when he came from the mountain with the Ten Commandments.

We concede that these great teachings are not perfectly lived up to today, but I would rather be a builder than a wrecker, hoping always that the structure of life is growing, not dying. May the destroyers who still persist in our midst decrease. They, like some of our enemies, have a long road to travel before they accept the ethics of humanity. Someday, in the distant future perhaps — but some day, it is certain — all of them will remember, with the Master, "Thou shalt love thy neighbour as thyself."

THE COLD WAR ERA

The passing of World War II saw the United States asked to bear enormous new geopolitical responsibilities. The world's most powerful nation was looked upon to lead the way in rebuilding Europe, in the transformation of Western economies from war to peace, and in the provision of collective security of not just Europe but much of the globe. As the Soviet Union transformed quickly from battlefield ally to ideological opponent, friends like Canada took sides.

In the post-war years the two countries worked in lockstep on everything from NORAD — the North American Aerospace Defence Command — to NATO. Canada also contributed mightily to the Korean War with the contribution of 26,000 soldiers to the U.N. force as well as naval destroyers, aircraft, and substantial logistical support.

At the same time, the theme of life in free societies, sustained by a culture of progress and by assured material prosperity, was taking hold. This theme was readily picked up to show the Canada-U.S. relationship as a model for the world. Speeches now looked more to the common culture of freedom and development than to a shared British ethnic heritage. Speakers now referred to common development projects — especially the economic promise of the St. Lawrence Seaway. And U.S. presidents no longer spoke of Canada diplomatically in the context of Great Britain, but instead as a U.S. partner in its own right.

Vietnam gave rise to tensions, but throughout the Cold War Canada was reliably warm with its southern neighbour.

President Harry S. Truman

Address to a Joint Session of Parliament
Ottawa, Ontario
June 11, 1947

Americans who come to know Canada informally, such as our tourists, as well as those whose approach is more academic, learn that Canada is a broad land — broad in mind, broad in spirit, and broad in physical expanse.

They find that the composition of your population and the evolution of your political institutions hold a lesson for the other nations of the Earth. Canada has achieved internal unity and material strength, and has grown in stature in the world community, by solving problems that might have hopelessly divided and weakened a less gifted people.

Canada's eminent position today is a tribute to the patience, tolerance, and strength of character of her people, of both French and British strains. For Canada is enriched by the heritage of France, as well as of Britain, and Quebec has imparted the vitality and spirit of France itself to Canada. Canada's notable achievement of national unity and progress through accommodation, moderation, and forbearance can be studied with profit by her sister nations.

Much the same qualities have been employed, with like success, in your relations with the United States. Perhaps I should say "your foreign relations with the United States." But the word "foreign" seems strangely out of place. Canada and the United States have reached the point where we no longer think of each other as "foreign" countries. We think of each other as friends, as peaceful and co-operative neighbours on a spacious and fruitful continent.

We must go back a long way, nearly a century and a half, to find a time when we were not on good terms. In the War of 1812, there was fighting across our frontier. But permanent good came of that brief campaign.

It shocked Canadians and Americans into a realization that continued antagonism would be costly and perilous. The first result of that realization was the Rush-Bagot Agreement in 1817, which embodied a spirit and an attitude that have permeated our relations to this day. This agreement originally was intended to limit and to regulate the naval vessels of both countries on the Great Lakes. It has become one of the world's most effective disarmament agreements, and it is the basis for our much-hailed unfortified frontier.

I speak of that period of history to make the point that the friendship that has characterized Canadian-American relations for many years did not develop spontaneously. The example of accord provided by our two countries did not come about merely through the happy circumstance of geography. It is compounded of one part proximity and nine parts goodwill and common sense.

[OPPOSITE]

President Harry S. Truman, the thirty-third president of the United States.

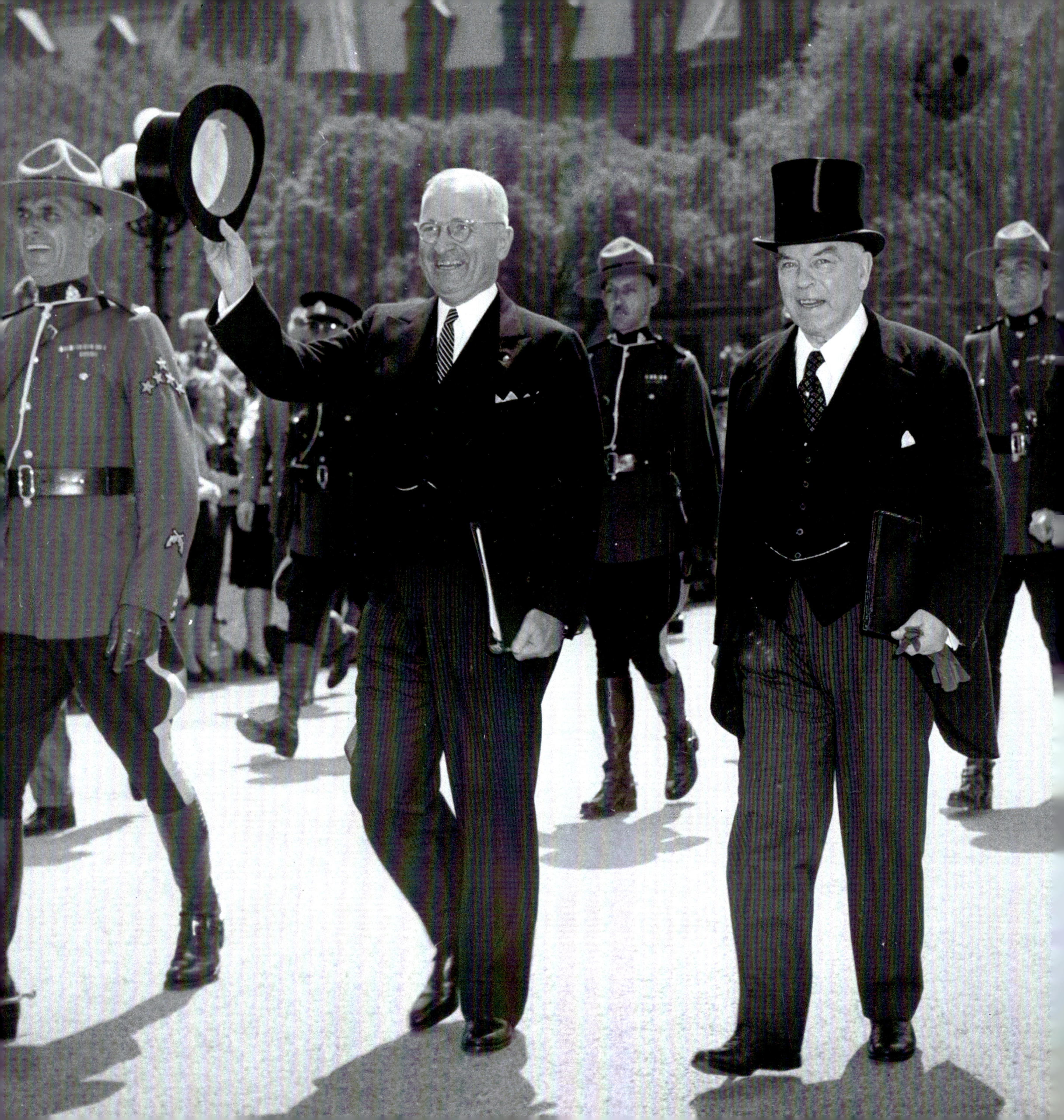

AT WAR

We have had a number of problems, but they have all been settled by adjustment, by compromise, and by negotiations inspired by a spirit of mutual respect, and a desire for justice on both sides. This is the peaceful way, the sensible way, and the fair way to settle problems, whether between two nations that are close neighbours, or among many nations widely separated.

This way is open to all. We in Canada and the United States are justifiably proud of our joint record, but we claim no monopoly on that formula. Canada and the United States will gladly share the formula, which rejects distrust and suspicion in favour of common sense, mutual respect, and equal justice with their fellow members of the United Nations. One of the most effective contributions our two countries can make to the cause of the United Nations is the patient and diligent effort to apply, on a global scale, the principles and practices which we have tested with success on this continent.

This is the peaceful way, the sensible way, and the fair way

to settle problems, whether between two nations that are close neighbours, or among many nations widely separated.

— PRESIDENT HARRY S. TRUMAN

Relations between Canada and the United States have emphasized the spirit of co-operation rather than the letter of protocol. The Rush-Bagot Agreement was stated in fewer than 150 words. From time to time, it has been revised by mutual agreement to meet changing conditions. It was amended as recently as last December. The last war brought our countries into even closer collaboration. The Ogdensburg Agreement of 1940 provided for the creation of the Permanent Joint Board on Defence. It was followed by the Hyde Park Agreement of 1941, which enabled us to coordinate our economic resources with increased efficiency.

Common interests, particularly after Pearl Harbor, required the creation of several joint agencies to coordinate our efforts in special fields. When victory ended the necessity for these agencies, they were quietly disbanded with a minimum of disturbance of the national economies of the two countries. Common sense again.

The Permanent Joint Board on Defence will continue to function. I wish to emphasize, in addition to the word "permanent," the other two parts of the title. The board is joint, being composed of representatives of each government. Canada and the United States participate on the basis of

[OPPOSITE]
President Harry S. Truman and Prime Minister Mackenzie King in Ottawa on June 11, 1947.

WITH FAITH & GOODWILL

equality, and the sovereignty of each is carefully respected. This was true during the gravest dangers of the war, and it will continue to be true, in keeping with the nature of all our joint undertakings.

The board was created, and will continue to exist, for the sole purpose of assuring the most effective defence for North America. The board, as you know, has no executive powers, and can only make recommendations for action. The record of the board provides another example of the truly co-operative spirit that prevails between our two countries.

The spirit of common purpose and the impressive strength which we marshalled for action on all fronts are the surest safeguard of continental security in the future. The people of the United States fully appreciate the magnificent contribution in men and resources that Canada made to the Allied war effort. The United States soldiers, sailors, and airmen in the heat of battle knew their Canadian comrades as valiant and daring warriors. We look back with pride on our association as staunch allies in two wars.

Today, our two nations are called upon to make great contributions to world rehabilitation. This task requires broad vision and constant effort. I am confident that we can overcome the difficulties involved, as we overcame the greater difficulties of the war. The national genius of our peoples finds its most satisfying expression in the creation of new values in peace. The record proves that in peaceful commerce, the combined efforts of our countries can produce outstanding results. Our trade with each other is far greater than that of any other two nations on Earth.

Gather 'round, boys. President Harry S. Truman holds a special news conference at Montebello, June 12, 1947. To the right of President Truman is U.S. Ambassador to Canada Ray Atherton.

Last year, the flow of trade in both directions across the border reached the record peacetime total of $2.25 billion. We imported from Canada more than twice the value of goods we received from the United Kingdom, France, China, and Russia combined. The United States' purchases from Canada were about six times our purchases from Great Britain, nearly ten times those from China, and eleven times those from France. We sold to Canada nearly as much as we sold to Britain and France together.

Gratifying as the volume of our trade now is, it is capable of even further expansion to our mutual benefit. Some of our greatest assets are still to be developed to the maximum. I am thinking

> The spirit of common purpose and the impressive strength which we marshalled for action on all fronts are the surest safeguard of continental security in the future.
>
> — President Harry S. Truman

of one particularly that holds tremendous possibilities: the magnificent St. Lawrence–Great Lakes System, which we share and which we must develop together.

The St. Lawrence project stirs the imagination long accustomed to majestic distances and epic undertakings. The proposal for taking electric power from the river and bringing ocean shipping 2,400 miles inland, to tap the fertile heart of our continent, is economically sound and strategically important. When this program is carried out, the waterway that is part of our boundary will more than ever unite our two countries. It will stimulate our economies to new growth, and will spread the flow of trade.

There have been times when short-sighted tariff policies on both sides threatened to raise almost insurmountable barriers. But the need to exchange goods was so imperative that trade flourished despite artificial obstacles. The Reciprocal Trade Agreements of 1936 and 1939 made possible a sensible reduction of tariff rates, and paved the way to our present phenomenal trade.

Something more than commercial agreements, however, is required to explain why Canada and the United States exchange more than $2 billion worth of goods yearly. Ambassador Atherton has aptly given the reason as not "free trade," but "the trade of free men." The record flow of goods and the high standard of living it indicates, on both sides of the border, provide a practical demonstration of the benefits of the democratic way of life and a free economy.

Wild about Harry! President Harry S. Truman receives a bouquet of flowers upon arrival at the Seigniory Club, June 12, 1947.

The benefits of our democratic governments and free economies operating side by side have spread beyond our countries to the advantage of the whole world. Both nations expanded their productivity enormously during the war, and both escaped the physical damage that afflicted other countries. As a result, Canada and the United States emerged from the war as the only major sources of the industrial products and the food upon which much of the world depends for survival.

Canada has responded as nobly to the challenge of peace as she did to that of the war. Your wheat has fed millions who otherwise would have starved. Your loan strengthened Britain in her valiant battle for recovery. The United States is particularly gratified to find Canada at our side in the effort to develop the International Trade Organization. We attach great importance to this undertaking, because we believe it will provide the key to the welfare and prosperity of the world in the years immediately ahead.

In sponsoring the International Trade Organization, the United States, with the co-operation of Canada and other countries, is making a determined effort to see that the inevitable adjustments in world trade as a result of the war will result in an expanding volume of business for all nations. Our goal is a vast expansion of agriculture and industry throughout the world, with freer access to the raw materials and markets for all nations, and a wider distribution of the products of the Earth's fields and factories among all peoples. Our hope is to multiply the fruitfulness of the Earth and to diffuse its benefits among all mankind.

At this critical point in history, we of the United States are deeply conscious of our responsibilities to the world. We know that in this trying period, between a war that is over and a peace that is not yet secure, the destitute and the oppressed of the Earth look chiefly to us for sustenance and support, until they can again face life with self-confidence and self-reliance.

We are keenly aware that much depends upon the internal strength, the economic stability, and the moral stamina of the United States. We face this

AT WAR

challenge with determination and confidence. Free men everywhere know that the purpose of the United States is to restore the world to health and to re-establish conditions under which the common people of the Earth can work out their salvation by their own efforts.

We seek a peaceful world, a prosperous world, a free world, a world of good neighbours, living on terms of equality and mutual respect, as Canada and the United States have lived for generations. We intend to expend our energies and to invest our substance in promoting world recovery, by assisting those who are able and willing to make their maximum contribution to the same cause.

We intend to support those who are determined to govern themselves in their own way, and who honour the right of others to do likewise. We intend to aid those who seek to live at peace with their neighbours, without coercing or being coerced, without intimidating or being intimidated.

We seek a peaceful world,
a prosperous world, a free world,
a world of good neighbours ...
— President Harry S. Truman

We intend to uphold those who respect the dignity of the individual, who guarantee to him equal treatment under the law, and who allow him the widest possible liberty to work out his own destiny and achieve success to the limit of his capacity. We intend to co-operate actively and loyally with all who honestly seek, as we do, to build a better world in which mankind can live in peace and prosperity.

We count Canada in the forefront of those who share these objectives and ideals. With such friends we face the future unafraid.

President Dwight D. Eisenhower

Address to a Joint Session of Parliament
Ottawa, Ontario
November 14, 1953

This day, I again salute the men and women of Canada. As I stand before you, my thoughts go back to the days of global war. In that conflict, and then through the more recent savage and grievous Korean battles, the Canadian people have been valorous champions of freedom for mankind. Within the framework of NATO, in the construction of new patterns for international security, in the lengthy and often toilsome exploration of a regional alliance, they have been patient and wise devisers of a stout defence for the Western world.

Canada, rich in natural gifts, far richer in human character and genius, has earned the gratitude and the affectionate respect of all who cherish freedom and seek peace.

I am highly honoured by the invitation of the Parliament that I address. For your invitation is rooted in the friendship — the sense of partnership — that for generations has been the hallmark of the relations between Canada and the United States. Your country, my country — each is a better and stronger and more influential nation because each can rely upon every resource of the other in days of crisis. Beyond this, each can work and grow and prosper with the other through years of quiet peace.

We, of our country, have long respected and admired Canada as a bulwark of the British Commonwealth, and as a leader among nations. As no Soviet wile or lure can divide the Commonwealth, nothing will corrupt the Canadian-American partnership.

We have a dramatic symbol of that partnership in the favoured topic of every speaker addressing an audience made up of both our peoples — our unfortified frontier. But though this subject has become shopworn and well-nigh exhausted as a feature of after-dinner oratory, it is still a fact that our common frontier grows stronger every year, defended only by friendship. Its strength wells from indestructible and enduring sources: identical ideals of family and school and church, and traditions which come to us from the common past. Out of this partnership has evolved a progressive prosperity and a general well-being, mutually beneficial, that is without parallel on Earth.

In the years ahead, the pace of our mutual growth will surely be no less. To strive, even dimly, to foresee the wonders of Canada's next generation, is to summon the utmost powers of the imagination. This land is a mighty reservoir of resources. Across it, at this moment, there moves an extraordinary drama of enterprise and endeavour — Canadians, rapidly building basic industries, converting waters into hydroelectric energy, scrutinizing your soil for new wealth, pushing into the barrens of the North for minerals and for oil. You, of Canada, are building a magnificent record of achievement. My country rejoices in it....

[OPPOSITE]
We like Ike! President Dwight Eisenhower addresses the Canadian Parliament in November 1953.

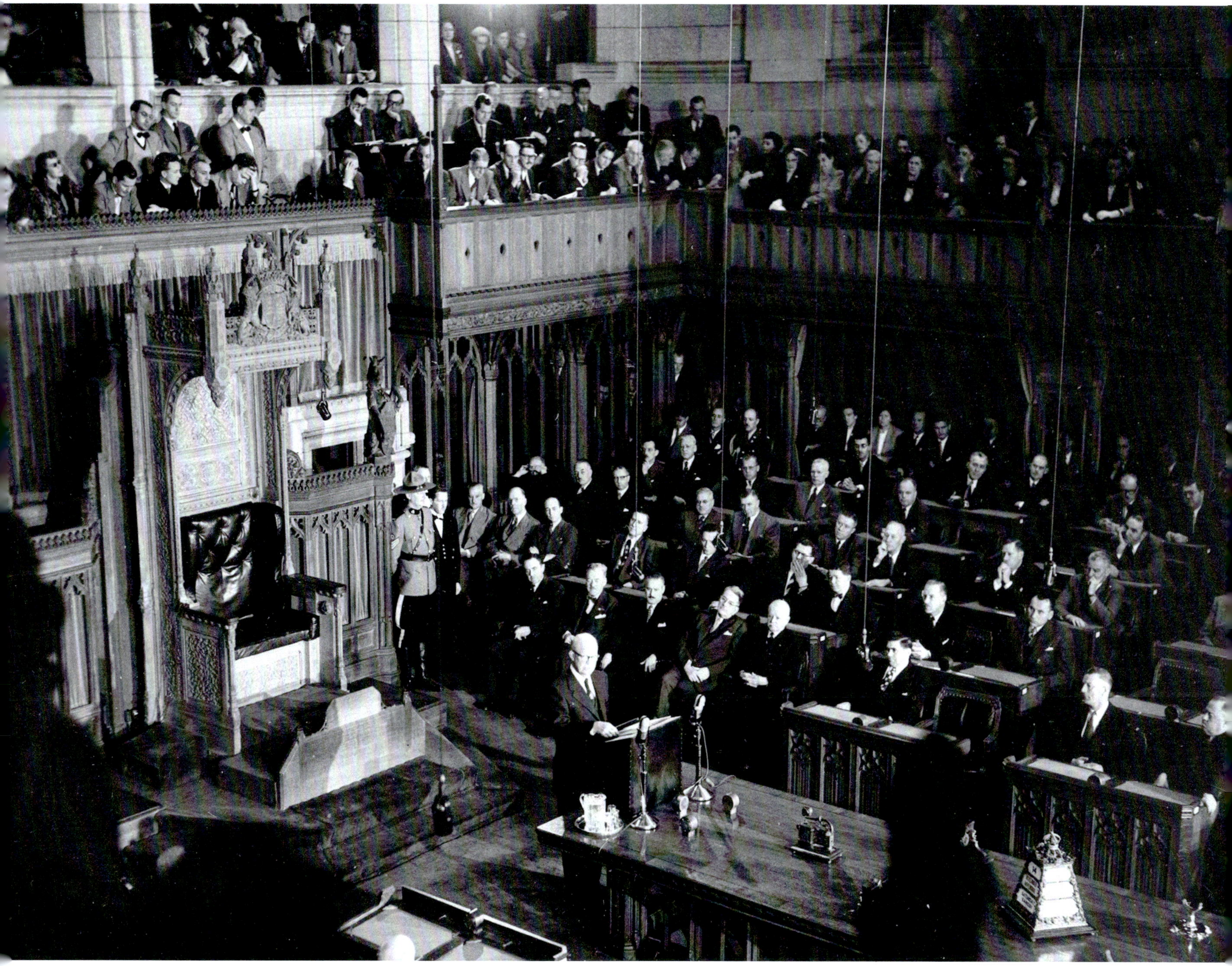

This Parliament is an illustrious symbol of a human craving, a human search, a human right to self-government. All the free legislatures of the world speak for the free peoples of the world. In their deliberations and enactments, they mirror the ideas, the traditions, the fundamental philosophies of their respective nations.

On the other hand, every free nation, secure in its own economic and political stability, reflects the responsible leadership and the wise comprehension which its legislature has brought to the management of public affairs.

Now, this continent uniquely has been a laboratory of self-government, in which free legislatures have been an indispensable force. What is the result? It is a mighty unity built

> Your country, my country —
> ## each is a better and stronger and more influential nation
> because each can rely upon every resource of the other in days of crisis.
> — President Dwight D. Eisenhower

of values essentially spiritual. This continent, of course, is a single physical and geographical entity. But physical unity, however, broken by territorial lines, fortress chains, and trade barriers, is a characteristic of every continent. Here, however, independent and sovereign peoples have built a stage on which all the world can see: first, each country's patriotic dedication to its own enlightened self-interest, but free from vicious nationalistic exploitation of grudge or ancient wrong; second, a joined recognition that neighbours, among nations as among individuals, prosper best in neighbourly co-operation, factually exemplified in daily life; third, an international will to cast out the bomb and the gun as arbiters and to exalt the joint search for truth and justice.

Here, on this continent, we present an example that other nations someday surely will recognize and apply in their relationships among themselves. My friends, may that day be close, because the only alternative — the bankruptcy of armament races and the suicide of nuclear war — cannot for long, must not for long, be tolerated by the human race.

Great has been our mutual progress. It foreshadows what we together can accomplish for our mutual good. Before us of Canada and the United States lies an immense panorama of opportunity in every field of human endeavour. A host of jobs to be done together confronts us. Many

[OPPOSITE]

Ike and Uncle Louis. Lester B. Pearson, on the left, and Secretary of State John Foster Dulles, on the right, join their bosses, President Dwight D. Eisenhower and Prime Minister Louis St. Laurent, on March 1, 1956.

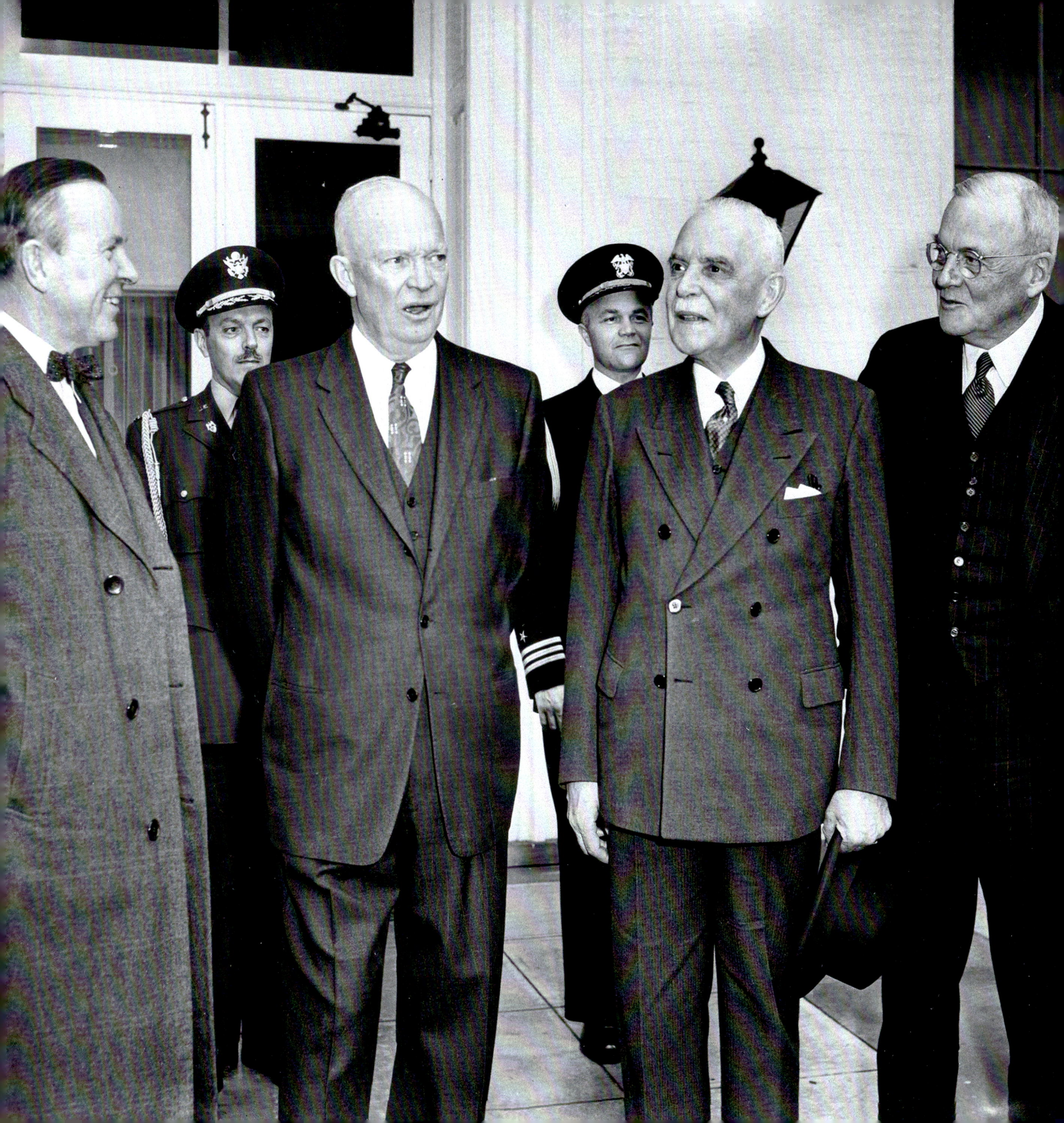

of them cry for immediate attention. As we examine them together in the work days ahead, we must never allow the practical difficulties that impede progress to blind our eyes to the objectives established by principle and by logic.

With respect to some aspects of our future development, I hope I may, without presumption, make three observations. The first is: the free world must come to recognize that trade barriers, although intended to protect a country's economy, often in fact shackle its prosperity. In the United States, there is a growing recognition that free nations cannot expand their productivity and economic strength without a high level of international trade. Now, in our case — yours and ours — our two economies are enmeshed intricately with the world economy. We cannot risk sudden dislocation in industry and agriculture and widespread unemployment and distress, by hasty decisions to accomplish suddenly what inevitably will come in an orderly economic evolution. "Make haste slowly" is a homely maxim with international validity.

Moreover, every common undertaking, however worthwhile it may be, must be understood in its origins, its application, its effects by the peoples of our two countries. Without this understanding, it will have negligible chance of success. Canadians and citizens of the United States do not accept government by edict or decree. Informed and intelligent co-operation is, for us, the only source of enduring accomplishment.

To study further the whole subject of United States foreign economic policy, we have, at home, appointed a special commission with wide representation, including members of the Congress as well as spokesmen for the general public. From the commission's studies will come, we hope, a policy which can command the support of the American people, and which will be in the best interest of the United States and the free world.

Toward the strengthening of commercial ties between Canada and the United States, officials of our two governments have, for some months, been considering the establishment of a joint economic and trade committee. This committee, now approved, will consist of Cabinet officers of both countries. They will meet periodically to discuss, in broad terms, economic and trade problems and the means for their equitable solution. I confidently believe that out of this process, the best interests of both our countries will be more easily harmonized and advanced.

The second observation is this: joint development and use of the St. Lawrence–Great Lakes Waterway is inevitable. It is sure and certain. With you, I consider this measure a vital addition to our economic and national security. Of course, no proposal yet made is entirely free from faults of some sort. But every one of them can be corrected — given patience and co-operation.

In the United States, my principal security advisers, comprising the National Security Council, favour the undertaking for national defence reasons. The Cabinet favours it on both security and economic grounds. A committee of the United States Senate has approved a measure authorizing it. This measure provides for the United States' participation in a joint development by both countries. The proposal now awaits action by the United States Senate which, I am confident, will act favourably on it or some similar measure. The ways and means for assuring American co-operation in this great project will, I hope, be authorized and approved during the coming session of the Congress.

I have noted with satisfaction the New York Power Authority's acceptance of the Federal Power Commission's licence. With this act, the stage is set for a start on the St. Lawrence Power Project which will add materially to the economic strength of both countries.

My third observation is this: you of Canada and we of the United States can and will devise ways to protect our North America from any surprise attack by air. And we shall achieve the defence of our continent without whittling our pledges to Western Europe or forgetting our friends in the Pacific.

The basic threat of Communist purpose still exists. Indeed, the latest Soviet communication to the Western world is truculent, if not arrogant, in tone. In any event, our security plans must now take into account Soviet ability to employ atomic attack on North America, as well as on

> These days demand ceaseless vigilance. We must be ready and prepared. The threat is present.
> — President Dwight D. Eisenhower

countries, friendly to us, lying closer to the borders of the U.S.S.R. Their atomic stockpile will, of course, increase in size, and means of delivery will increase as time goes on.

Now, each of our two nations seeks a secure home for realization of its destiny. Defence of our soil presents a challenge to both our peoples. It is a common task. Defensively, as well as geographically, we are joined beyond any possibility of separation. This element in our security problem is an accepted guide of the service leaders, government officials, and legislatures on both sides of the border. In our approach to the problem, we both realize that purest patriotism demands and promotes effective partnership. Thus we evolve joint agreements on all those measures we must jointly undertake to improve the effectiveness of our defences, but every arrangement rests squarely on the sovereign nature of each of our two peoples.

Canada and the United States are equal partners, and neither dares to waste time. There is a time to be alert and a time to rest. These days demand ceaseless vigilance. We must be ready and prepared. The threat is present. The measures of defence have been thoroughly studied by official bodies of both countries. The Permanent Joint Board on Defence has worked assiduously and effectively on mutual problems. Now is the time for action on all agreed measures.

Steps to defend our continent are, of course, but one part of the world-wide security program. The North Atlantic Treaty Organization, for example, is an essential defence of Ottawa, and of Washington, and of our neighbours to the south, as well as of communities thousands of miles to the east. Implicit in the consultations and detailed studies which must continue, and in the defences which we have already mounted, is the need for worldwide vigilance and strength. But the purpose is defence. We have no other aim.

In common with others of the free world, the United States does not rely on military strength alone to win the peace. Our primary reliance is a unity among us forged of common adherence to moral principles. This reliance binds together in fellowship all those who believe in the spiritual nature of man, as the child of God. Moreover, our country assuredly claims no monopoly on wisdom. We are willing — nay, anxious — to discuss with friends and with any others all possible paths to peace. We will use every means — from the normal diplomatic exchange to the forum of the United Nations — to further this search. We welcome ideas, expressions of honest difference, new proposals, and new interpretations of old ones — anything and everything honestly offered for the advancement of man's oldest aspiration.

There are no insoluble problems. Differences can be resolved; tensions can be relieved. The free world, I deeply believe, holds firmly to this faith, striving earnestly towards what is just and equitable.

My friends, allow me to interpolate here merely an expression of my own personal faith. I call upon all of those who are in responsible position, either in civil government or in the

[OPPOSITE]
John and Olive Diefenbaker and President Dwight Eisenhower at a state dinner, June 3, 1960. First Lady Mamie Eisenhower was hospitalized at Walter Reed Army Hospital at the time of the dinner and was unable to attend.

[THIS PAGE]
John likes Ike, too! President Dwight Eisenhower and Louis St. Laurent's successor, Prime Minister John Diefenbaker, in June 1960.

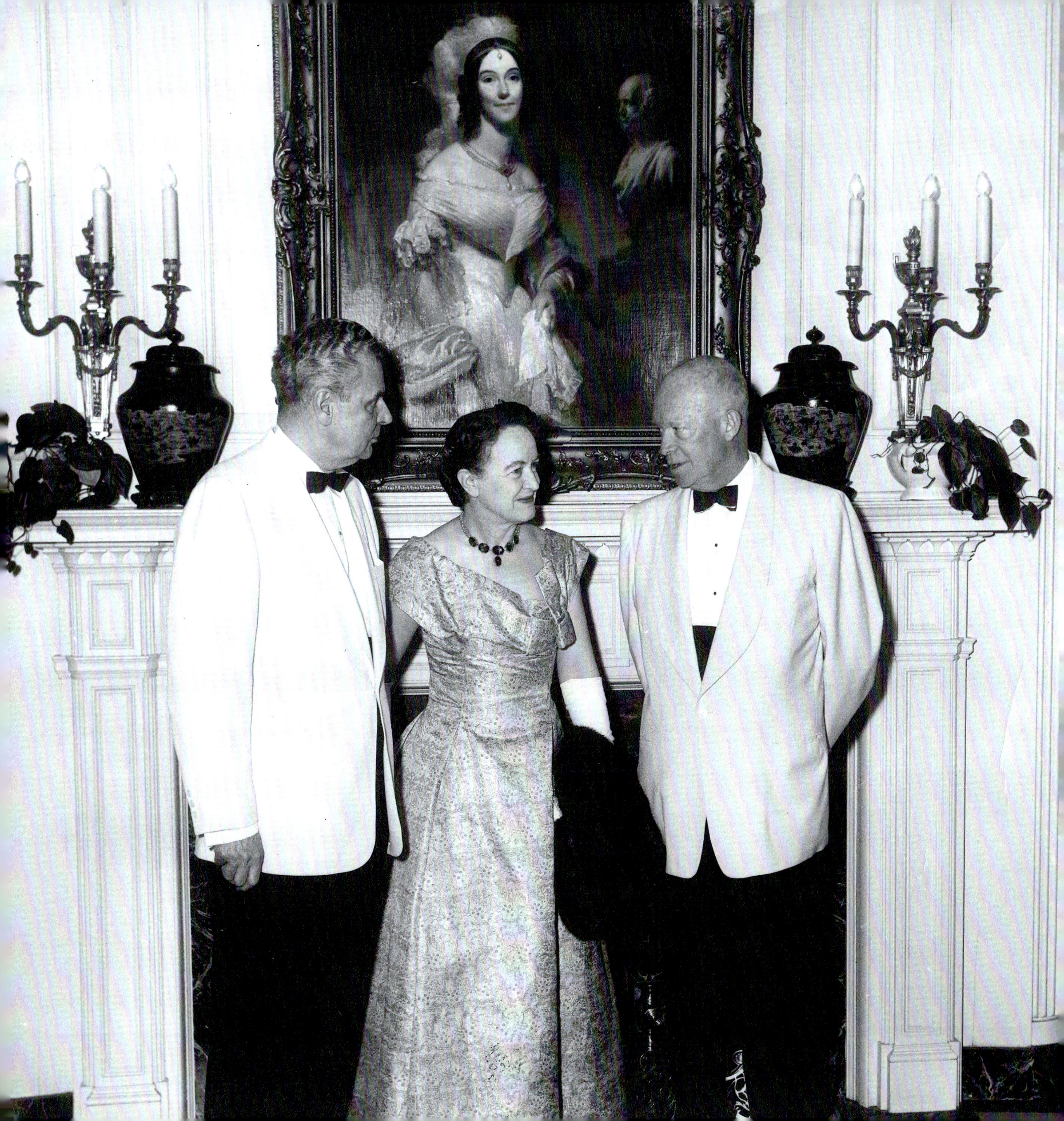

military world. In the dark days of 1940 and 1941 and 1942, there seemed no place from which to start to conquer the enemy that bid fair to enslave us all. Already he had put most of Europe under his heel. When I stop to think of the bewilderment of our people — the fears of our people in those days, and then how in a few short years we were coming home to celebrate that great victory that we thought could at last mark the end of all wars, we see how fast human affairs, human outlooks can change, from one of despondency — almost of despair, in many quarters — to one of exultation.

Now today, as we fail to understand the intransigence that we feel marks others, as we try to colour every proposal we make with what we believe to be reason, understanding — even sympathy, as we are nonplussed as to why these offers are never taken up, let us never despair that faith will not win through.

Beyond the shadow of the atomic cloud, the horizon is bright with promise.

— President Dwight D. Eisenhower

The world that God has given us is, of course, material in its values, intellectual and spiritual. We have got to hand on to those who come after us this balance — this balance of values — and particularly the certainty that they can enjoy the same kind of opportunity in this spiritual, intellectual, and material world that we, who will then be their ancestors, enjoyed before them.

That, it seems to me, is the real problem that Canada and the United States today have to meet. And it is the one reason I get such a thrill every time I come to this country, because here I sense in the very atmosphere your determination to work in that direction, not acknowledging defeat, certain that we can win because there are values that man treasures above all things else in the world that are now at stake.

The free world believes that practical problems can be solved practically; that they should be solved by orderly procedure, step by step, so that the foundation for peace, which we are building in concert with other nations, will be solid and unshakable. I deem it a high privilege to salute, through this their Parliament, the Canadian people for the strength they have added to this faith — and for the contribution they are making toward its realization.

Beyond the shadow of the atomic cloud, the horizon is bright with promise. No shadow can halt our advance together. For we, Canada and the United States, shall use carefully and wisely the God-given graces of faith and reason as we march together toward it — toward the horizon of a world where each man, each family, each nation lives at peace in a climate of freedom.

[OPPOSITE]
Prime Minister Paul Martin and President George W. Bush share a laugh while posing for the official group photo of the 2005 APEC summit with Vietnamese President Tran Duc Luong, South Korean President Roh Moo-hyun, and Chilean President Ricardo Lagos, in Busan, South Korea.

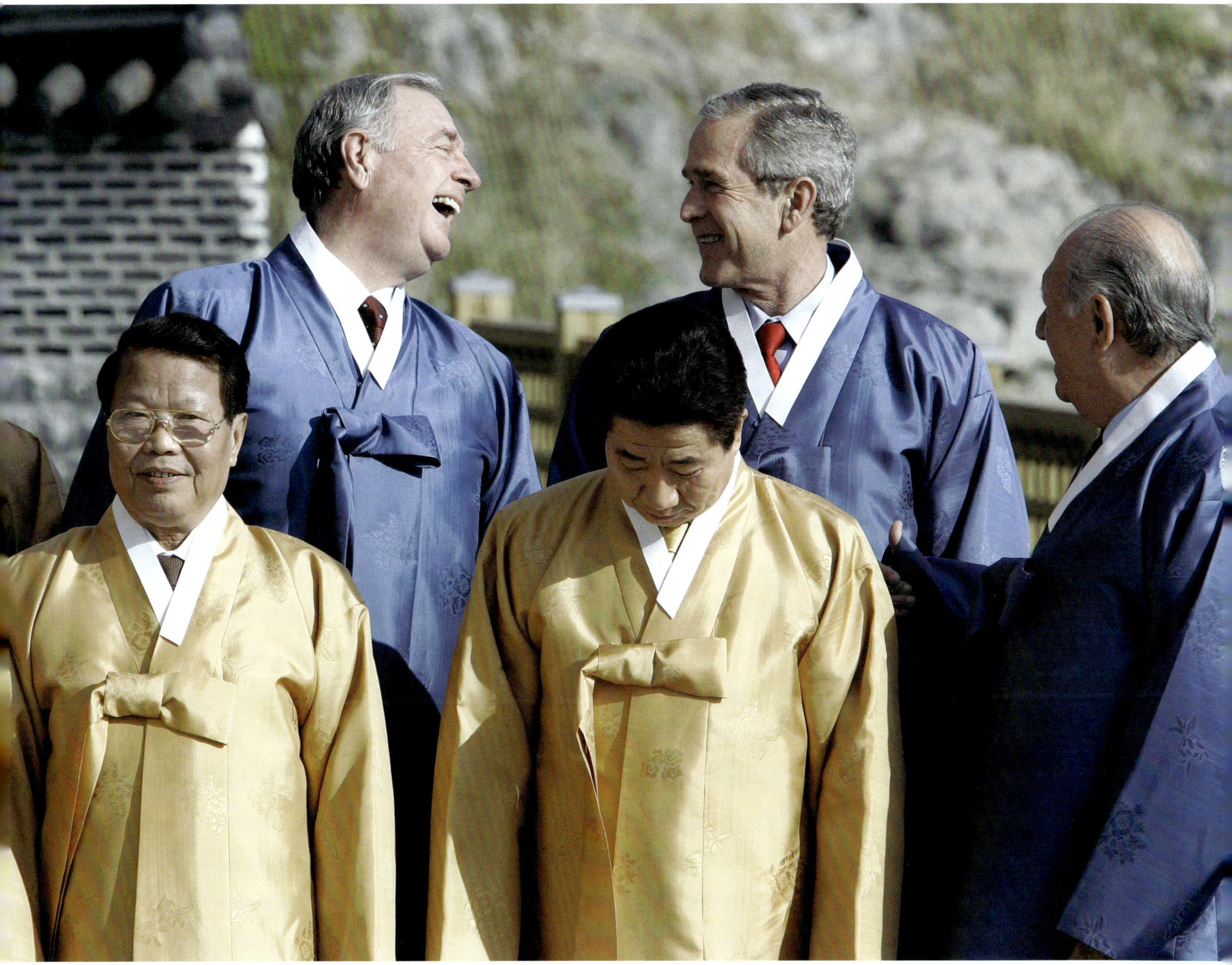

A NEW WORLD ORDER

Since the fall of the Berlin Wall, the world has become a markedly more unpredictable place — which inevitably adds complexity to the relationship between Canada and the United States. State aggression has been augmented by less defined but not less dangerous threats. The events of 9/11 shook the United States, and Canada was shaken alongside it.

In the shadow of terror, the two countries came together once again with common cause. Operation Yellow Ribbon saw the people of Gander, Newfoundland, receive thirty-eight flights and play host to 6,500 U.S. citizens after the Twin Towers went down. The two countries were also in lockstep as they went to Afghanistan — although they differed over the war in Iraq. The changes that followed in terms of shared security, coordinated intelligence, and collective defence of North America brought profound cultural and economic impacts.

Prime Minister Jean Chrétien

National Day of Mourning
Parliament Hill, Ottawa, Ontario
September 14, 2001

Mr. Ambassador [U.S. Ambassador to Canada Paul Cellucci], you have assembled before you, here on Parliament Hill and right across Canada, a people united in outrage, in grief, in compassion, and in resolve; a people of every faith and nationality to be found on Earth; a people who, as a result of the atrocity committed against the United States on September 11, 2001, feel not only like neighbours but like family.

At a time like this words fail us. We reel before the blunt and terrible reality of the evil we have just witnessed. We cannot stop the tears of grief. We cannot bring back lost wives and husbands. Sons and daughters. American citizens, Canadian citizens, citizens from all over the world. We cannot restore futures that have been cut terribly short. At a time like this, the only saving grace is our common humanity and decency. At a time like this, it is our feelings, our prayers, and our actions that count. By their outpouring of concern, sympathy and help, the feelings and actions of Canadians have been clear. And, even as we grieve our own losses, the message they send to the American people is equally clear: Do not despair; you are not alone; we are with you — the whole world is with you.

At a time like this words fail us.
We reel before the blunt and terrible reality of
the evil we have just witnessed.

— Prime Minister Jean Chrétien

The great Martin Luther King, in describing times of trial and tribulation, once said that "in the end, it is not the words of your enemies that you remember, it is the silence of your friends."

Mr. Ambassador, as your fellow Americans grieve and rebuild, there will be no silence from Canada. Our friendship has no limit. Generation after generation, we have travelled many difficult miles together. Side by side, we have lived through many dark times, always firm in our shared resolve to vanquish any threat to freedom and justice. And together, with our allies, we will defy and defeat the threat that terrorism poses to all civilized nations.

Mr. Ambassador, we will be with the United States every step of the way — as friends, as neighbours, as family.

President George W. Bush

Toast Delivered at Gatineau, Quebec
November 30, 2004

Our common bond of values and mutual respect [has] created an alliance that is unsurpassed in strength and depth and potential. Ours is one of the largest trading relationships in the world. We depend on each other to secure the energy resources that help our economies expand. We work together to protect the land and waters of our beautiful continent. Most importantly, our nations work together to protect our people from harm.

> On September 11, it was a Canadian general, holding the chair at NORAD, who **gave the order to initiate our defences.**
> — President George W. Bush

For nearly fifty years, the military personnel of your nation and mine have worked together as a single unit at NORAD to monitor the air approaches to North America and to protect us from attack. On September 11, it was a Canadian general, holding the chair at NORAD, who gave the order to initiate our defences. In an era of new threats, American and Canadian law enforcement and intelligence agencies are working more closely than ever before, and our peoples are more secure because of it.

We also share the mission of spreading the blessings of liberty around the world. In October of this year, millions of Afghans, including millions of women, voted peacefully to elect a leader of moderation. We're working together for stability and prosperity in Haiti and the Sudan. With Canada's generous contribution, the reconstruction of Iraq will help that nation become a peaceful democracy.

Our efforts in these troubled regions are driven by our faith, faith in the ability of liberty to unite different cultures, races, and religions, and faith in the ability of liberty to lift up people, to offer an alternative to hate and violence, and to change the world for the better.

STANDING TOGETHER AGAINST TYRANNY

―――

The impact of 9/11 quickly drew international attention to Afghanistan. For nearly two decades, Canadian and U.S. forces fought alongside each other, joined by NATO allies, to confront terrorist threats. In the summer of 2021, those forces finally left and the prospect of democratic rule for the people of Afghanistan ended with the return of the Taliban. But the sacrifice of Americans and Canadians, along with their allies among the people of Afghanistan, will never be forgotten.

Prime Minister Stephen J. Harper

Speech to Canadian Soldiers
Kandahar, Afghanistan
May 23, 2007

―――

Thank you for proving to Canadians and to people around the world that when Canada makes a commitment, Canada follows through. And when we all work together — Canada, NATO, and Afghanistan — we achieve real results.... Not just Canadians but all the NATO and allied soldiers who are here with the United Nations helping the Afghan people reclaim and rebuild their war-ravaged country.

I don't have to tell you the story, the link between Afghanistan and the attacks of 9/11, the oppression and brutality endured under the Taliban, and the risk that terrorism will come home if we don't confront it here.

You also know the progress we have made since the beginning of the mission over five years ago.

WITH FAITH & GOODWILL

This progress hasn't all been achieved by men and women in uniform. But none of it could have been achieved unless you had put yourselves on the line.

Because of you, the people of Afghanistan have seen the institution of democratic elections, the stirring of human rights and freedoms for women, the construction of schools, healthcare facilities, and the basic infrastructure of a functional economy.

Still, you know that your work is not complete. You know that we cannot just put down our arms and hope for peace. You know that we can't set arbitrary deadlines and simply wish for the best. And you must also know that your hard work is making a real difference to real people and their families....

Canada has no friends among America's enemies.
And America has no
better friend than Canada.

— Prime Minister Stephen J. Harper

AT WAR

Friends, you are helping the Afghan people make a better life for themselves and their children.

I saw it yesterday morning at the Aschiana School in Kabul, where Canada is partnering to ensure that children who, because of war, tragedy, and chaos, were left out of the school system are now getting an education. I learned of it through discussions in Kabul with Canadians who are assisting with vaccination programs, reaching nearly two hundred thousand children and women in this country.

Canadians who are working with Afghans on over twenty-seven thousand reconstruction projects now underway, including clean water, sanitation, and electrical power.

Such achievements come only through the secure environment you are building here. Now, friends, I know your mission has been at times very difficult. And the nature of your tasks and the sheer brutality of your foe mark inherent dangers along the road to a lasting peace and reconstruction in Afghanistan....

[OPPOSITE AND BELOW] Prime Minister Stephen Harper undertook a secret trip to Afghanistan in 2007 to thank Canadian troops serving on the frontlines of that conflict in person.

You're Canada's sons and daughters and your country, as much as this country, owes you a debt of gratitude and its unwavering support.

As Canadians, we have tremendous pride in our great country and its values. But we truly show our belief in our values only when we put them on the line — only when we are prepared to share them with those less fortunate than ourselves.

I don't have to tell you the story, the link between Afghanistan and the attacks of 9/11, the oppression and brutality endured under the Taliban, and the risk that terrorism will come home if we don't confront it here.

— Prime Minister Stephen J. Harper

Every day, you personify these values and virtues here in Afghanistan. You are the diligent neighbours and the compassionate workers. You are the courageous warriors and the loyal friends. You're the very best our country has to offer.

I am proud of you. Canadians are proud of you. And I'm here to tell you that we are behind you. Your government will continue steadfastly supporting the men and women of the Canadian Forces as the most professional, disciplined, and effective soldiers in the world.

We will let no one diminish all that you have achieved here for Canada. I thank you for all that you are doing. God bless you in the work that lies ahead. God bless your loved ones at home. And God bless Canada.

Prime Minister Stephen J. Harper

Joint Declaration on the Border with President Barack Obama
Washington, D.C.
February 4, 2011

———

A THREAT TO THE UNITED STATES IS A THREAT TO CANADA, TO OUR TRADE, TO OUR interests, to our values, and to our common civilization. Canada has no friends among America's enemies. And America has no better friend than Canada.... While a border defines two peoples, it need not divide them. That is the fundamental truth to which Canadians and Americans have borne witness for almost two centuries, and through our mutual devotion to freedom, democracy, and justice, at home and abroad, it is the example we seek to demonstrate for all others.

Keeping the Canada-U.S. border secure and combatting terrorism were key parts of the talks held between Prime Minister Stephen J. Harper and President Barack Obama at the White House in February 2011.

AT WORK

IN GOD WE TRUST

T HERE ARE EXACTLY 3,987 MILES — OR 6,416 KILOMETRES — OF undefended border between Canada and the United States. That much geography gives rise to a great many issues and an awful lot of work. In the long history of our nation-to-nation relationship, few issues have been more important than trade, and no issue has produced more work at the negotiating table, as well as on the factory floor and in the office suite. In usual times, the movement of goods and services between our two countries generates $2 billion per day and is responsible for countless jobs.

Never was the importance of border issues felt more acutely than when it was contested by the arrival of Covid-19. But with determined effort, even that threat was managed, attesting to the deep commitment on both sides to preserve safe and secure commercial relations under the most difficult of circumstances. Trade is far from the only matter to occupy the two countries. But in some ways, its history is a history of the relationship itself.

Sir John A. Macdonald, Canada's first prime minister, helped to create the National Policy — a system of tariffs that protected industry in Ontario and Quebec. For Macdonald, this wasn't just an economic policy — it had deep cultural resonance, as he demonstrated during his final election campaign in the winter of 1891. His Liberal opponent, Wilfrid Laurier, was advocating a free trade agreement with the United States. Macdonald would have none of it. Using the most famous election poster in Canadian history — "The Old Flag, The Old Policy, The Old Leader," it proclaimed — Macdonald called the idea "veiled treason" and shouted proudly, "A British subject I was born. A British subject I will die!"

[PREVIOUS PAGE]
Prime Minister Brian Mulroney addresses a joint session of Congress, April 1988.

I have been attacked as an imperialist and as an anti-imperialist.

I am neither.

I am just a Canadian, a Canadian first, last, and all the time.

— Prime Minister Wilfrid Laurier

Twenty years later, Laurier achieved his dream. He was able to negotiate a free trade agreement — known then as reciprocity — with William Howard Taft's administration. Laurier placed it before the people and all hell broke loose. His Tory opponent, Robert Borden, took a page from Sir John A.'s book and waved the British flag before English Canadians. He combined this tactic with a brilliant appeal to Quebec nationalists, and Laurier went down to defeat. "I have been attacked as an imperialist and as an anti-imperialist. I am neither. I am just a Canadian, a Canadian first, last, and all the time," Laurier said sadly in one speech.

"You'll never die, Sir John!" Sir John A. Macdonald, the first prime minister of Canada.

Like his negotiating partner Wilfrid Laurier, President Taft was also saddened by the deal's defeat. "I have just been informed that reciprocity has failed in Canada," Taft told the press. "For me it is a great disappointment. I had hoped that it would be put through to prove the correctness of my judgment that it would be a good thing for both countries. It takes two to make a bargain, and if Canada declines, we can still go on doing business at the old stand."

Almost eighty years later, Prime Minister Brian Mulroney would experience first-hand how riled up Canadians can get when a federal campaign turns on an issue like free trade.

Like Laurier, Mulroney successfully negotiated a free trade agreement with an American administration. This time it was Ronald Reagan in the Oval Office. After one of the most raucous elections in Canadian history, Mulroney was re-elected in 1988 and the Canada-U.S. Free Trade Agreement came into effect. Where Laurier had failed, the boy from Baie-Comeau, Quebec, prevailed.

Three decades later, new pressures and new politics led to an updating of that accord, and the United States-Mexico-Canada Agreement (USMCA) came into being after a challenging set of negotiations. President Donald Trump's protectionist bent and mercurial manner tested Prime Minister Justin Trudeau and his team thoroughly. But the deep, historical tug of mutual self-interest triumphed, and the USMCA was proclaimed on November 30, 2018. That was followed a little more than two years later by a new U.S. president and a new blueprint for bilateral co-operation in the face of a sweeping pandemic. Working collaboratively, President Joe Biden and Prime Minister Trudeau were able to put into place a roadmap in February 2021 that reached beyond the USMCA to include areas such as public health protocols, climate change, defence, and co-operative security.

Prime Minister Justin Trudeau meets virtually with newly inaugurated President Joe Biden on February 23, 2021.

BUILDING BRIDGES — AND HIGHWAYS AND SEAWAYS AND …

The middle of the twentieth century saw the United States and Canada caught up in a post-war boom that exploded the populations and infrastructure of both countries. At times, it seemed as though the entire continent was under construction, with national highways, new bridges, and corridors created to link the two countries together and from within.

Such expansion required the contribution of the private sector and, often, the enthusiastic involvement of the public sector as well. Political leaders have always seen bridges and railways, seaways and airports as a metaphor for new opportunity and, even more important, new jobs and growth.

Prime Minister William Lyon Mackenzie King

Opening of the Peace Bridge
Buffalo, New York
August 7, 1927

On behalf of the government and people of Canada, I thank His Excellency, the governor of the state of New York for the welcome he has extended to the guests of our country, His Royal Highness the Prince of Wales, his Royal Highness Prince George, and the prime minister of Great Britain, and for the welcome which through his words, and the distinguished presence of the vice president and the secretary of state, comes from the people of the United States to all who are here from Canada today.

You will notice that I have referred to our distinguished visitors as our guests. We are all part of the same family. We are all of the same British household united by a common allegiance to the Crown, which is represented here today in the person of His Royal Highness the Prince of Wales. We are united, too, by common political institutions based upon those of the mother of parliaments, which also happily is represented here in the person of Mr. Baldwin. As members of the British household have grown up, scattered as they are throughout different parts of the world, they have come to possess on different continents their own individual households, while remaining members of the one British family. We of Canada are greatly pleased to have the privilege of having with us some of the older members of the family, and having them see how we live among ourselves and how we live with our neighbours.

We are delighted to have the opportunity of bringing our royal and distinguished visitors to a part of the international frontier which is unparalleled in its scenic beauty. It is a source of even greater pleasure to be able to show them a frontier whose history is unique in the annals of the world — an international frontier across which, for over one hundred years, not a single shot has been fired, not a single sword has been drawn, and along the whole of which,

A royal greeting. Prince Edward (later King Edward VIII) and Vice President Charles G. Dawes, top-hatted on the right, heading to the ceremonies for the dedication of the Peace Bridge on the American side, August 7, 1927.

a distance of nearly four thousand miles, there is today not a single fort. Where at one time, more than a century ago, near the place where we are now assembled, there were two forts, one on this side of the Niagara River, and the other on the Canadian shore opposite, there are today the two great supports of the international bridge which has just been formally opened, and which stands as a symbol of international amity, international goodwill, and international peace. This is the great object lesson which we of the New World have to give to those who come to us from the Old.

In the one hundred years of peace we have enjoyed on this continent, we have sought to develop a method of adjusting our differences which would make reason supreme over force. While we recognize that peace stands rooted in the instinctive goodwill of our peoples, we know it is due also in no small part to the conscious planning of those who strive for peace. The Rush-Bagot Agreement of 1817 laid the foundations. The International Joint Commission, which was appointed in 1911 as the result of legislation by the governments of the two countries, has, through the careful judgment of wise and thoughtful men and the influence of public opinion, been the means of settling practically all the boundary questions which of recent years

[OPPOSITE]
Edward, Prince of Wales (left), and his brother, Prince George, at the ceremonies.

[THIS PAGE]
Vice President Charles Dawes shakes hands with the Prince of Wales.

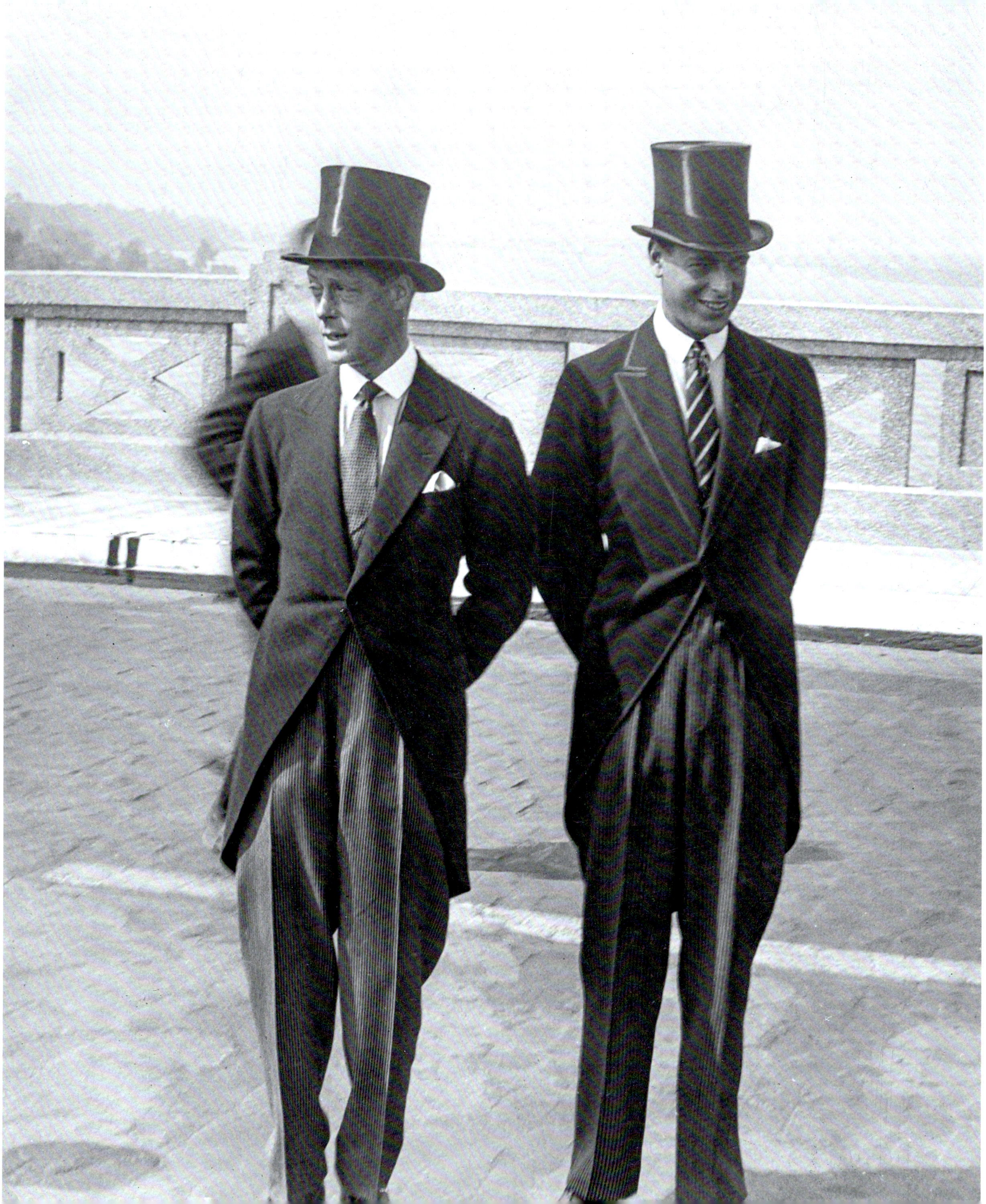

have arisen, and which were likely to lead to serious controversy. Therein lies an assurance and a means of peace which we shall not only cherish for ourselves, but which we hope may prove of value in wider fields. We believe that in the years to come, the International Joint Commission will continue to carry on its work with equal success. But we hope, nay, we believe, that it will not be confined to settle questions which may arise between Canada and the United States, but that empowered as it is to deal with any question which may be referred to it by agreement, it will prove a helpful model for the adjustment of all international differences which may arise between English-speaking peoples.

> In the one hundred years of peace we have enjoyed on this continent, we have sought to develop a method of adjusting our differences which would make reason supreme over force.
>
> — Prime Minister William Lyon Mackenzie King

We of this continent have taken this year yet another forward step, of which this bridge may well stand as a symbol. We have sought, by an exchange of ministers, to throw a bridge of international goodwill from the one capital to the other. The presence on this occasion of the newly appointed ministers adds significance to this ceremony. The appointment by the United States of a minister to Canada and the appointment by Canada of a minister to the United States had the full approval and concurrence of the British government and of His Majesty the King. The appointment of our minister means a more direct representation of Canada at Washington. It will mean, as well, a closer co-operation on the part of Canada with the British Embassy at Washington in questions affecting the relations between the United States and the whole British Empire. We believe that this further exchange of personal relationships in international affairs will help to perpetuate the peace which the English-speaking peoples have enjoyed for more than a century; a peace which it is our hope today may be continued for all time.

This is indeed an occasion which we may well remember, an occasion for thanksgiving, an occasion of dedication. We thank a wise and kind Providence which has given us in the New World this friendly border, the most precious of our common heritages; and which has inspired New-World methods of settling matters of international dispute.

Vice President Charles Dawes

From Notes as Vice President
A Day at the Peace Bridge
August 7, 1927

———

WE STOPPED AT BUFFALO, NEW YORK, FOR THE DEDICATION OF THE PEACE BRIDGE. The ceremony took place on the centre of the bridge where the two official groups met. The prince and I shook hands and exchanged informal greetings over a ribbon stretched across the bridge; Mrs. Dawes then cut the ribbon with a pair of gilt scissors. Both parties next rode to a platform on the American side, where an audience estimated at seventy-five thousand was gathered. When the prince and I stepped from our car, I insisted that he precede me to the platform, as that appealed to me as the proper courtesy to show our guest. When he and I went through formal affairs later in the afternoon on the Canadian side, he insisted that I precede him. I

Best show in town! The crowd at the ceremonies — an estimated one hundred thousand people — witnessed the dedication of the Peace Bridge.

mention this merely because some American papers criticized at length this proceeding on the American side as indicating that our government was improperly taking a back seat because I did not step ahead. Washington indulges in much discussion of questions of personal precedence, and to such a degree is offense sometimes taken if the precedents are not followed that the State Department undertakes to give advice in the matter, especially in connection with official dinners and other official occasions. I suppose this saves a lot of petty and undignified quarreling. But I do not think the American people care a "whoop" about these things.

The principal addresses were made by the Prince of Wales, Premier Baldwin, Premier King, Secretary Kellogg, Governor Smith, and myself. In my address, as the Geneva Naval Disarmament

> The speech was referred to by some of the newspaper correspondents as "undiplomatic"; but it was not so. Common sense is never undiplomatic.
> — Vice President Charles Dawes

Conference had just ended in a failure to agree, and this was a peace celebration, I commented upon the result.

The speech was referred to by some of the newspaper correspondents as "undiplomatic"; but it was not so. Common sense is never undiplomatic. Premier Baldwin asked me to sign my reading copy as a souvenir for him and the Canadian minister told me afterward that his government had indicated its agreement with its conclusions. The editorial comments on both sides of the boundary line were commendatory, and I think it expressed the common sentiments of the English-speaking peoples....

President Dwight D. Eisenhower

Opening of the St. Lawrence Seaway
June 26, 1959

———

This waterway, linking the oceans of the world with the Great Lakes of the American continent, is the culmination of the dreams of thousands of individuals on both sides of our common Canadian-United States border. It is the latest event in a long history of peaceful parallel progress by our two peoples.

Side by side we have grown up together. Long ago we found solutions for many of the problems characteristic of pioneering peoples. We have built nations out of vast stretches of virgin territory and transformed a wilderness into one of the most productive areas on Earth. We are still developing better means of production and communication and supporting measures needed for the welfare of our respective peoples.

A notable spirit of co-operation has been responsible for major steps in our past progress. That spirit animates both countries today. We enjoy between us a larger volume of reciprocal trade than do any other two nations in the world. Our peoples move freely back and forth across a boundary that has known neither gun nor fortress in over a century. Our citizen-soldiers have three times fought together in the cause of freedom and today we are as one in our determination to defend our homelands. We have lived in peace with each other for nearly a century and a half. We cherish this record.

There have been and are still problems to solve between us. But in the past, as now, we have never faltered in our conviction that these problems must be settled by patient and understanding negotiation, never by violence.

So today, our two nations celebrate another triumph in peaceful living. The St. Lawrence Seaway presents to the world a 2,300-mile waterway of locks, lakes, and man-made channels. Its completion is a tribute to those far-sighted and persevering people who across the years pushed forward to their goal despite decades of disappointments and setbacks. We pause to salute all those who have shared in this task, from the architects and the planners to the artisans and the workers who have spent countless hours in its construction. Included among those who made possible this great development are statesmen and political leaders of the major parties of both countries, beginning with the administrations of Prime Minister Bennett of Canada and President Herbert Hoover of the United States.

The parade of ships already passing through the Seaway on their way to and from the heart of the continent strikingly demonstrates the economic value of this new channel. But the Seaway is far more than a technical and commercial triumph. It has more significance than could

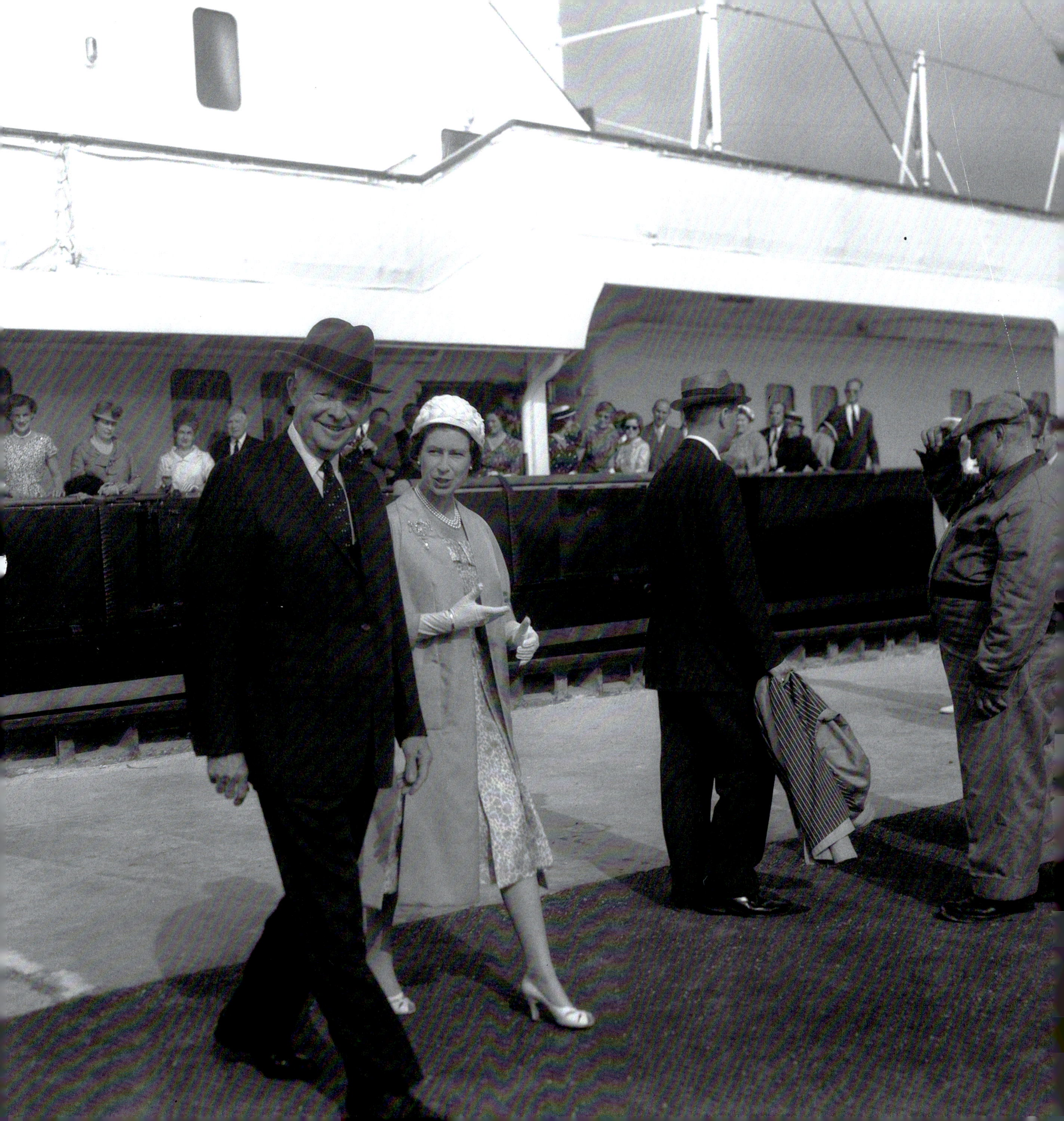

AT WORK

Our citizen-soldiers have three times fought together in the cause of freedom and today we are as one in our determination to defend our homelands.

— President Dwight D. Eisenhower

just the successful construction of even this notable aid to commerce and navigation. It is, above all, a magnificent symbol to the entire world of the achievements possible to democratic nations peacefully working together for the common good.

So may this example be never forgotten by us, and may it never be ignored by others. For in the reasonable resolution of the acute international problems of our time rests the single hope for world prosperity and happiness in peace, with justice for all.

[OPPOSITE]
Another royal good time! Her Majesty Queen Elizabeth II and President Eisenhower at the opening of the St. Lawrence Seaway, June 26, 1959.

[THIS PAGE]
Realizing a bilateral dream. The official party at the opening of the St. Lawrence Seaway. His Royal Highness Prince Philip (front left), Her Majesty Queen Elizabeth II, President Eisenhower, First Lady Mamie Eisenhower (far right).

FREE TRADE: TAKING THE LEAP OF FAITH

As long as there has been a Canada, there has been a political debate about its economic relationship with the United States. From the country's earliest days, Canadian leaders have suggested, defended, and sometimes been defeated in service to the idea of more open borders and freer trade between the two nations. For its part, the United States has always looked upon the vast natural resources of its northern neighbour with a desire to widen commerce and create jobs — although the subject of free trade today seems more politically combustible in U.S. politics than it does in Canada's.

Three hard runs at what was then known as reciprocity were taken in Canada's early days. Both times they turned elections — electing one of its greatest prime ministers, Sir John A. Macdonald, in the first example and defeating another of its formative leaders in Sir Wilfrid Laurier on the second turn. Mackenzie King, who had been defeated as a young MP while running under Laurier's trade-with-America banner, later as prime minister backed away from pursuing advance negotiations with the United States when a deal was probably achievable.

Dogged by the sluggish economy of the 1970s, a new breed of leaders took power in the decade to follow with a determination to unleash the fuller force of private enterprise. Leaders like Ronald Reagan and Brian Mulroney were willing to wrestle with the complicated details and brave the political wrath that came from opening the door again to reciprocity in trade between the two nations, which by the 1980s had been relabelled "free trade."

Years of negotiations, an army of experts, divided opinion, and a defining single-issue election campaign in Canada gave birth to the Canada-U.S. Free Trade Agreement in the late 1980s. By the early 1990s its reach had been stretched to include Mexico, with the signing of NAFTA. The economic and identity issues it unleashed remain a feature of politics to this day.

President Ronald Reagan

Address to a Joint Session of Parliament
Ottawa, Ontario
April 6, 1987

———

IT'S TRULY AN HONOUR TO HAVE A SECOND OPPORTUNITY TO ADDRESS THIS AUGUST body, this great democratic legislature that has been witness to, and shaper of, so much of the history of freedom. I remember those days not so very long after the attack on Pearl Harbor had once again united our two nations in a world conflict, when Winston Churchill stood where I am standing today.

Wake Island had fallen just a week before. On Christmas Day, after a heroic defence by Canadian troops, Hong Kong was captured by the Axis. Manila was soon to be swallowed up as well. But those who might have been expecting a picture of democracy in retreat got something very different from that indomitable spirit. "We have not journeyed all this way across the centuries," he said, "across the oceans, across the mountains, across the prairies, because we're made of sugar candy." Churchill was speaking of the members of the British Commonwealth, most specifically of the people of Canada — but I confess we Americans have always flattered ourselves that, though the thought was unspoken, he had us in mind, too. *[Laughter.]*

As two proud and independent peoples, there is much that distinguishes us one from the other, but there is also much that we share: a vast continent, with its common hardships and uncommon duties; generations of mutual respect and support; and an abiding friendship that grows ever stronger. We are two nations, each built by immigrant refugees from tyranny and want, pioneers of a new land of liberty. The first settlers of this New World, alone before the majesty of nature, alone before God, must have been thrown back on first principles, must have realized that it was only in their most basic values that they would find the wisdom to endure and the strength to triumph. And so, a dedication was formed, as hard as the granite of the Rockies, a dedication to freedom, a commitment to those unalienable human rights and their only possible guarantee: the institutions of democratic government.

A shared history, yes, but more than that, a shared purpose. It must have seemed to Churchill, besieged and isolated as he was in the one corner of Europe still clinging to freedom, that this American continent and his two great friends and one-time colonies had been placed here by a wise and prescient God, protected between two vast oceans, to keep freedom safe. In the crisis of the moment, Churchill said it was not then time to "speak of the hopes of the future, or the broader world which lies beyond our struggles and our victory. We must first," he said, "win that world for our children."

In a very real sense, that is still our imperative today: to win the world for our children, to win it for freedom. Today, our task is not merely the survival of liberty but to keep the peace while we extend liberty to a world desperately in need. Today, we still contend against war, against a foreign expansionism, and I will speak to that in a moment.

But I wish first to talk about a second struggle, one that must occupy an equal place in our attentions: the struggle against the plagues of poverty and underdevelopment that still ravage so much of mankind. Our two nations have committed many resources to that struggle, but we have it within our power at this moment to take a historic step toward a growing world economy, and an expanding cycle of prosperity that reaches beyond the industrialized powers even to the developing nations.

We are two nations, each built by immigrant refugees
from tyranny and want, pioneers of a new land of liberty.
— President Ronald Reagan

We can lead, first, by our powerful example, specifically by the example of Prime Minister Mulroney's farsighted proposal to establish a free trade agreement that would eliminate most remaining trade barriers between Canada and the United States. After the allied victory over the Axis powers, America and Canada combined their efforts to help restore Europe to economic health. Those were golden years of international economic co-operation that saw the creation of GATT, which knocked down the tariff barriers that had so damaged the world economy; the International Monetary Fund; and, thirty years ago last month, the creation of the Common Market. The theme that ran through it all was free and fair trade. Free and fair trade was the lifeblood of a reinvigorated Europe, a revitalized free world that saw a generation of growth unparalleled in history.

We must keep these principles fixed in our minds as we move forward on Prime Minister Mulroney's free trade proposal, a proposal that I'm convinced will prove no less historic. Already, our two nations generate the world's largest volume of trade. The United States trades more with the province of Ontario alone than with Japan. United States citizens are by far the principal foreign investors in Canada, and Canadians on a per capita basis are even greater investors in our country. This two-way traffic in trade and investment has helped to create new jobs by the millions, to expand opportunity for both our peoples, and to augment the prosperity of both our nations.

Prime Minister Mulroney's proposal would establish the largest free trade area in the world, benefiting not only our two countries, but setting an example of co-operation to all nations that now wrestle against the siren temptation of protectionism. To those who would hunker down behind barriers to fight a destructive and self-defeating round of trade battles, Canada and the United States will show the positive way. We will overcome the impulse of economic isolationism with a brotherly embrace — an embrace, it is not too much to hope, that may someday extend throughout the Americas and ultimately encompass all free nations. We can look forward to the day when the free flow of trade, from the southern reaches of Tierra del Fuego to the northern outposts of the Arctic Circle, unites the people of the Western hemisphere in a bond of mutually beneficial exchange, when all borders become what the U.S.-Canadian border so long has been: a meeting place, rather than a dividing line.

We recognize that the issues facing us are many and difficult. And, just as this proud Parliament is watching our negotiations, so, too, is the United States Congress. A comprehensive, balanced agreement that provides open trade and investment on a comprehensive basis, an agreement in which both sides are winners — that is our goal. Augmenting the spirit of the Uruguay trade negotiations, prelude to our economic summit in Venice this June, our free trade discussions here will be a model of co-operation to the world. Mr. Prime Minister, this will be a pioneering agreement worthy of a pioneering people, a visionary strategy worthy of the elected head of one of the world's greatest democracies. Mr. Prime Minister, we salute you, and I pledge to you now that, for our part, we shall commit ourselves and the resources of our administration to good-faith negotiations that will make this visionary proposal a reality. And on this, the Canadian people and the members of Parliament have my word.

Freedom works. The democratic freedoms that secure the God-given rights of man, and the economic freedoms that open the door to prosperity — they are the hope and, we trust, the destiny of mankind. If free trade is the lifeblood, free enterprise is the heart of prosperity. Jobs, rising incomes, opportunity — they must be created, day to day, through the enterprise of free men and women.

We've had to learn and relearn this lesson in this century. In my own country, we have witnessed an expansion and strengthening of many of our civil liberties, but too often we have seen our economic liberties neglected, even abused. We have protected the freedom of expression of the author, as we should; but what of the freedom of expression of the entrepreneur, whose pen and paper are capital and whose profits and whose literature is the heroic epic of free enterprise, a tale of creativity and invention that not only delights the mind but has improved the condition of man, feeding the poor with new grains, bringing hope to the ailing with new cures, vanquishing ignorance with wondrous new information technologies….

And free markets, low tax rates, free trade — this is the most valuable foreign aid we can give to the developing nations of the Third World. These are the weapons of peace we must deploy in the struggle to win a future of liberty for mankind. So many have come to Canada and the United States in hope; let us now give that hope to the world.

Throughout our history, our two nations have keenly felt our international responsibilities. Instrumental in founding and maintaining the NATO alliance, through co-operative efforts in

NORAD, Canada has taken a leading role in defence of the free world. And meanwhile, we have co-operated in extending every effort to lessen the dangers of a nuclear-armed world. Over the past six years, the United States, working closely with Canada and our other allies, has sought to achieve deep reductions in Soviet and American nuclear arms. Thanks to the firmness shown by the alliance, we are moving toward a breakthrough agreement that would dramatically reduce an entire class of weapons: American and Soviet longer-range, intermediate-range, INF missiles in Europe and Asia.

We've travelled far to get here, from past treaties that only codified the nuclear buildup, to the point where we may soon see the dismantling of thousands of these agents of annihilation. We're hopeful, we're expectant, but we face many difficulties still. As our negotiators continue to work toward a sound agreement, we are not going to abandon our basic principles or our allies' interests for the sake of a quick fix, an inadequate accord. We will work for truly verifiable reductions that strengthen the security of our friends and allies in both Europe and Asia, and that cannot be circumvented by any imbalance in shorter-range INF systems.

In short, America will stand where she has always stood: with her allies in defence of freedom and the cause of peace....

On the border between Canada and the United States stands a plaque commemorating over a century and a half of friendship. It calls the border "a lesson of peace to all nations." And that's what it is: a concrete, living lesson that the path to peace is freedom, that the relations of free peoples — no matter how different, no matter how distinct their national characters — those relations will be marked by admiration, not hostility.

> So many have come to Canada and the United States in hope; let us now give that hope to the world.
> — President Ronald Reagan

Go stand along the border at the beginning of July. You'll see the Maple Leaf and the Stars and Stripes mixed in a swirling cloud of visitors and celebrants. As a Canadian writer once put it: "What's the difference between Dominion Day and July Fourth? About forty-eight hours." *[Laughter.]*

Yes, we have differences, disputes, as any two sovereign nations will; but we're always able to work them out, *entre amis* [between friends].

One area of particular concern to all Canadians, I know, is the problem of acid rain. When the prime minister and I met in Quebec two years ago, we appointed two distinguished envoys,

Bill Davis and Drew Lewis, to examine the problem. They issued a joint report, which we have endorsed, and we're actively implementing many of their recommendations. The first phase of our clean coal technology program is underway, the beginning of a $6 billion commitment through 1992, and I have asked Congress for the full share of government spending recommended by the envoys, $2.5 billion, for the demonstration of innovative pollution control technologies over the next five years. Literally thousands of firms and millions of jobs will be affected by whatever steps we take on this problem, so there are no quick and easy answers. But working together, we have made an important start, and I am convinced that, as in the past, our disputes will bring us closer as we find a mutual accord. Our differences will become only another occasion for co-operation.

> This is the chosen place in history our two nations occupy: a land where the mind and heart of man is free, a land of peace, a land where indeed anything is possible.
> — President Ronald Reagan

Let me assure you that your concerns are my concerns. I was struck recently by the words of a Canadian — a Hungarian-Canadian you might call him — who came to this country, as so many before him, to escape oppression. "I wanted to stretch," he said. "I needed a place where I could move mountains or carry larger stones than Sisyphus, and here was the place for it. Nobody telling me what I'm supposed to believe, as a Canadian, gave me a kind of freedom for my mind and my spirit and my creative energies that I had never experienced before in life. And I found that for me anyhow, anything could be possible here."

This is your Canada, and our continent. This is the chosen place in history our two nations occupy: a land where the mind and heart of man is free, a land of peace, a land where indeed anything is possible.

Let me add a word, if I can, about our discussions today on two issues of critical interest to our two countries. The prime minister and I agreed to consider the prime minister's proposal for a bilateral accord on acid rain, building on the tradition of agreements to control pollution of our shared international waters. The prime minister and I also had a full discussion of the Arctic waters issue, and he and I agreed to inject new impetus to the discussions already underway. We are determined to find a solution based on mutual respect for sovereignty and our common security and other interests.

Prime Minister Brian Mulroney

Address to the U.S. Congress
Washington, D.C.
April 27, 1988

———

We are two independent nations, each with its own national interests and unique character. You have one official language; we have two. Your system of governments is congressional; ours is parliamentary. Neither of our countries is without its inequities and its imperfections. But we are, each in our own way, building caring societies that give our citizens remarkable opportunities for education and employment, enabling them and our countries to make dramatic social and economic progress. We each have sovereign interests to assert, national interests to uphold. And we can have different views of the world, just as we clearly have different responsibilities in the world.

You know, it is fashionable in some circles to suggest that America is growing weary of its role, and that its influence is in decline in the world. The evidence to the contrary is all about you, in the Silicon Valley of California, in the Sun Belt of the South, in your great agricultural heartland, in the new high technology corridor of the Northeast, in the towers of Manhattan, and throughout this splendid capital.

The world still looks to America not only as a model of liberty, but as a source of persuasive international leadership. The world counts as well on the strength and independence of this Congress, a legislature of unprecedented influence and capacity for good which has endured for over two hundred years, and which stands proudly as a cornerstone of this impressive democracy.

Mr. Speaker, when I sought the leadership of my party five years ago, and it was then that I acquired a deep respect for everyone everywhere who has had to run in a primary, but when I sought the leadership of my own party, I said that Canada and the United States were one another's best friend and greatest ally. Nothing in my experience in government (and we have known tensions and serious disagreement) has led me to revise my views about the profound value of an exemplary relationship between two of the world's great democracies.

Our common democratic values and our shared commitment to defend them are but one worthy example of neighbourliness and leadership. The protection of our environment is another. As President Reagan has said: Our two countries should work together on all matters of environment, because entrusted to us is the care of a very unique and a very beautiful continent, and all of us share the desire to protect this for generations of Canadians and Americans yet to come....

[OPPOSITE]

"Did you hear the one about the Irishman?" Prime Minister Brian Mulroney and President Ronald Reagan share a laugh as Mulroney departs the White House after a visit, March 24, 1986.

AT WORK

In terms of resources, Canada plays a major role in the world. With the seventh largest economy in the free world, Canada has had, since 1984, the strongest growth rate of the economic summit countries. We are the world's largest exporter of metals and lumber, the world's second largest exporter of wheat, and we supply fully one-third of the world's newsprint (I am not responsible for the editorials).

Canada and the United States conduct vital energy trade. Canada is the most important foreign supplier of oil, gas, and electricity. This is just one component of the world's largest trading partnership, in which two million jobs in each country depend on exports to the other. Consider

> Our common democratic values and our shared commitment to defend them are but one worthy example of neighbourliness and leadership.
> — Prime Minister Brian Mulroney

this: three-quarters of our exports come to the United States; fully one-quarter of your exports go to Canada. We buy, as Canadians, twice as much from you as Japan, and we buy ten times as much on a per capita basis. Canada buys more from the United States of America than the United Kingdom, France, West Germany, and Italy combined, and I tell you, that is the record of a fair and good trader. May Margaret Thatcher forgive me, but, in point of fact, as you already know, we are your best customers. We are good partners. We are fair traders.

The Free Trade Agreement presents our two countries with a historic opportunity to create new jobs and [develop] enduring prosperity. This won't surprise you, but there are those in our country who say that in these negotiations, we gave up too much. There are those in your country, perhaps even in this chamber, who contend that we conceded too little. The agreement is not everything either side would have wanted, but as Franklin Roosevelt once observed: "Nations are co-equals, and therefore any treaty must represent compromises."

This is a good, balanced, and fair agreement, the most important ever concluded between two trading partners. Quite apart from phasing out all tariffs, which I think you will agree is an achievement in itself, we've established a number of important firsts: for trade in services, for financial services, for bilateral investment. And we've established a unique dispute settlement mechanism.

My administration has the majority to enact this agreement, and we shall. In the Congress, you will vote it up or down, as you see the interest of your fellow citizens. It is there, on the table, for both of us to ratify: a dream as old as the century, a dream that has eluded successive generations of leaders for a hundred years, a dream that is now clearly within our grasp.

Now is the time to send a powerful signal to our other trading partners, to give strong impetus to the GATT, to give new hope to those poorer nations who desperately need more liberalized trade and more generous access to our markets.

We stand at the threshold of a great new opportunity for all our citizens. This is more than simply a commercial agreement between two countries. The Free Trade Agreement for you and for me is a call to excellence. It is a summons to our two peoples to respond to the challenge of comparative advantage in the twenty-first century. A nation's productivity may end on the assembly line, but it begins in the classroom. The imperatives of education are compelling and clear. Canadians know we have learned that the growth areas of our economy, the areas of technology and innovation and the service sector, will demand, for example, higher math scores, higher reading and reasoning skills, and greater language proficiency, if we are to remain competitive.

The demands of trade have obliged us, as a smaller country with twenty-five million people, to learn to be lean and aggressive, but fair, and in becoming more competitive in the world, I think we have become more knowledgeable upwardly.

And so, Mr. Speaker, that is the challenge of the Pacific. This is not a mystery. This is the challenge of the Pacific. That is the challenge of the European community, 320 million strong, in 1992. That is the challenge of developing nations who cannot meet their financial obligations if they cannot sell their goods. If the poorest nations cannot get that crippling burden of debt off their backs, they can't do business with either of our great countries.

From the age of the Phoenicians, to the age of Venice, to our own era, civilizations have always been enriched by trade. And that is my judgment, and I fought for this, and I have carried our share of responsibility, and others in this chamber have as well. That is what the Free Trade Agreement is about — a magnificent opportunity for a new decade and a new century. The challenges and the choices for both our nations are clear: to guarantee our continued security; to ensure an environment in which our children can inherit both a standard of living and a standard of life; to provide for their education and development in a manner which will assure, years from now, their well-being and their competitiveness and their prosperity. And most of all, you and I as legislators and as leaders of our respective countries, must continue to build distinctive and independent societies on the North American continent that reflect both the excitement of change and the strength of immutable values.

Mr. Speaker, and Mr. Vice President, and members of the Congress, succeeding generations of Americans have known the wisdom of the philosopher Ralph Waldo Emerson, who wrote: "The way to have a friend is to be one." Our two peoples, our two countries, have met that test in the past. We do so today, and I know that we shall in the future. I am confident — there is not the slightest doubt in my mind — I am confident that in the relationship between Canada and the United States of America, we will know difficulties, we will know moments of strain, we will know moments of crisis and tensions, but there is not the slightest doubt in my mind that, rooted as we are in fundamental values and democratic traditions, this relationship will always be, as Winston Churchill described it more than a half a century ago, "an example to every country, and a pattern for the future of the world."

WITH FAITH & GOODWILL

President George H.W. Bush

At the Air Quality [Acid Rain] Agreement Signing Ceremony
West Block, Parliament Hill
Ottawa, Ontario
March 13, 1991

———

Long after he left office Brian Mulroney was named Canada's "greenest" prime minister by a non-partisan group of Canadians that included Elizabeth May, the former leader of Canada's Green Party. Mulroney's success in forging a bilateral agreement between Canada and the United States to battle the continent's scourge of acid rain is a proud part of Mulroney's environmental legacy and also a credit to the leadership of George H.W. Bush. This 1991 address reminds us that while they were preoccupied with negotiating free trade agreements between the two nations, our governments also pursued worthy environmental goals.

. . .

This agreement that we're fixing to sign is added proof that the challenges we face require a new partnership among nations. Last year at the Houston economic summit, we agreed to give this effort real priority. Our negotiators gained momentum with the passage in the U.S. of our landmark environmental legislation, the Clean Air Act of 1990.

Beyond our common interest in our shared environment, this agreement says something about our overall relationship. The fact that Canada and the United States were able so quickly to craft a wide-ranging and effective agreement on such a complex subject says a lot about the extraordinarily strong relationship between our two countries.

Mr. Prime Minister [Brian Mulroney], I do recall our own discussions on environmental issues, and especially our meeting before I became president, back in January of 1987. I made a comment then that made its way into more than a few Canadian news reports, that I'd gotten "an earful" from you on acid rain. That was the understatement of the year. *[Laughter.]* So now, I came up here to prove to you that I was listening, and that all of us on the American side were listening. And again, we appreciate your strong advocacy, your articulate advocacy of this principle that I think will benefit the American people, the Canadian people. And I like to think it goes even beyond the borders of our two great countries.

[OPPOSITE]
Prime Minister Brian Mulroney and President George H.W. Bush meet in the Prime Minister's Office in March 1991. Joining them are Derek H. Burney and General Brent Scowcroft.

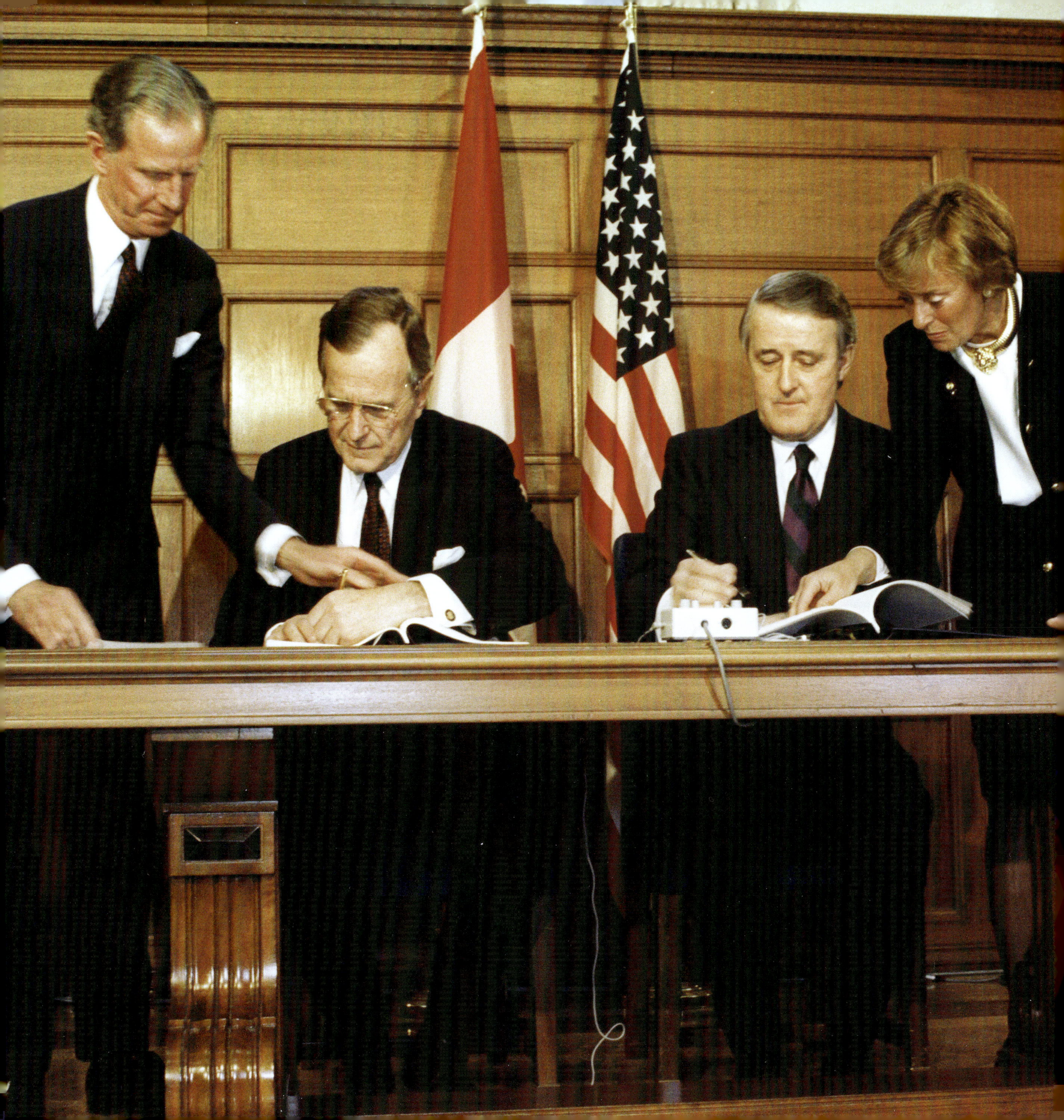

AT WORK

> The fact that Canada and the United States were able so quickly to craft a wide-ranging and effective agreement on such a complex subject says a lot about the **extraordinarily strong relationship between our two countries.**
>
> — President George H.W. Bush

So, thank you very much. The treaty that we sign today is testimony to the seriousness with which both our countries regard this critical environmental issue. And here is one that did take "two to tango." Here is one where each had to come give a little and take a little, and it's been worth it. And I think we're doing something good and sound and decent today.

[OPPOSITE]
Combatting acid rain. President George H.W. Bush and Prime Minister Brian Mulroney signing the 1991 Air Quality Agreement, March 31, 1991.

President George H.W. Bush

At the Initialling Ceremony for the North American Free Trade Agreement (NAFTA)
San Antonio, Texas
October 7, 1992

This meeting marks a turning point in the history of our three countries. Today, the United States, Mexico, and Canada embark together on an extraordinary enterprise. We are creating the largest, richest, and most productive market in the entire world, a $6 trillion market of 360 million people that stretches five thousand miles from Alaska and the Yukon to the Yucatan Peninsula.

NAFTA, the North American Free Trade Agreement, is an achievement of three strong and proud nations. This accord expresses our confidence in economic freedom and personal freedom, in our peoples' energy and enterprise.

The United States, Mexico, and Canada have already seen the powerful and beneficial impact of freer trade and more open markets. Over the past five years, as President Salinas reduced trade barriers under his bold reform program and as Prime Minister Mulroney and I implemented the United States–Canadian Free Trade Agreement, trade between our three countries has soared. In 1992 alone, that trade will reach an estimated $223 billion, up $58 billion just since 1987.

If anyone doubts the importance of trade for creating jobs, they should come to this great state, come to the Lone Star State. In 1991, Texas exports totalled $47 billion, just from this state. And of that amount, over $15 billion went to Mexico, almost two and a half times as much as five years ago. This export boom goes well beyond one state, well beyond Texas. Virtually every state has increased exports to Mexico in the past five years.

NAFTA means more exports, and more exports means more American jobs. Between 1987 and 1991, the increase in our exports to Mexico alone created over 300,000 new American jobs. These are high-wage jobs. In the case of merchandise exports, those jobs pay a worker a full 17 percent more than the average wage.

Free trade is the way of the future. I've set a goal for America to become, by the early years of the next century, the world's first $10 trillion economy, and NAFTA is an important element in reaching that goal. With NAFTA, as more open markets stimulate growth, create new products at competitive prices for consumers, we'll create new jobs at good wages in all three countries.

NAFTA will do these things and remain consistent with our other international obligations, our GATT trade obligations. Let me be clear that I remain committed to the successful conclusion of the Uruguay round of trade negotiations this year.

But NAFTA's importance is not limited to trade. We've taken particular care that our workers will benefit and the environment will be protected. As a result of NAFTA, the United States and Mexico are working more closely than we ever have to strengthen co-operation on such important labour issues as occupational health and safety standards, child labour, and labour-management relations.

Then, on the environment, an issue of critical concern for all three leaders here today, we have agreed on practical, effective steps to address urgent issues such as border pollution, as well as longer-term problems, such as preventing countries from lowering environmental standards to attract foreign investment.

I know for some, NAFTA will be controversial precisely because it opens the way to change. Some of NAFTA's critics will fight the future, throw obstacles in the way of this agreement, to mask a policy of protectionism. But history shows us that any nation that raises walls and turns inward is destined only for decline. We cannot make that choice for ourselves or for our children. We must set our course for the future, for free trade.

Take that, Ross Perot! North American leaders gather for the signing of the North American Free Trade Agreement in October 1992. Left to right, back row: Mexican President Carlos Salinas de Gortari, President Bush, Prime Minister Mulroney. Left to right, front row: Mexican Secretary of Commerce and Industrial Development Jaime Serra Puche, U.S. Trade Representative Carla Hills, Canadian Minister of International Trade Michael Wilson.

THE QUEBEC QUESTION

It is said often that Canada is a mosaic and the United States is a melting pot. It's difficult to know if that generalization remains apt in contemporary terms. But there can be no question that Quebec's presence within Canada is one of the great and unique differences between the two countries.

In October 1995, Quebec's future was subject to a fierce debate thanks to a referendum on whether it should seek to become an independent country. Quebec would stay within Canada — but only barely. One of the more unexpected and eloquent voices in the Quebec referendum's aftermath was that of a U.S. president. Bill Clinton's exploration of federalism, tribalism, and the benefits of community was as powerful a statement as any made during the earlier referendum campaign — and all the more fascinating coming from an outsider.

President Bill Clinton

Address to the Forum of Federations Conference
Mont-Tremblant, Quebec
October 8, 1999

I think when a people think it should be independent in order to have a meaningful political existence, serious questions should be asked: Is there an abuse of human rights? Is there a way people can get along if they come from different heritages? Are minority rights, as well as majority rights, respected? What is in the long-term economic and security interests of our people? How are we going to co-operate with our neighbours? Will it be better or worse if we are independent, or if we have a federalist system?

In a way, we've become more of a federalist world when the United Nations takes a more active role in stopping genocide in places in which it was not involved, and we recognize mutual responsibilities to contribute and pay for those things.

AT WORK

For a united Canada. U.S. Ambassador Gordon Giffin, Canadian Ambassador Raymond Chrétien, President Clinton, and Prime Minister Chrétien before the Forum of Federations Conference in Quebec, October 1999.

President Bill Clinton and Prime Minister Jean Chrétien chat during a working visit to Ottawa in October 1999.

So I believe we will be looking for ways, over and over and over again (the prime minister and I have endorsed the Free Trade Area of the Americas), we'll be looking for ways to integrate our operations for mutual interest, without giving up our sovereignty. And where there are dissatisfied groups in sections of countries, we should be looking for ways to satisfy anxieties and legitimate complaints without disintegration, I believe.

That's not to say that East Timor was wrong. If you look at what the people in East Timor have been through, if you look at the colonial heritage there, if you look at the fact that the

> We are fortunate because **life is more interesting and fun** when there are different people who **look differently and think differently** and find their way to God differently.
> — President Bill Clinton

Indonesians offered them a vote, they took it, and nearly 80 percent of them voted for independence, it seems that was the right decision there.

But let us never be under the illusion that those people are going to have an easy path, assuming that those of us who are trying to support and help them — assuming we can stop all the pro-integrationist militias from oppressing the people, and we can get all the East Timorese back home, and they'll all be safe — there will still be less than a million of them, with a per capita income among the poorest in the world, struggling to make a living for their children in an environment that is not exactly hospitable.

Now, does that mean they were wrong? No. Under the circumstances they faced, they probably made the only decision they could have. But wouldn't it have been better if they could have found their religious, their cultural, their ethnic, and their economic footing — and genuine self-government — in the framework of a larger entity which would also have supported them economically? And reinforced their security instead of undermined it? It didn't happen; it's too bad.

But I say this because I don't think there are any general rules; I think that, at the end of World War I, when President Wilson spoke, there was a general assumption, because we were seeing empires break up (the Ottoman Empire, the Austro-Hungarian Empire; there was the memory of the Russian Empire; British colonialism was still alive in Africa, and

[OPPOSITE]
President Bill Clinton, Prime Minister Jean Chrétien, and staff in Ottawa at the time of Clinton's famous address about federalism, October 1999.

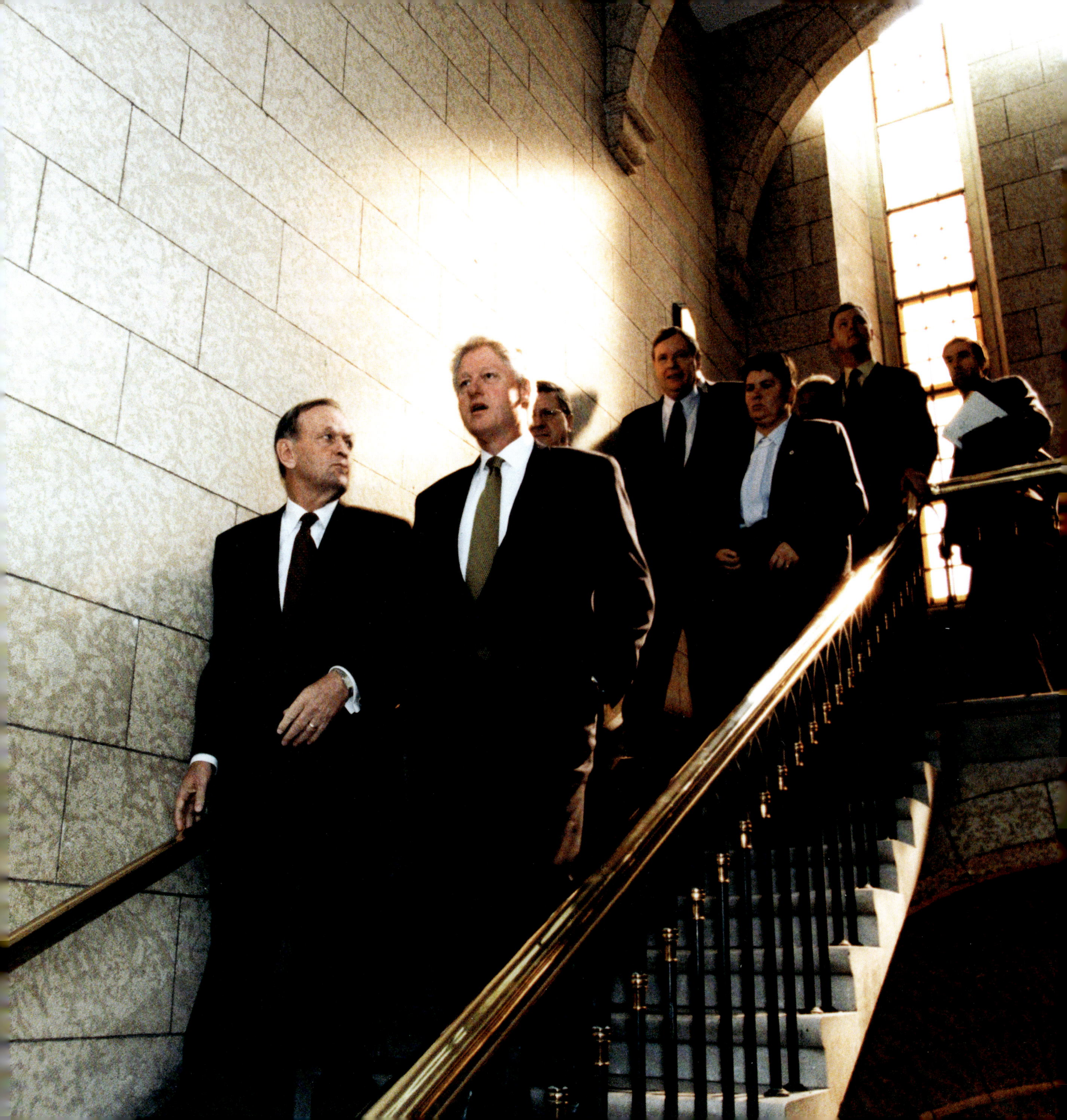

> We all have to grow and learn when we
> confront people who are different than we are, and
> # instead of looking at them in fear
> # and hatred and dehumanization,
> we look at them and see a mirror of ourselves and our common humanity.
>
> — President Bill Clinton

so was French colonialism) and at that time, we all assumed, and the rhetoric of the time imposed the idea that the only way for people to feel any sovereignty or meaning was if they were independent. And I think we've spent a lot of the twentieth century minimizing the prospects of federalism. We all have recoiled, now, so much at the abuse of people because of their tribal, racial, and religious characteristics that we tend immediately to think that the only answer is independence.

But we must think of how we will live after the shooting stops, after the smoke clears, over the long run. And I can only say this, in closing: I think the United States and Canada are among the most fortunate countries in the world because we have such diversity; sometimes concentrated, like the Inuit in the north; sometimes widely dispersed within a certain area, like the diversity of Vancouver. We are fortunate because life is more interesting and fun when there are different people who look differently and think differently and find their way to God differently. It's an interesting time.

And because we all have to grow and learn when we confront people who are different than we are, and instead of looking at them in fear and hatred and dehumanization, we look at them and see a mirror of ourselves and our common humanity. I think if we will keep these questions in mind: What is most likely to advance our common humanity in a smaller world? What is the arrangement of government most likely to give us the best of all worlds, the integrity we need, the self-government we need, the self-advancement we need, without pretending that we can cut all the cords that bind us to the rest of humanity? I think more and more and more people will say, "This federalism, it's not such a bad idea."

"A PERMANENT REALITY"

Living alongside one another has involved Canada and the United States in countless matters over the years beyond the terms of bilateral trade and shared commercial interest. Some, such as agreements over the common waters that link our countries, have clear effects that are there for anyone to see. Others, such as encouraging higher learning or working to forge a multilateral peace, are less tangible or visible to the eye — albeit no less important. They are borne of interwoven values and they come together to make our countries' partnership what a young senator from Massachusetts once called "a permanent reality."

The remarks below not only reflect the variety of other issues that occupy our leaders, they highlight the contributions that come constantly from those other than heads of government.

Senator John F. Kennedy

Convocation Address, University of New Brunswick
Fredericton, New Brunswick
October 8, 1957

While I am grateful for the personal satisfaction this has accorded me, I know that this is simply another demonstration of the continued strengthening of the common ties that bind together Canada and the United States, New Brunswick and Massachusetts — ties of history, ties of kinship, and ties of an inseparable destiny.

Both New Brunswick and Massachusetts border on the Atlantic Ocean, with rich maritime and fishing traditions. Both were instrumental in the formation of their nations, New Brunswick being one of the four provinces united in the Dominion in 1867, and Massachusetts being one of the thirteen united to form the American Union of 1787. Throughout the history of Massachusetts, a large proportion of its residents have traced their origins to New Brunswick and the other Canadian provinces. Indeed, of all the many residents of my state of Massachusetts who were born outside of the United States, a much larger percentage — more than one out of four — were born in Canada than in any other country.

New Brunswick, too, has many residents who can trace their ancestry back to the United States and Massachusetts — although in many instances this relates to an unhappy period in the history of our two countries. Following the Revolutionary War, the so-called Tories who had remained loyal to the British Crown did not fare well in America. The freshly victorious colonists were proud in their new independence, and angry at those who had not joined them during the bitter years of struggle. Their patience and tolerance, I am afraid, were limited — and so harshly were some Tories treated that they were forced to flee the country. One of the favourite havens of refuge for those coming from Massachusetts was the province of New Brunswick.

Incidentally, when the United States in cooler times offered amnesty to these exiles, one Charles Wentworth Upham, born in New Brunswick of parents who had fled from Boston, returned to the ancestral home of Massachusetts and settled in Salem. His distinguished career included service as president of the Massachusetts Senate and as one of my early predecessors in the Massachusetts delegation to the United States House of Representatives, and, interestingly enough, by marrying the sister of Oliver Wendell Holmes, Sr., this native of New Brunswick became an uncle of one of the most distinguished sons of our commonwealth and one of the most famous of our nation's Supreme Court's justices.

At the moment we see and hear much about a "new chapter" in the relations between the United States and Canada. Unquestionably the new Canadian government under Prime Minister Diefenbaker has received a mandate to explore means by which Canada may renew a closer trade connection with Great Britain and take a new compass-bearing on international economic policies. But in reading the statements made by your prime minister on several recent occasions, both in this country and in the United States, it is quite apparent that the main outlines of Canadian policy are but little altered. Both of our peoples delude themselves if they believe that there is some new and previously unexplored line of policy which Canada can now explore. It does no service, either, to suppose that Canada has a closed option between a "pro-British" and a "pro-American" approach to foreign policy and trade. Canada can neither be an extension of the Cornish coastline nor is she a mere northern vestibule to the United States. Canada has achieved a national strength and prestige which simply does not allow any portrayal of the country as an appendage of either Great Britain or the United States. To be sure, Canada has some special links with each of these two English-speaking nations, but it possesses most certainly a national destiny of its own to which it is well and timely to give foremost recognition.

The United States and Canada are more than ever continental partners. Not only do they share Atlantic and Pacific coastlines; they now also have a long common coast along the St. Lawrence Seaway, which is opening up new maritime centres on both sides of the border.

[OPPOSITE]
Less than five years after addressing the crowd of graduates at the University of New Brunswick as a U.S. senator, JFK would give another well-received speech before a Canadian audience. Here he is as the newly elected President of the United States addressing a joint session of the Canadian Parliament in 1961.

AT WORK

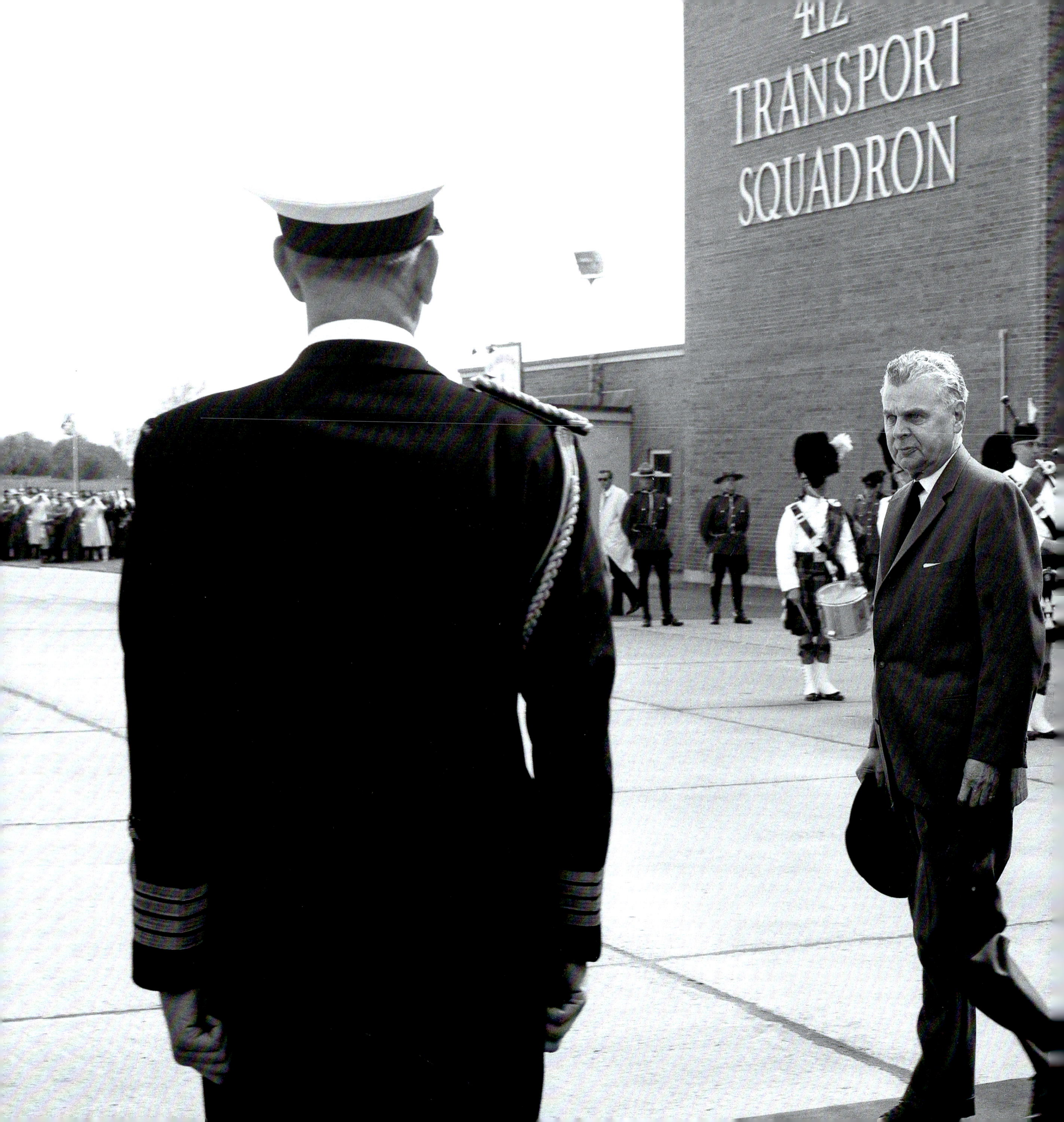
412
TRANSPORT
SQUADRON

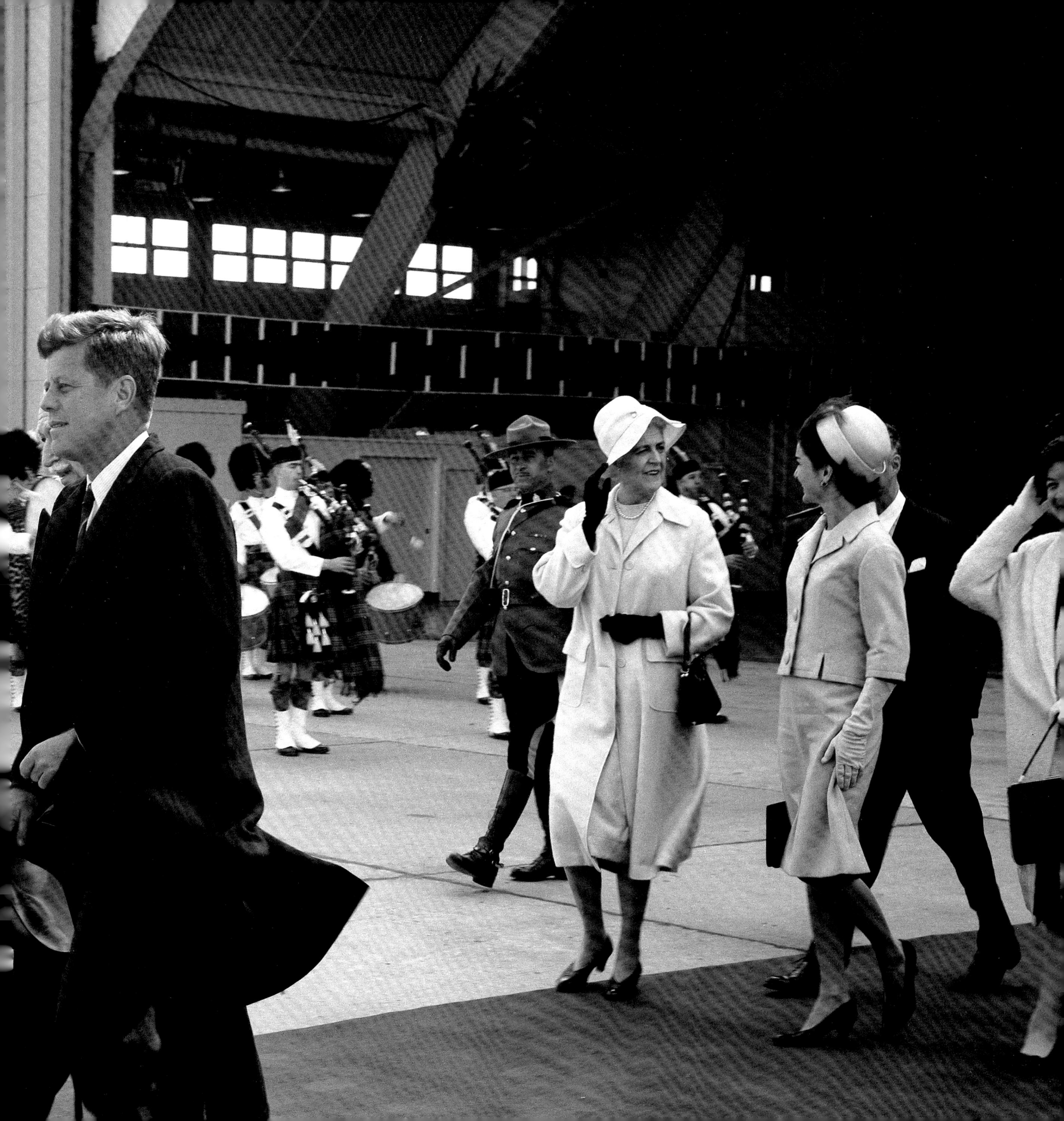

Natural conditions decree that we share common interests in hydroelectric power, natural gas, high sea fisheries. Our defence perimeters have merged all the way to the Arctic. Our agricultural economies have common characteristics and weaknesses born of abundance. This common heritage gives strength to both of our countries, but we must frankly concede that

> Today, if the United States and Canada, with their common language, common history, common economic and political interests, and other close ties, cannot live peacefully with one another, then what hope is there for the rest of the world?
>
> — Senator John F. Kennedy

the very closeness of our interests and national aspirations have recently brought new frictions and irritations to the surface. The resilience and buoyancy of our two economies have been accompanied by understandable collisions and misunderstandings.

For example, our natural resources should not be neatly compartmentalized nationally. We must soon resolve the disputes which have arisen over the uses to which some of the waters of the Columbia, Yukon, and St. John Rivers are to be put. There remain some unresolved questions about the St. Lawrence Seaway, especially regarding the level of tolls. Fisheries have been a classical issue in the relations between our two countries, whereas the methods by which we dispose of agriculture surpluses have become a new source of tension. The deep penetration of American venture capital and business management into Canadian enterprises in such sectors as mining and fuels has aroused natural fears among Canadians. And there are more than a few Canadians who are appalled that the hopes for a distinctively national cultural tradition are being suffocated by a loud cacophony south of the border.

These are examples of the types of tensions which suggest that we should improve the machinery of joint consultation and management. A small beginning is being made in the business sphere by the committee on economic relations established by the National Planning Association under the chairmanship of former Ambassador R. Douglas Stuart and Mr. R.M. Fowler of Montreal. This committee will make special inquiry into the questions of U.S. domination in Canadian

[PREVIOUS PAGE]
President Kennedy walks with Prime Minister John Diefenbaker as he and First Lady Jacqueline Kennedy depart Ottawa following a state visit on May 18, 1961. President Kennedy's trip to Ottawa and address to Parliament was the first official state visit of his presidency.

enterprise and the dumping of agricultural surpluses. In my judgment, however, our two nations should devise far better permanent consultative channels so that each new problem does not have to be dealt with on an ad hoc and individual emergency basis. Fortunately, our two governments are able to carry on a frank dialogue.

Today, if the United States and Canada, with their common language, common history, common economic and political interests, and other close ties, cannot live peacefully with one another, then what hope is there for the rest of the world? We have a responsibility to demonstrate to all peoples everywhere that peaceful and stable existence, by powerful countries side by side, can remain a permanent reality in today's troubled world.

Today, for example, the Arabs and the Israelis would do well to recall the tense relations and boundary disputes which divided the United States and Canada over a century ago — of how finally the Webster-Ashburton Treaty of 1842 was devised to settle these differences, with some concessions by both parties, and of how unpopular that treaty was on both sides of the line, with both Mr. Webster of Massachusetts and Lord Ashburton being repeatedly denounced for having sacrificed the rights of their people. (Indeed, Webster and Ashburton finally convinced the Senate and Parliament respectively, it is said, only after each had used a different map to pretend that he had in reality cheated the other.) And yet the peace and prosperity to both countries flowing from that much-abused settlement for more than a century have been worth several thousand times as much as the value of all the territory that was in dispute.

I do not mean to imply that the relations between our two nations are so close as to encourage domination or subservience. This has not been a case where, in terms of the old saying, "familiarity breeds contempt." On the contrary, a co-operative friendship of such meaning and solidarity permits a full and frank discussion of issues of mutual interest, even when that discussion may jar sensitive ears on the other side of the border. Your prime minister, I believe, has done well to remind both countries of the issues and potential areas of conflict that our two countries must not neglect. A friendship such as ours, moreover, encourages healthy competition in international trade; it requires that neither take the other for granted in international politics. "Good fences," reads a poem by one of our most distinguished New England poets, Robert Frost, "make good neighbours." Canada and the United States have carefully maintained the good fences that help make them good neighbours.

In the final analysis, the elimination of these various tensions and misunderstandings on both sides of the border cannot depend upon any treaty or mechanical formula or ancient statute, but must rely upon the wisdom, understanding, and ability of the leaders and officials of our two nations, upon the thought and effort they are willing to give to clearing up these misunderstandings. It will require in both Canada and America political leaders of patience, tact, and foresight — dedicated, responsible men who can look beyond the problems of the next election to see the problems of the next generation. Where, in the future, are those leaders to come from? Primarily from

WITH FAITH & GOODWILL

the University of New Brunswick and the University of Massachusetts, from all of the colleges and educational institutions of our two nations. In the long run, it is upon these colleges and the type of graduates they produce that the continuation of Canadian-American friendship depends.

I do not say that our international relations, or our political and public life, should be completely turned over to college-trained experts who ignore public opinion. Nor would I adopt for my own country the provision from the Belgian Constitution of 1893, giving three votes instead of one to college graduates (at least not until more Democrats go to college). Nor do I suggest that the University of New Brunswick be given a seat in Parliament as our William and Mary College was once represented in the Virginia House of Burgesses.

But I do urge that each of you, regardless of your chosen occupation, consider entering the field of politics at some stage in your career, that you offer to the political arena, and to the critical problems of our society which are decided therein — including the delicate problems of Canadian-American co-operation — the benefits of the talents which society has helped to develop in you. I ask you to decide, as Goethe put it, whether you will be an anvil or a hammer. The formal phases of the "anvil" stage will soon be completed for many of you, though hopefully you will continue to absorb still more in the years ahead. The question now is whether you are to be a hammer — whether you are to give to the world in which you are reared and educated the broadest possible benefits of that education.

This is a great university, the University of New Brunswick. Its establishment and continued functioning, like that of all great universities, has required considerable effort and expenditure. I cannot believe that all of this was undertaken merely to give the school's graduates an economic advantage in the life struggle. "A university," said Professor Woodrow Wilson, "should be an organ of memory for the state for the transmission of its best traditions. Every man sent out from a university should be a man of his nation, as well as a man of his time." And Prince Bismarck was even more specific — one-third of the students of German universities, he once stated, broke down from overwork; another third broke down from dissipation; and the other third ruled Germany. (I leave it to each of you to decide which category you fall in.)

But if you are to be among the rulers of your land, from alderman to prime minister, if you are willing to enter the abused and neglected profession of politics, then let me tell you, as one who is familiar with the political world, that our profession in all parts of the world stands in serious need of the fruits of your education. We do not need political scholars whose education has been so specialized as to exclude them from participation in current events — men like Lord John Russell, of whom Queen Victoria once remarked that he would be a better man if he knew a third subject, but he was interested in nothing but the Constitution of 1688 and himself. No, what we need are men who can ride easily over broad fields of knowledge and recognize the mutual dependence of our two worlds, men like my nation's Thomas Jefferson, whom a contemporary described as "A gentleman of 32, who could calculate an eclipse, survey an estate, tie an artery, plan an edifice, try a case, break a horse, dance a minuet, and play the violin."

[OPPOSITE]
President John F. Kennedy's motorcade in Ottawa during his state visit on May 17, 1961. President Kennedy can be seen sitting in the back seat of the rear car.

I realize that politics has become one of our most neglected, our most abused, and our most ignored professions. It ranks low on the occupational list of a large share of the population; and its chief practitioners are rarely well or favourably known. No education, except finding your way around a smoke-filled room, is considered necessary for political success. "Don't teach my boy poetry," a mother recently wrote the headmaster of Eton; "he's going to stand for Parliament." The worlds of politics and scholarship have indeed drifted apart.

But it is here, I repeat, that the foundations for future Canadian-American relations must be laid, here in this citadel of learning, from which you can take with you upon graduation all the accumulated knowledge and inspiration you may need to face the future. I am assuming, of course, that you are taking something with you, that you do not look upon this university as Dean Swift regarding Oxford. Oxford, he said, was truly a great seat of learning; for all freshmen who entered were required to bring some learning with them in order to meet the standards of admission — but no senior, when he left the university, ever took any learning away; and thus it steadily accumulated.

We want from you not the sneers of the cynics or the despair of the faint-hearted. Of that we already have an abundance. We ask that you bring enlightenment, vision, and illumination to a troubled world, where the rock of our two nations' friendship must always stand firm.

President Kennedy with embassy personnel at the United States Embassy Chancery in Ottawa, during his state visit. U.S. Ambassador to Canada Livingston T. Merchant stands at the far right.

AT WORK

We ask that you bring enlightenment, vision, and illumination
to a troubled world, where the rock of our two nations' friendship must always stand firm.

— Senator John F. Kennedy

In his book, *One Man's America*, Alistair Cooke tells the story which well illustrates this point. On the nineteenth of May, 1780, as he describes it, in Hartford, Connecticut, the skies at noon turned from blue to grey and, by mid-afternoon had blackened over so densely that, in the religious age, men fell on their knees and begged a final blessing before the end came. The Connecticut House of Representatives was in session. And as some men fell down in the darkened chamber and others clamoured for an immediate adjournment, the speaker of the house, one Colonel Davenport, came to his feet. And he silenced the din with these words: "The Day of Judgment is either approaching — or it is not. If it is not, there is no cause for adjournment. If it is, I choose to be found doing my duty. I wish, therefore that candles may be brought."

Students of the University of New Brunswick, we who are here today concerned with the dark and difficult task ahead, I ask once again that you bring candles to illuminate our way.

ONE CANADA

Almost twenty years before President Clinton's 1995 speech on federalism, a Canadian prime minister, Pierre Trudeau, had assured Americans that Canada would not divide. Trudeau's remarks came during his address to the U.S. Congress in February 1977. Only weeks before, René Lévesque's separatist Parti Québécois had earned a majority mandate in the 1976 Quebec election. Prime Minister Trudeau reassured both Americans, and Canadians, that a united Canada would prevail.

Prime Minister Pierre Elliott Trudeau

Address to a Joint Session of the United States Congress
Washington, D.C.
February 22, 1977

We in Canada, facing internal tensions with roots extending back to the seventeenth century, have much to gain from the wisdom and discipline and patience which you, in this country, in this generation, have brought to bear to reduce racial tensions, to broaden legal rights, and to provide opportunity to all....

The accommodation of two vigorous language groups has been, in varying fashion, the policy of every Canadian government since Confederation. The reason is clear. Within Quebec, over 80 percent of the population speak French as their first or only language. In Canada as a whole, nearly one-fifth of the people speak no language but French. Thus from generation to generation there has been handed down the belief that a country could be built in freedom and equality with two languages and a multitude of cultures.

There will have to be changes in some of our attitudes; there will have to be a greater comprehension of one another across the barrier of language difference. Both English-speaking and

Prime Minister Pierre Elliott Trudeau and Quebec Premier René Lévesque arrive at Government House (Rideau Hall) in Ottawa on January 4, 1979.

French-speaking Canadians will have to become more aware of the richness that diversity brings and less irritated by the problems it presents. We may have to revise some aspects of our constitution so that the Canadian federation can be seen by six and a half million French-speaking Canadians to be the strongest bulwark against submersion by some 220 million English-speaking North Americans.

These very figures illustrate dramatically the sense of insecurity of French Canada. But separation would not alter the arithmetic; it would merely increase the exposure.

Nor would the separation of Quebec contribute in any fashion to the confidence of the many cultural minorities of various origins who dwell throughout Canada. These communities have been encouraged for decades to retain their own identities and to preserve their own cultures. They have done so and flourished nowhere more spectacularly than in the prairie provinces of Alberta, Saskatchewan, and Manitoba. The sudden departure of Quebec would signify the tragic failure of our pluralist dream, the fracturing of our cultural mosaic, and would likely remove much of the determination of Canadians to protect their cultural minorities.

WITH FAITH & GOODWILL

Vice President Walter Mondale greets President Jimmy Carter in Washington, D.C., on the occasion of Prime Minister Pierre Elliott Trudeau's 1977 address to Congress. To the president's right are Prime Minister Trudeau, First Lady Rosalynn Carter, and the prime minister's wife, Margaret Trudeau.

Problems of this magnitude cannot be wished away. They can be solved, however, by the institutions we have created for our own governance. Those institutions belong to all Canadians, to me as a Quebecker as much as to my fellow citizens from the other provinces. And because those institutions are democratically structured, because their members are freely elected, they are capable of reflecting changes and of responding to the popular will.

I am confident that we in Canada are well along in the course of devising a society as free of prejudice and fear as full of understanding and generosity, as respectful of individuality and beauty, as receptive to change and innovation, as exists anywhere.

I am confident it can be done.

I say to you with all the certainty I can command that
Canada's unity will not be fractured.

— PRIME MINISTER PIERRE ELLIOTT TRUDEAU

NEW CHALLENGES, NEW APPROACHES

THE 2010S BROUGHT A HOST OF NEW CHALLENGES TO THE CANADA-U.S. relationship. After decades of global trade liberalization, the political pendulum swung back toward protectionism, especially in the United States. The U.S. Congress grew more agitated about offshoring of jobs and loss of industry. Donald Trump's arrival in the White House signalled a new militancy on such issues, and it became necessary to pound out a new, updated accord on trade between the three North American nations.

At the same time, new geopolitical tensions arose as multilateral institutions such as NATO came under pressure and China pursued a far more aggressive foreign policy. The need for a new blueprint to help move the Canada-U.S. relationship forward in the face of new economic, trade, and other challenges became clear — with the necessity to co-operate constructively growing more important when Covid-19 struck in early 2020. Again, it fell to leaders on both sides of the border to find the faith and goodwill to work together and identify solutions.

Mexican President Enrique Peña Nieto, President Donald Trump, and Prime Minister Justin Trudeau sign the USMCA on November 30, 2018.

WITH FAITH & GOODWILL

Speaker of the U.S. House of Representatives Nancy Pelosi

Floor Speech in Support of Transformed USMCA
Washington, D.C.
December 19, 2019

———

I PROUDLY RISE TO JOIN MY COLLEAGUES ON THIS EXCITING DAY, AS THE HOUSE PASSES a historic trade agreement that is truly worthy of the American people: a new and dramatically improved United States-Mexico-Canada Agreement....

> We just can't come up with a bill that's a little sugar on top and say this is better, because the impact on workers would be felt for a long time. We knew we could do better.
>
> — NANCY PELOSI, SPEAKER OF THE U.S. HOUSE OF REPRESENTATIVES

Democrats knew that hard-working Americans needed more from the USMCA than just a broken NAFTA with better language but no real enforcement. That was my concern. We just can't come up with a bill that's a little sugar on top and say this is better, because the impact on workers would be felt for a long time. We knew we could do better.

The original USMCA draft put forward by the [Trump] Administration fell far short than where it is now: [it] still left many American workers exposed to losing their jobs to Mexico, included [an] unacceptable provision locking in high drug prices, came up short on key environmental standards, critically lacked the tough, effective ... enforcements that are essential to protecting American jobs and holding our trading partners accountable to their promises.

After months of Democrats working with the Trade Representative, we have key changes to the USMCA that make this a truly transformative agreement for America's workers.

[OPPOSITE]
Speaker Nancy Pelosi delivered an enthusiastic speech in support of the USMCA on December 19, 2019, on the floor of the U.S. House of Representatives.

Now, with Democrats' changes, the USMCA now has the strongest enforcement mechanisms of any U.S. trade agreement.

Again, in contrast to the original USMCA draft, which would have allowed nations who did not live up to their obligations to stop enforcement complaints from even being heard, Democrats' changes prevented nations from "panel blocking."

For workers: while the Administration's draft stacked the deck against labour violation claims, our changes enact new rules and monitoring tools to protect American workers, prosecute labour violations, and ensure that Mexico is complying with labour reforms.

For the environment:
whereas the [Trump] Administration's draft had weak environmental rules and tilted the playing field against violation claims,
Democrats have strengthened the rules and enforcement tools
and are lowering pollution and increasing resilient infrastructure.

— Nancy Pelosi, Speaker of the U.S. House of Representatives

Including — another point is for the workers — including by establishing Labour Attachés based in Mexico that will provide on-the-ground information about Mexico's labour practices, and by creating facility-specific rapid response labour enforcement mechanism to stop trade in goods that violate this agreement.

This is — these are not technical changes. These make a big difference.

For the environment: whereas the Administration's draft had weak environmental rules and tilted the playing field against violation claims, Democrats have strengthened the rules and enforcement tools and are lowering pollution and increasing resilient infrastructure.

Sadly, while the Administration refuses to acknowledge the existence, let alone the urgency of the climate crisis, our changes in the USMCA set a firm footing for progress when we have a President who brings us back to the Paris Accord. And by the way, while we were in Spain on this subject, our large bicameral delegation's team was, "We are still in," when it came to the Paris Accord.

And on lowering prescription drug costs: the White House draft contained unacceptable giveaways for Big Pharma that would have locked in high prescription drug prices.

Democrats have eliminated these unfair hand-outs to big corporations, and secured provisions to lower drug costs and improve access to life-saving medicines.

The changes House Democrats have secured in the USMCA make this a truly transformational trade agreement.

As the AFL-CIO wrote in their letter of support last week, "We have secured an agreement that working people can proudly support."

"Working people," this is still their quote, "are responsible for a deal that is a vast improvement over both the original NAFTA and the flawed proposal brought forward in 2017. For the first time, there truly will be enforceable labour standards.

"The USMCA also eliminates special carve outs for corporations like the giveaway to Big Pharma in the Administration's initial proposal and loopholes designed to make it harder to prosecute labour violations.

"The USMCA is far from perfect…. But there is no denying that the trade rules in America will now be fairer because of our hard work and perseverance. Working people have created a new standard for future trade negotiations."

I think that this is in conclusion. I may have another thought.

Labour groups and trade organizations, I'll submit to the record. Farmers, growers and ranchers, groups representing businesses around the country, social justice and faith-based organizations, such as NETWORK. The list goes on and on, and it will be part of the statement that I submit to the record.

This is a strong agreement that honours our promises For The People to make — give us bigger paycheques, and makes a difference for millions, with all the respect in the world for our neighbours. I respect the greatness of Mexico as our neighbour and the friendship that we have and want to engender and our neighbour to the north, Canada, with respect to them. Our responsibility was to have a trade agreement that lifted all workers in our hemisphere, our first responsibility was to American workers….

In December 2019, Democratic Chair of the U.S. House of Representatives Ways and Means Committee Richard Neal and Speaker of the House Nancy Pelosi announced agreement with President Donald Trump on the USMCA.

AT PLAY

HOLIDAYING IN
EACH OTHER'S NATION

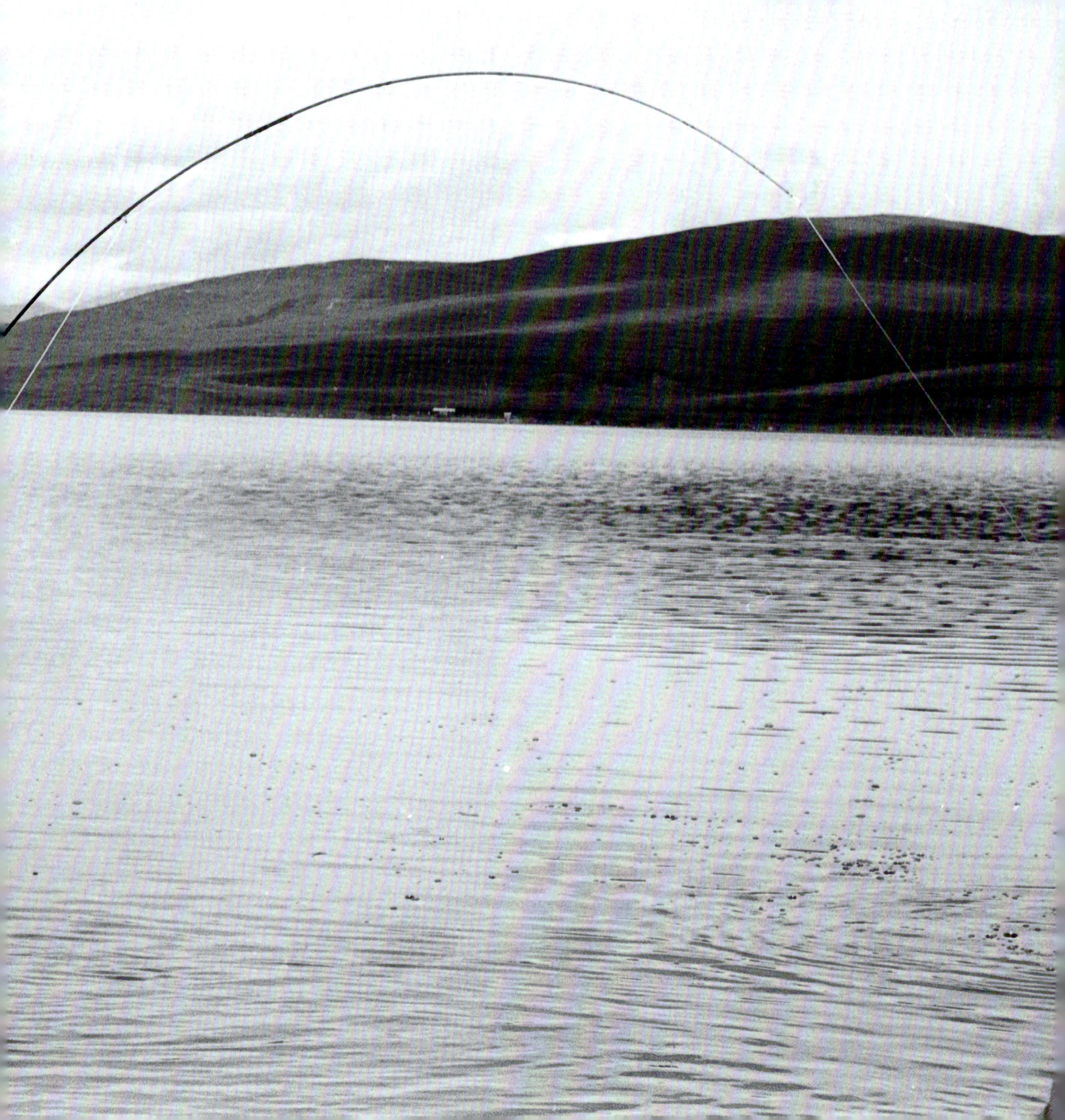

A S THE THIRD-PARTY CANDIDATE DURING AMERICA'S 1912 ELECTION, Teddy Roosevelt, the world's most famous hunter, rancher, naturalist, writer, and ex-president, was shot just before a campaign speech. But his would-be assassin and the entire world soon discovered that it would take more than a bullet to slow Roosevelt down. "It takes more than that to kill a bull moose," Roosevelt told his audience, and the nickname of Teddy Roosevelt's party, the "Bull Moose" party, was born.

Only a few years later, while on a hunting holiday in Canada, Teddy would prove he knew what he was talking about when it came to confronting a bull moose in the wild. Where else but Canada would Roosevelt, the man who explored the Amazon and hunted big game in Africa, come under attack by the very animal that was his political namesake? "Even in Africa I have never known anything but a rogue elephant or buffalo, or an occasional rhinoceros, to attack so viciously or with such premeditation when itself neither wounded nor threatened," Teddy later wrote of his encounter with Canadian wildlife.

Canadian and American leaders have a long history of holidaying in each other's country. President Chester A. Arthur, for example, held a Canadian salmon fishing record in the 1870s and secretly crossed into Canadian waters in search of fish while on a presidential holiday in the 1880s. Herbert Hoover and Jimmy Carter both spent many days on Canadian lakes and rivers in their quest for angling greatness. And in 1997, after fishing for Arctic char in what is now Nunavut, George H.W. Bush was so thrilled to fish in Canadian waters that he wrote a detailed column about his experiences for a Northwest Territories weekly paper.

[PREVIOUS PAGE]
President Jimmy Carter has been a frequent visitor to Canada over the years and has fished on both Canadian coasts.

Canadian prime ministers dating back to Sir John A. Macdonald have often sought rest and relaxation — and sun and warmth during Canadian winters — south of the border. And at times our leaders have holidayed together, with Pierre Trudeau skiing with Gerald Ford, and Brian Mulroney and George H.W. Bush spending each Labour Day weekend together at Kennebunkport, Maine. Bull Mooser Teddy Roosevelt sent his daughter for a private holiday in Canada, where she was hosted by Sir Wilfrid and Lady Laurier.

Probably the most famous vacation spot of all in the American-Canadian relationship is a small island in New Brunswick. Franklin Roosevelt spent many summers on Campobello as a boy and a young man, and even returned there as president to stay in his family's cottage. It is now the site of Roosevelt Campobello International Park, a site jointly administered by Canadians and Americans and itself a tribute to friendship between nations.

[THIS PAGE]

The conservation president. Delegates to the North American Conservation Conference, including Clifford Sifton, Canada's Minister of the Interior under Sir Wilfrid Laurier, and President Theodore Roosevelt.

[OPPOSITE]

All men are equal before fish. President Hoover during a fishing trip in 1936. President Hoover was an avid fly fisherman in his post-presidential years, with many successful fishing expeditions in Canada. He even published a book on his experiences — *Fishing for Fun and to Wash Your Soul* — shortly before his death in 1964.

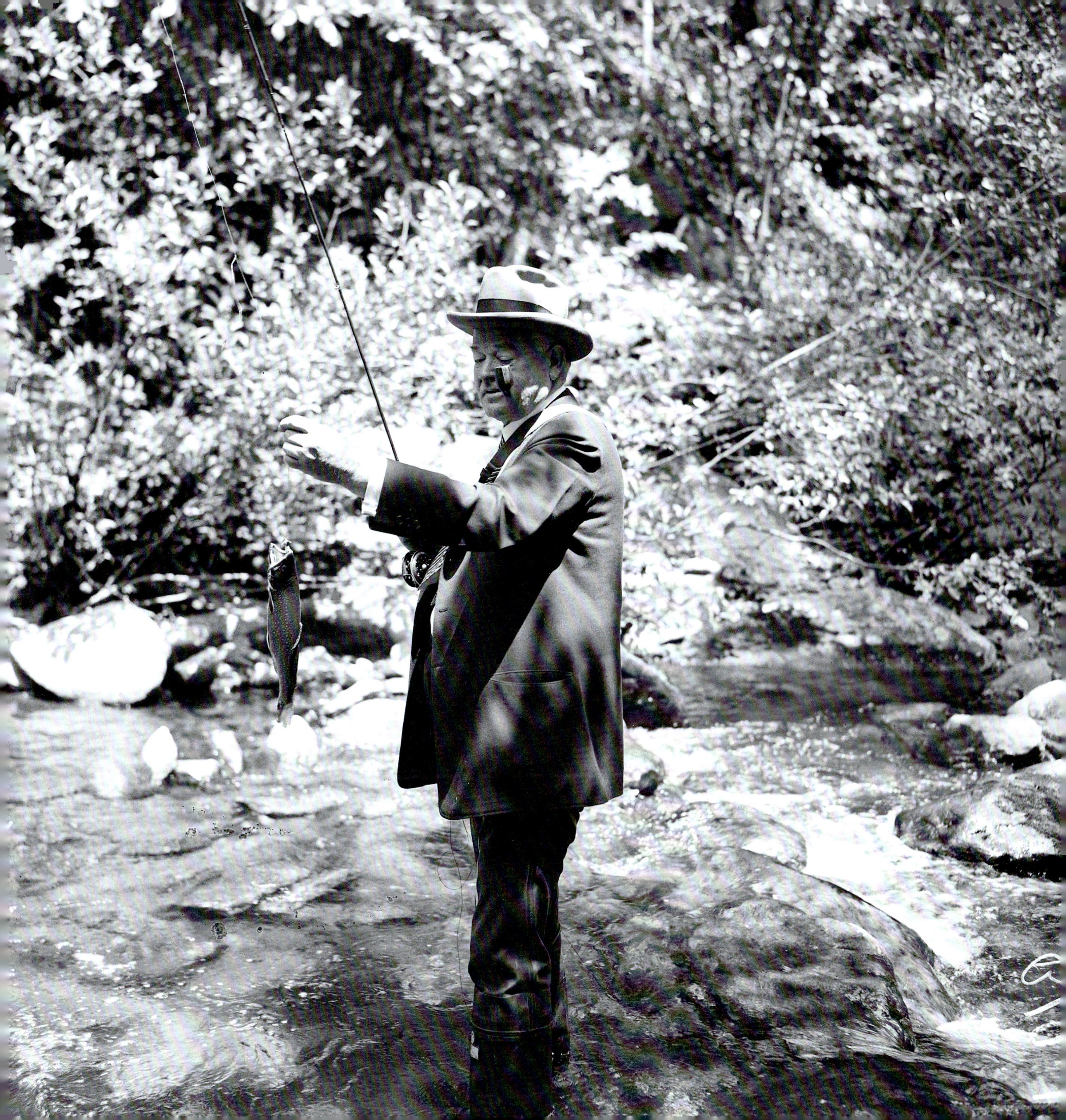

President Theodore Roosevelt

Excerpt from A Book-Lover's Holidays in the Open, *1916*

———

In 1915, I spent a little over a fortnight on a private game reserve in the province of Quebec. I had expected to enjoy the great northern woods, and the sight of beaver, moose, and caribou; but I had not expected any hunting experience worth mentioning. Nevertheless, toward the end of my trip, there befell me one of the most curious and interesting adventures with big game that have ever befallen me during the forty years since I first began to know the life of the wilderness....

When half a mile from the landing we saw a big bull moose on the edge of the shore ahead of us. It looked and was — if anything — even bigger-bodied than the one I had shot in the morning, with antlers almost as large and rather more palmated. We paddled up to within a hundred yards of it, laughing and talking, and remarking how eager we would have been if we had not already got our moose. At first it did not seem to notice us. Then it looked at us but paid us no further heed. We were rather surprised at this but paddled on past it, and it then walked along the shore after us. We still supposed that it did not realize what we were. But another hundred yards put us to windward of it. Instead of turning into the forest when it got our wind, it merely bristled up the hair on its withers, shook its head, and continued to walk after the canoe, along the shore.

I had heard of bull moose, during the rut, attacking men unprovoked, if the men were close up, but never of anything as wanton and deliberate as this action, and I could hardly believe the moose meant mischief, but Arthur said it did; and obviously we could not land with the big, evil-looking beast coming for us — and, of course, I was most anxious not to have to shoot it. So we turned the canoe round and paddled on our back track. But the moose promptly turned and followed us along the shore. We yelled at him, and Odilon struck the canoe with his paddle, but with no effect....

He vented his rage on a small tree, which he wrecked with his antlers. We continued to paddle round the head of the bay, and he followed us; we still hoped we might get him away from the portage, and that he would go into the woods. But when we turned he followed us back, and thus went to and fro with us. Where the water was deep near shore we pushed the canoe close in to him, and he promptly rushed down to the water's edge, shaking his head, and striking the earth with his fore hoofs.

We shouted at him, but with no effect. As he paraded along the shore he opened his mouth, lolling out his tongue; and now and then when he faced us he ran out his tongue

[OPPOSITE]
Are there any bull moose around here? Former President Theodore Roosevelt with Vancouver Mayor L.D. Taylor, during a visit to Vancouver in August 1914.

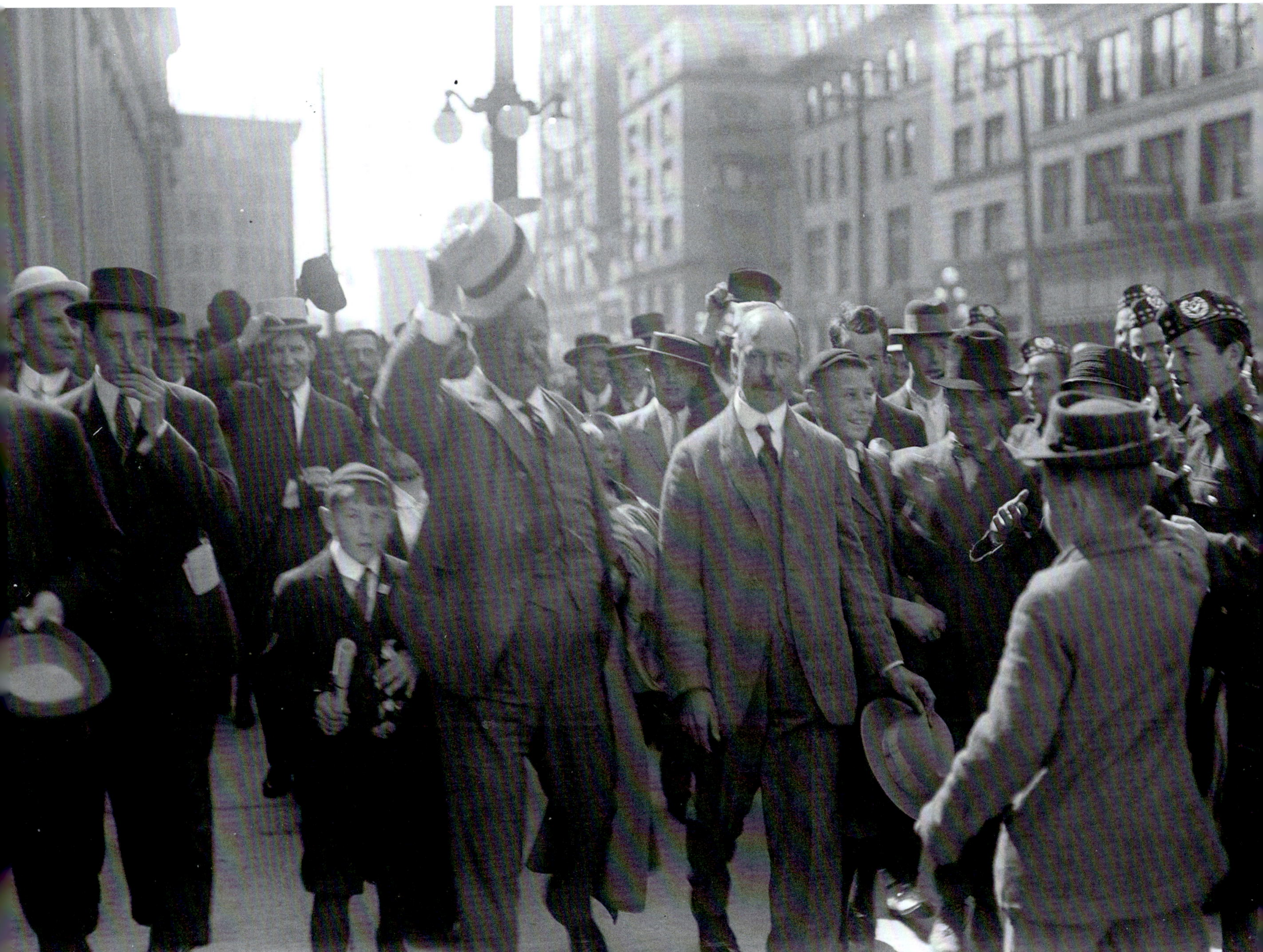

Altogether the huge black beast looked like a formidable customer,
and was evidently in a most evil rage
and bent on man-killing.
— President Theodore Roosevelt

and licked the end of his muzzle with it. Once, with head down, he bounded or galloped round in a half circle; and from time to time he grunted or uttered a low, menacing roar. Altogether the huge black beast looked like a formidable customer, and was evidently in a most evil rage and bent on man-killing. For over an hour he thus kept us from the shore, running to meet us wherever we tried to go.

The afternoon was waning; a cold wind began to blow, shifting as it blew. He was not a pleasant-looking beast to meet in the woods in the dusk. We were at our wits' ends what to do. At last he turned, shook his head, and with a flourish of his heels galloped — not trotted — for fifty yards up beside the little river which paralleled the portage trail. I called Arthur's attention to this, as he had been telling me that a big bull never galloped. Then the moose disappeared at a trot round the bend. We waited a few minutes, cautiously landed, and started along the trail, watching to see if the bull was lying in wait for us; Arthur telling me that if he now attacked us I must shoot him at once or he would kill somebody.

A couple of hundred yards on, the trail led within a few yards of the little river. As we reached this point a smashing in the brush beyond the opposite bank caused us to wheel; and the great bull came headlong for us, while Arthur called to me to shoot. With a last hope of frightening him I fired over his head, without the slightest effect. At a slashing trot he crossed the river, shaking his head, his ears back, the hair on his withers bristling ... and when the bull was not thirty feet off I put a bullet into his chest, in the sticking point. It was a mortal wound, and stopped him short; I fired into his chest again, and this wound, too, would by itself have been fatal. He turned and re-crossed the stream, falling to a third shot, but as we approached he struggled to his feet, grunting savagely, and I killed him as he came toward us.

I was sorry to have to kill him, but there was no alternative. As it was, I only stopped him in the nick of time, and had I not shot straight at least one of us would have paid forfeit with his life in another second. Even in Africa I have never known anything but a rogue elephant or buffalo, or an occasional rhinoceros, to attack so viciously or with such premeditation when itself neither wounded nor threatened.... On reaching Lambert's camp, Arthur and Odilon made affidavit to the facts as above set forth, and this affidavit I submitted to the secretary of mines and fisheries of Quebec, who approved what I had done.

[OPPOSITE]
Walk softly and carry a big gun.
Teddy Roosevelt.

[THIS PAGE]
A "Bully" president, Theodore Roosevelt.

President William Howard Taft

"Mr. Taft's Murray Bay" [Quebec]
The New Yorker, *September 4, 1926*

———

As he has done for twenty-five out of the last thirty-five years, Mr. William Howard Taft has been spending the summer at Murray Bay in Quebec. His sixty-ninth birthday on September 15 will find him looking some years less than that, a little less stout than he once was, but as jovial and as much a part of the Canadian colony as ever.

Earlier in the summer he was ill, but now once again sees him on the golf course, which skirts the St. Lawrence River, and hears him laughing easily and heartily as a good shot, exclaiming "Piffle" or "Posh" at a bad one.

His unpretentious cottage, on the same grounds as his brother's, is between the railroad on the shore and the highway higher up the side of the hill. The porch overlooks the river, which is twelve miles wide at Pointe au Pic.

The Chief Justice is almost an unofficial mayor of Murray Bay. His interest is deep in this small scale Newport of Canada. One realizes it when seeing him stroll with Mrs. Taft down the main street and pass the two general merchandise stores. His stops to chat about this and that are numerous, but it is noteworthy that they are almost exclusively with the older generations. A great many of the younger generation do not recognize the only living ex-president of the United States.

As a matter of fact he has but to return to his cottage to be very much in the younger set. Almost always one or more of his three children are there and most of his ten grandchildren. His life is quite simple; in his establishment there are his secretary and a few well-trained servants....

Weekends are unknown; guests come for fortnights, each household carefully scheduling its summer. Canadians and Americans are numerically almost equal. There is an old-school air about the place. The general custom of picnics is preserved; so also the dogcart. On the porch of each house overlooking the golf course, hangs a telescope or an opera glass through which to seek the lord and master when luncheon is on the horizon.

There are polite dances at the hotel which last only until midnight. The two trains a day and the river steamer's stops are events. Conversation is easy, intimate, and usually about golf.

[OPPOSITE]
President William Howard Taft with family in Quebec.

AT PLAY

Sir Robert Borden

Atlantic City, New Jersey
March–April 1934

———

Last winter we remained in Ottawa without going south. This year we left for Atlantic City on March 15, and returned April 4. During March, Atlantic City greeted us with two snow-blizzards; and twice during our visit the snowplough was required to clear the boardwalk. Easter arrived April 1; and as the weather had become somewhat milder, the crowds at Atlantic City exceeded anything I had ever known. The press reported 500,000 people on Easter Sunday; but this, I think, was a very great exaggeration. However, the boardwalk, on that day, was a mass of slowly moving humanity.

Sir Robert Borden

Holiday in the South (From Letters to Limbo*)*
April 4, 1936

———

Today I returned from a six-week holiday of which all, except one week, was spent at the Cloister Hotel, Sea Island, Georgia, a most delightful resort. The lawns, herbaceous borders, flowers, birds, and the sunshine made our visit most enjoyable.

On my way south, I was entertained ... in New York at a luncheon. Besides myself, the guests numbered fifteen, of whom all were prominent; either from business, finance, or economics. [There was] a straw vote as to who would be the next president. Sixteen ballots were handed in with the following result: Dickinson — 1; Hoover — 2; Landon — 3; Roosevelt — 10.

This was significant, as probably there was no supporter of Roosevelt at the table....

Leaving Sea Island on March 29, we reached the Biltmore on the following day (Monday) and during our stay in New York we saw *First Lady* (Jane Cowl); *Saint Joan* (Katharine Cornell and Brian Aherne); *Call It a Day* (Gladys Cooper and Philip Merivale and Jeanne Dante); *Victoria Regina* (Helen Hayes); and *Libel*, a play by Edward Wooll.

AT PLAY

HOME AWAY FROM HOME

There was no one who loomed larger — who had a more shaping influence or a more lasting impact — on the life of Franklin Delano Roosevelt than his mother, Sara Delano. And there was no place on the planet that Sara Delano felt more at home with her son than the family's impressive summer retreat on Campobello Island in Canadian waters.

Campobello Island is where a young FDR learned to sail and where, in adulthood, he would be diagnosed with polio. Wedged between the province of New Brunswick and the state of Maine, Campobello Island is more than the most famous Canadian landmark in American history. It is a geographical metaphor for the relationship between Canada and the United States — a place that hovers just near, if not astride, the border. A place where the values and people of the two countries are separated by little more than the tide and sunset. FDR unquestionably belonged to America. But, during a lifetime of summers, Campobello Island made certain to leave Canada's imprint on one of America's greatest leaders.

President Franklin D. Roosevelt

Informal Remarks Delivered at Campobello Island
New Brunswick
June 29, 1933

I think that I can only address you as my old friends of Campobello — old and new. I was figuring this morning on the passage of time and I remembered that I was brought here because I was teething, forty-nine years ago. I have been coming for many months, almost every year until about twelve years ago, when there was a gap.

It seems to me that memory is a very wonderful thing, because this morning when we

WITH FAITH & GOODWILL

were beginning to come out of the fog off Quoddy Head, the boys on the lookout in the bow called out "land ahead." Nevertheless, memory kept me going full speed ahead because I knew the place was the Lubec Narrows.

That was one of the things I learned up here, one of the things I learned, for instance, from Ed Lank, from John Calder, and from old Captain Mitchell who, by the way, gave me a few minutes ago a very delightful photograph of my father's first old boat away back in the early [1890s]. I am mighty glad to have it.

I was thinking also, as I came through the Narrows and saw the line of fishing boats and the people on the wharves, both here at Welchpool and also in Eastport, that this reception here is probably the finest example of friendship between nations — permanent friendship between nations — that we can possibly have.

I was glad that I had with me the American delegate to the Disarmament Conference in Geneva, Mr. Norman Davis, because he will go back to Geneva and will be able to tell them that he has seen with his own eyes what a border-line without fortifications means between two great nations.

I hope and am very confident that if peace continues in this world and that if the other nations of the world follow the very good example of the United States and Canada, I shall be able to come back here for a holiday during the next three years.

A young Franklin Roosevelt sailing in Campobello with his mother, Sara Delano Roosevelt, in 1904.

This reception here is probably the finest example of friendship between nations —
permanent friendship between nations — that we can possibly have.

— President Franklin D. Roosevelt

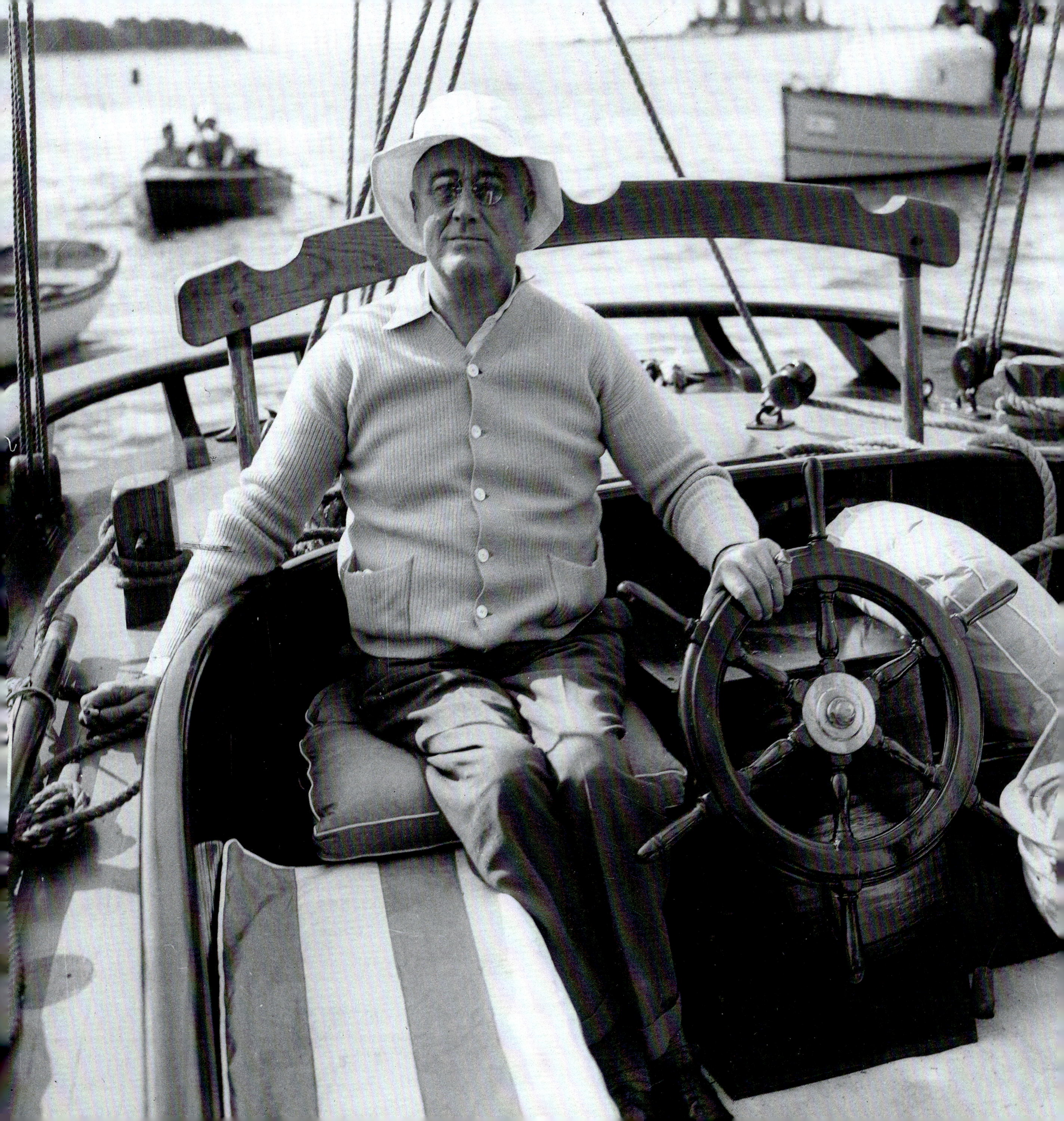

President Richard Nixon

Presidential Toast,
Ottawa, Ontario
April 13, 1972

———

I have been to Picton. Now, most Americans will not know what Picton is, but you Canadians will know. Or maybe you don't.

But in the year 1957, the secretary of state [William Rogers] and I — I was then vice president and he was attorney general of the United States — were invited by the publisher of the Rochester paper, Mr. Paul Miller, to sail … and to go over to the Canadian side and see the beauties of Canada. It was to be a wonderful trip.

But the incident which I would like to leave on this occasion with our friends from Canada was what happened in Picton [Ontario] that day. It was a Saturday night. We had played golf earlier in the day. We were still in sports clothes, in sports jackets — and we decided to go to one of the local pubs, just as we were.

We went in and sat down. We had no Secret Service at that time with us, and the waiter looked us all over, and some way he seemed to think he recognized me, but he wasn't sure.

We noted, or Secretary Rogers at least noted — he was then attorney general and is supposed to note such things — that the waiter was talking to the bartender after serving us. The bartender was looking over and saying, "No, it can't be, it can't be."

After we had finished — he was a very polite waiter — after we had finished and were ready to leave, the waiter came up and said, "Sir, if you don't mind, I have a bet with the bartender, and you can help me win it or I might lose it." I said, "What is the bet?" He said, "I bet him $5 that you are Vice President Nixon."

I said, "Well, call him over and we will confirm it." So the bartender came over and said, "Is it true?" I said, "Yes." He said, "I would never have believed it."

He gave him the $5, and as we started to move on, I heard him mumble to the waiter, "You know, he doesn't look near as bad in person as he does in his pictures."

[PREVIOUS PAGE]

President Roosevelt on the *Amberjack II* while sailing from Marion, Massachusetts, to Campobello, New Brunswick, June 16, 1933.

President George H.W. Bush

"The Thrill of Fishing in Arctic Canada"
Fort Simpson, Northwest Territories
Deh Cho Drum, *August 31, 1997*

―――

I love fishing the Tree River. Way above the treeline, the fast-flowing Tree River pours its rushing green-grey waters into the Arctic Ocean, about a mile or two from where I fished for char. As the waters race over the boulders and rocks, you can catch an occasional glimpse of the majestic char, struggling to continue their fight against the current, their quests to reach their destiny, up-river quest. If thirsty, you can cup your hands and drink of these pristine waters. Yes, there are some mosquitoes around, but not enough to detract from the joys of fishing. Even a mild breeze seems to keep the critters away.

This year the weather was perfect. We fished in T-shirts, needing a sweater or jacket only in the early morning or late afternoon. The weather up there is variable, and it can get wet and very cold even in August, but not this year. There were a lot of char in those fast-running waters, a lot of big, strong fish. My thirteen-year-old grandson, Jeb, from Miami, Florida, got a twenty-five to thirty-pound fish on his Magog Smelt fly, a brown, wet fly that was very productive over the course of our whole trip. He fought the fish for forty-five minutes, following our guide Andy's instruction to perfection. The big red, finally tiring, came into the shallow waters just above some rapids, and then, with one ultimate surge of energy, he flipped over the edge of the pool into the white-water rapids, broke the twenty-pound test tippet, and swam to freedom.

My grandson, not an experienced fly fisherman, had fought the fish to perfection. He did nothing wrong. All the fishing experts who were watching told him so, but those big fish are strong and tough and they never give up.

I had forty-three fish on my fly rod, only to bring two into the shore. Don't laugh; I was proud to have kept the fly in the water, kept on casting, having the thrill of having that many fish, even for a moment, on my No. 9 rod. I used an L.L. Bean reel. As for flies, I found that the Mickey Finn, the Blue Charm, and the Magog Smelt all worked well. So did some others, the names of which escape me even as I write. I tried some dry flies but they produced zilch in the way of action. I found that I got most of my fish when the fly was drifting downstream, though I got two or three hits the instant the fly hit the water.

One pool was narrow, right next to the fastest part of the river. I'd throw the fly out into the white-capped waves and it would be rushed by the current into the pool. When it left the raging water and hit the more placid pool, the fish would strike.

Miscellaneous observations: I did better on getting the fly unhooked from the rocks this year, though I did lose a tiny number of flies when they were claimed by some especially craggy rocks. I learned that the way to get lots of fish on the line is to keep the hook in the water. Obvious. Well, maybe, but a lot of fishermen seem to hang out waiting for someone else to catch one before they'd do serious fly casting. The rocks were very slick and, at seventy-three years of age, my balance is less than perfect. Put it this way: I can't turn very well and I slip a lot. The felt-bottom boots help. Better still are the felt-bottom boots with little, diamond-hard spikes.

I fish a lot, but my advice is "get a good guide." I had one in Andy, who in a very gentlemanly way pointed out mistakes and helped me in every way. He was a good net man, a great fly adviser, and he got as big a kick when I got a fish as if he had taken it himself.

Last observation: I found myself getting intolerant of those fishermen using hardware. There is something more sporting, more competitive, more difficult, more challenging about using a fly rod.

I know that the *Deh Cho Drum* paper is not quite the size of Toronto papers or the *New York Times*, but you know what? I bet the eight hundred or nine hundred readers of your paper know a hell of a lot more about fishing than the readers of those big city papers. That made me hesitant about sharing these amateurish observations with you. But, on the other hand, maybe your readers will better be able to sense the exhilarating joy I felt when standing out there, knee-deep in the ice-cold waters of the Tree River pools, communing with nature, counting my blessings, thanking God, and catching some char, too.

I am a very happy and a very lucky man now. Because of time spent fishing and the chance that fishing gives me to relax and think freely, now more than ever I see clearly just how blessed I really am. I served my country. I have a close family and a wonderful wife to whom I have been married for fifty-two-and-a-half years, and yes, I went to the Tree River and caught char. Tight lines to all you fisherman! Submitted by this most enthusiastic amateur, to whom Canada has given such joy.

[OPPOSITE]

All men are equal before fish II. President Bush and Prime Minister Mulroney on the *Fidelity* near Kennebunkport, Maine, in August 1990.

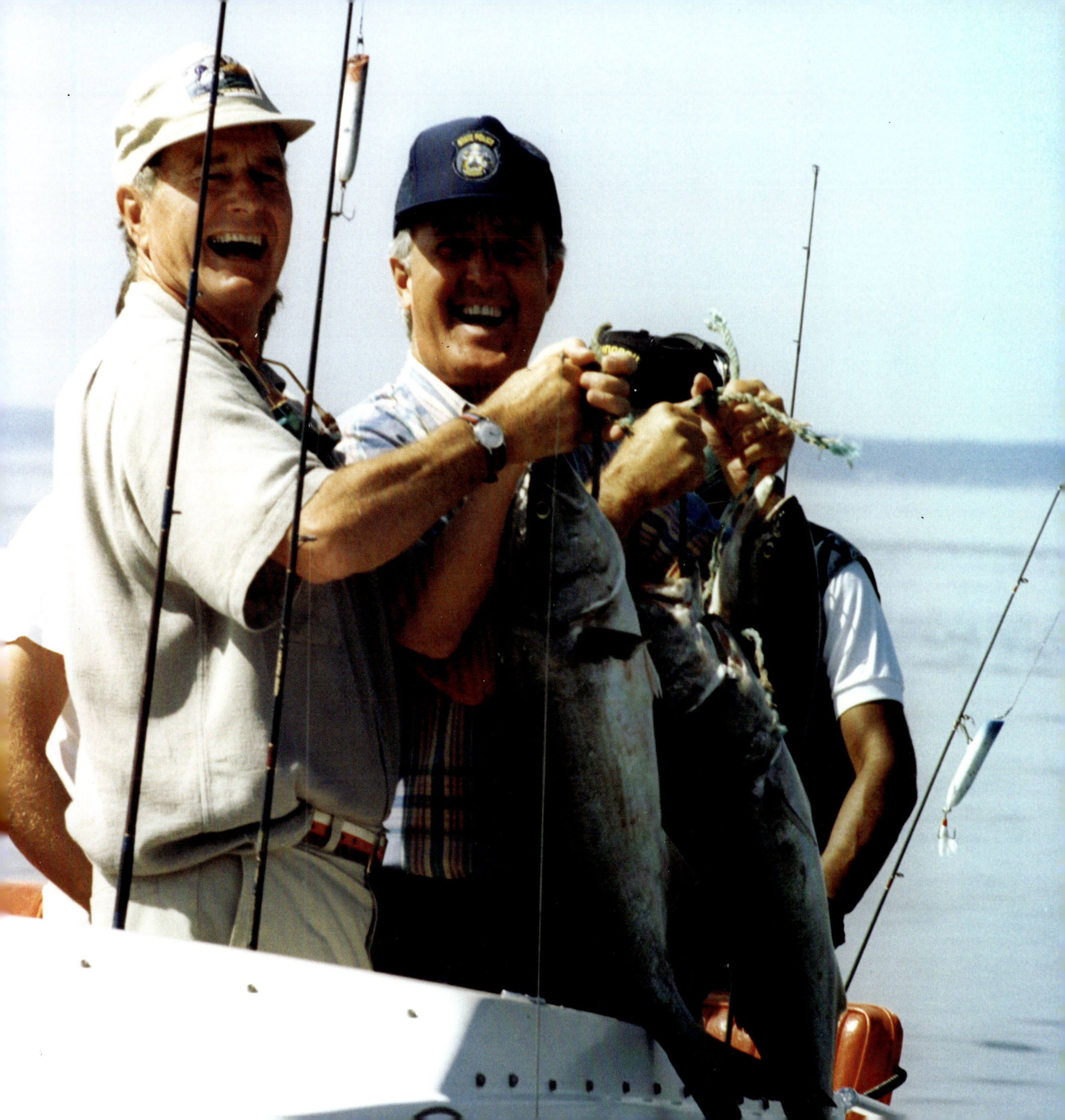

TOASTS AND TRIBUTES

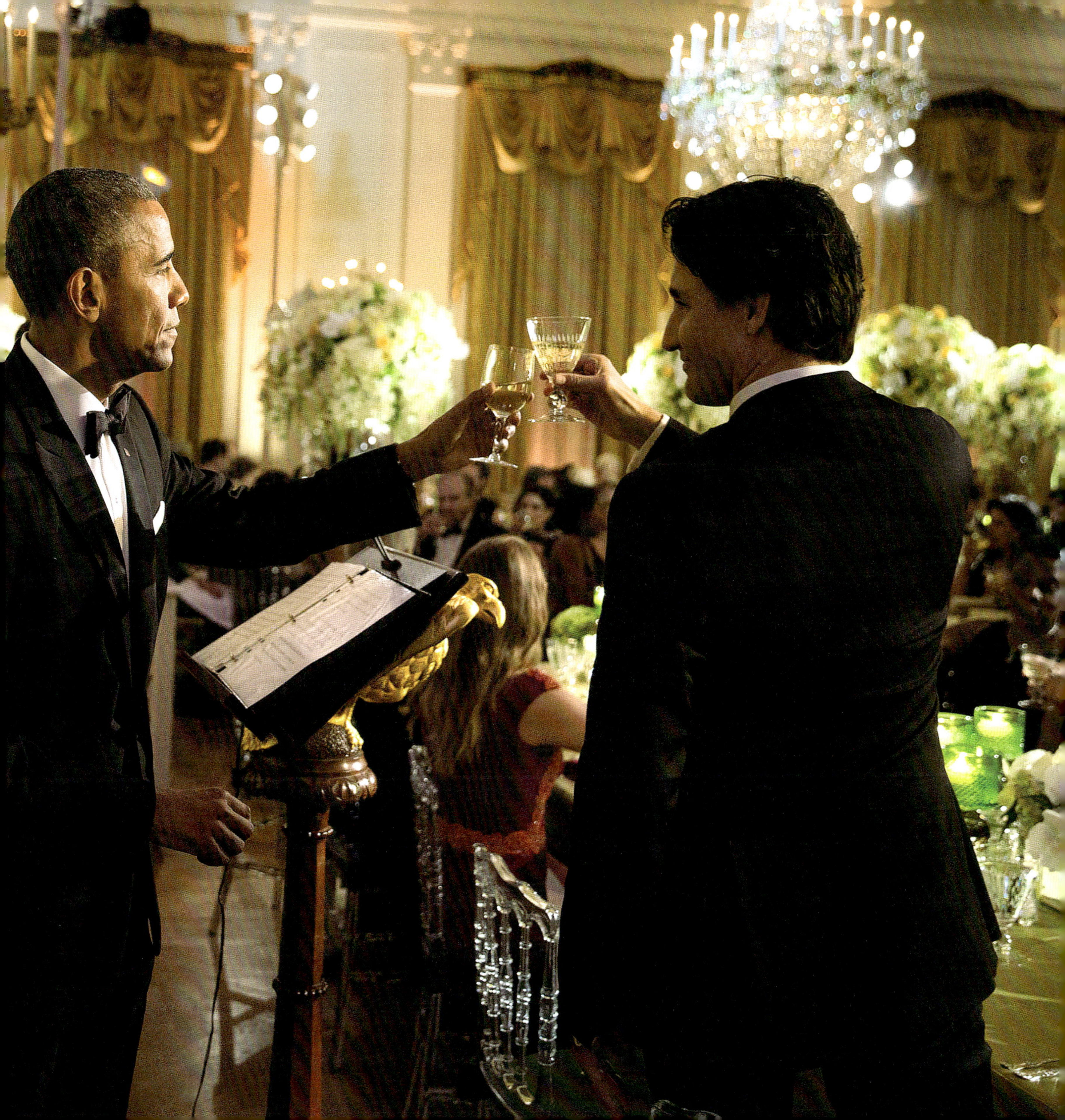

THE ART OF THE TOAST AND TRIBUTE IS ONE THAT ALL LEADERS MUST master. It is an art that comes more naturally to some than to others. Over the years, in times of challenge and times of cheer, American and Canadian leaders have remarked upon the achievements, the friendship, the boldness and, sadly, the passing of one another. Usually brief, these remarks frequently betray the most honest of emotions — sometimes during the most difficult of moments.

President George W. Bush visited Halifax, Nova Scotia, three years after September 11, 2001, and the dark days when Canada offered comfort and safety to thousands of Americans stranded after the skies over the United States were closed. His mission was to offer his nation's thanks. "You opened your homes and your churches to strangers," he said. "You brought food, you set up clinics, you arranged for calls to their loved ones, and you asked for nothing in return.

[PREVIOUS PAGE]
President Barack Obama delivers remarks and a toast during the state dinner for Prime Minister Justin Trudeau and Madame Sophie Grégoire-Trudeau in the East Room of the White House, March 10, 2016.

My heart is overwhelmed at the outpouring of Canadian compassion.
How does a person say
thank you to a nation?

— PRESIDENT GEORGE W. BUSH, QUOTING AN AMERICAN CITIZEN

One American declared, 'My heart is overwhelmed at the outpouring of Canadian compassion. How does a person say thank you to a nation?' Well, that's something a president can do. And so let me say directly to the Canadian people and to all of you here today who welcomed Americans, thank you for your kindness to America in an hour of need."

So when the politics, bilateral and world issues, and so much else is put aside, we are reminded that American-Canadian relations are really about just that — people. Bill Clinton put it best. During a speech in Ottawa while president, he reminded his audience that Canadians and Americans must forever reconfirm our common humanity. "That, to me," he said, "is the true story of our long friendship."

And whatever divides our peoples politically and socially and culturally, in our own country or in the other, we can all agree on that.

President Franklin Roosevelt is welcomed to Kingston, Ontario, by Prime Minister Mackenzie King in August 1938.

Prime Minister Wilfrid Laurier

On Abraham Lincoln
House of Commons, Ottawa, Ontario
May 26, 1898

ABRAHAM LINCOLN, UNKNOWN TO FAME WHEN HE WAS ELECTED TO THE PRESIDENCY, exhibited a power for the government of men which has scarcely been surpassed in any age. He saved the American union, he enfranchised the black race, and for the task he had to perform, he was endowed in some respects almost miraculously. No man ever displayed a greater insight into the motives, the complex motives, which shape the public opinion of a free country, and he possessed almost to the degree of an instinct, the supreme quality in a statesman of taking the right decision, taking it at the right moment, and expressing it in language of incomparable felicity.

Lincoln, the Great Emancipator.

TRIBUTES AT A TIME OF LOSS

Ambassador Lester B. Pearson
On the Death of President Franklin Roosevelt
Washington, D.C.
April 1945

Franklin D. Roosevelt was more than a great president of a great land. He was a leader of free men in every land in their fight against oppression and aggression and evil. He was a leader of the United Nations and as such he belonged to us all. So tonight we share with you the grief and tragedy of his loss. With you we take pride in the majesty of his achievements; we stand humble before the inspiration of his vision.

My country is Canada. We Canadians knew the president well and he knew us. He was, in fact, close to us, in a sense that no other president ever was. He spent his summers on our shores. He fished our northern streams. His fireside chats were heard in our homes; his ringing declarations uplifted our hearts. He understood our problems and our possibilities.

It was at his Hyde Park home that he and our prime minister worked out an enduring scheme for solidarity in war and peace between two friendly neighbours. It was at Quebec that he and that other great leader of embattled democracy, Winston Churchill, worked out those plans of victory which are now on the threshold of fulfillment.

Above all, we Canadians, conscious now of the sure approach of total triumph, remember what the great president meant to us when we were passing through the valley of the shadow of defeat. He held ever before us the hope of final victory and he backed his hope with help. At this time, above all times, we do not forget.

Now the president has joined the gallant company of those who fought and won and fell. We, from all the United Nations, can pay the best tribute to his memory and offer the highest homage to his greatness by carrying forward the fight from the point where he fell; the unslackening fight to win the war, the determined fight to win a peace worthy of him and all those other valiant souls who have died for it.

[OPPOSITE]
Former First Lady Jacqueline Kennedy departs the White House for JFK's funeral procession to the Capitol Building, November 25, 1963.

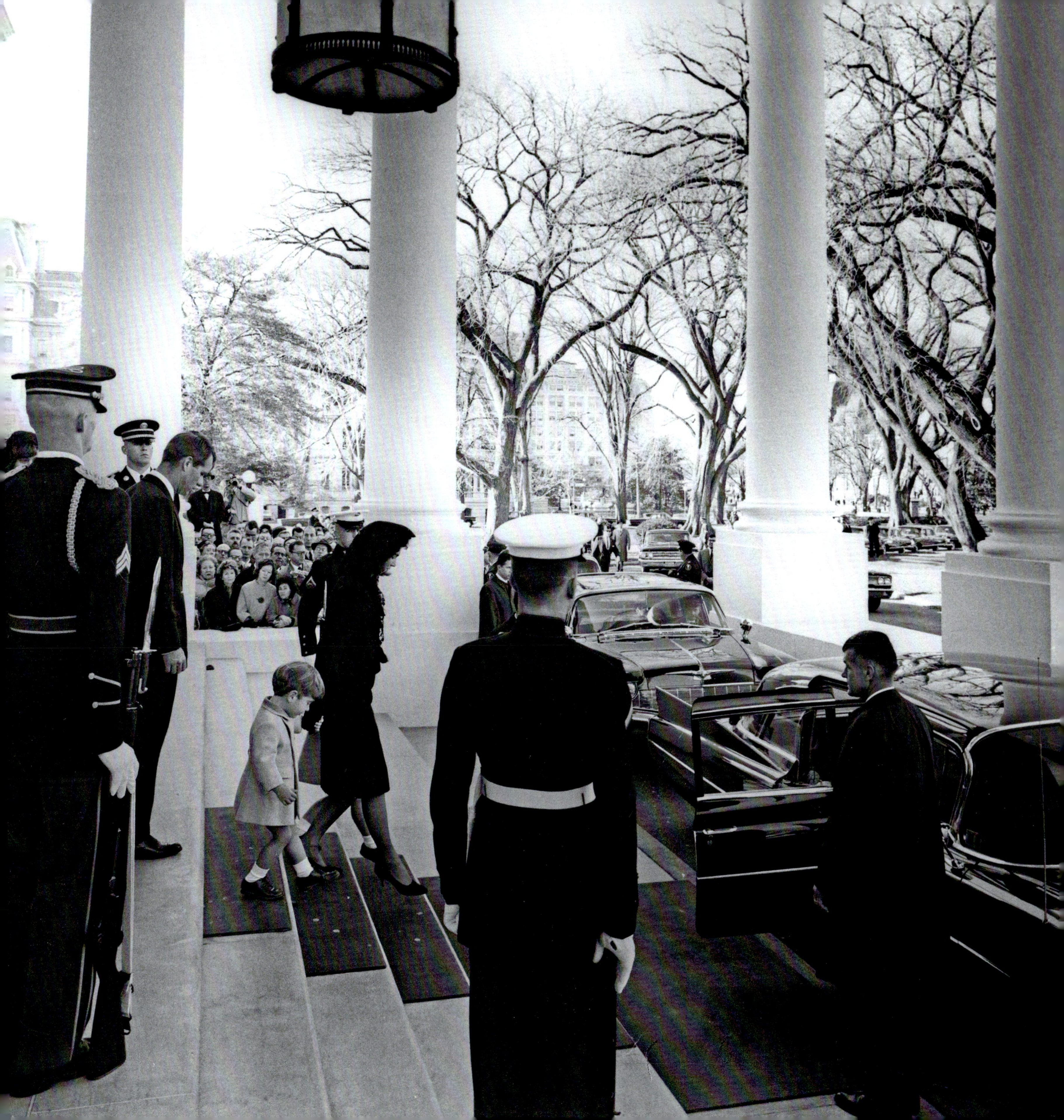

Prime Minister Lester B. Pearson

On the Death of President Kennedy
House of Commons
Ottawa, Ontario
November 22, 1963

I rise, Mr. Speaker, to express if I may, the feelings of shock and grief felt by all of us at the news of the attack on the life of the president of the United States. I would also like to express our sympathy and convey to the wives and the families of the president and governor of Texas [John Connally] ... I am sure that when the news came over the air our first thought was for them. I was about to add that with this sympathy for their recovery, but I have just received a message that President Kennedy died at 2 p.m. [the prime minister began his remarks just after 2:30 p.m.].

> A heartbreaking tragedy has occurred. The world can ill afford at this time in our history to lose a man of his courage, a courage which he displayed in both war and peace.
> — Prime Minister Lester B. Pearson

[OPPOSITE]
Former First Lady Jacqueline Kennedy receives condolences from Prime Minister Lester B. Pearson during a reception following JFK's funeral.

A heartbreaking tragedy has occurred. The world can ill afford at this time in our history to lose a man of his courage, a courage which he displayed in both war and peace. It can ill afford to lose a man of his wisdom, his determination to advance the cause of freedom in his own country and the world.

This is a tragedy not only for the president's family and for his people; it is a tragedy for all of us. No people outside the United States will share more deeply in this tragedy than the people of Canada, the neighbour of the United States.

It is difficult for me to say anything more than this. Our hearts are filled with sadness.

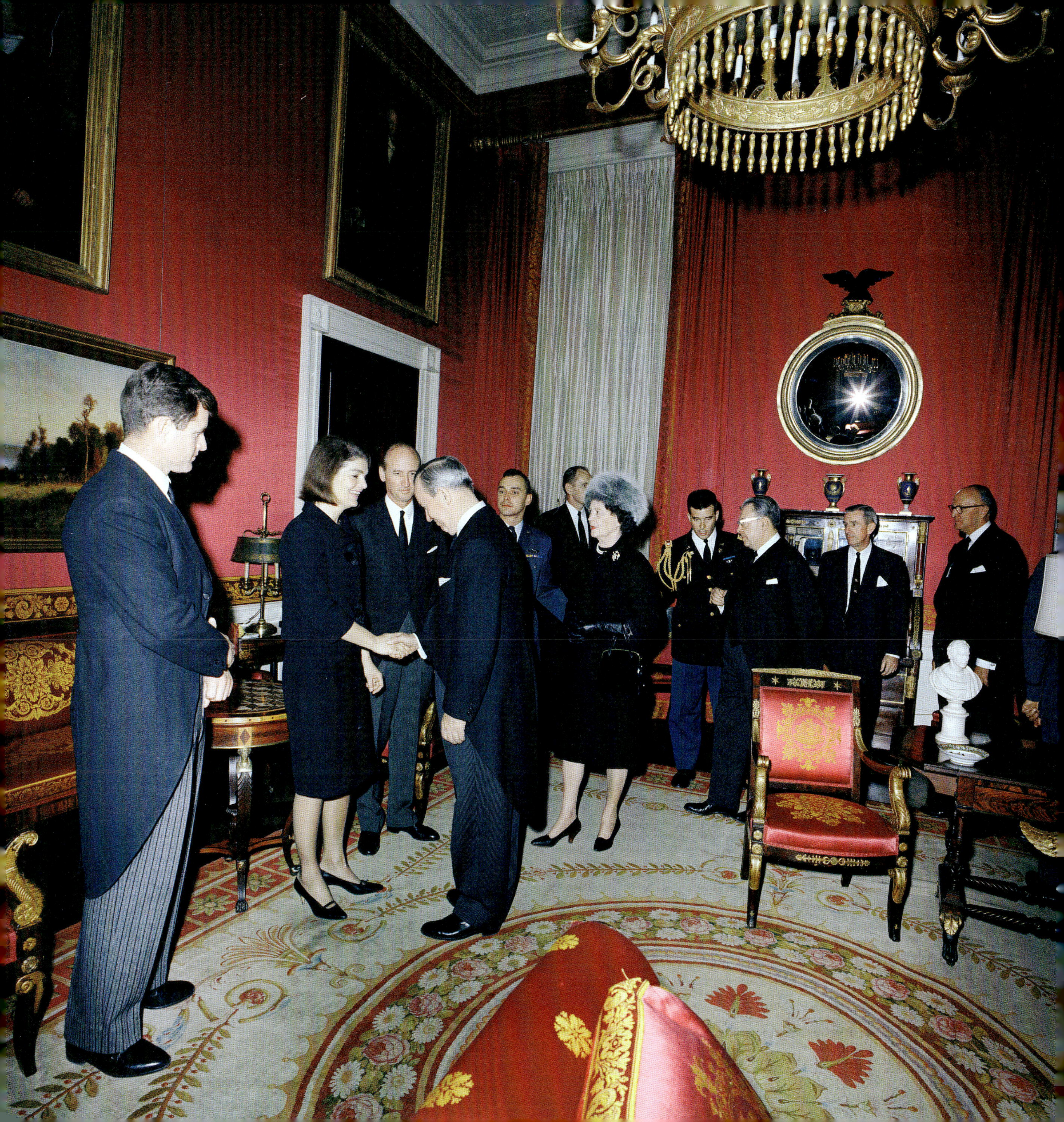

NDP Leader Tommy Douglas

On the Death of President Kennedy
House of Commons
Ottawa, Ontario
November 22, 1963

———

Mr. Speaker, I am sure that all of us [in the House], like all the people of Canada, are stunned at the news of the assassination of the young and far-seeing president of the United States. President Kennedy was a good friend of the people of Canada, and I think the people of Canada had a high regard for him. I think they watched with deep sympathy his endeavours to bring about racial integration and a better understanding among the people of his own country with regard to the problem of minority groups.

This tragedy is all the more pronounced since it has taken place in a democracy; because in democracies there are constitutional and peaceful means to bring about changes of government. It is a reflection on a democracy when an assassination like this takes place.

TOASTS AND TRIBUTES

President Richard Nixon

On the Death of Lester B. Pearson
December 28, 1972

Lester B. Pearson, former prime minister of Canada, will be remembered as one of the twentieth century's most untiring and effective workers in the cause of world peace. For four decades, as diplomat, statesman, and Nobel Peace Prize laureate, he gave unstintingly of himself in the service of Canada and the world community. The record of his accomplishments as an outstanding post-war leader has few equals.

Canada has lost a great leader. We in the United States have lost a firm friend. The world has lost a great statesman and a wise counsellor. His life illustrates in a profound way how much one man, by virtue of hard work, high principle, and a sympathetic understanding of his fellow man, can accomplish in the cause of peace and freedom.

As one who has had the privilege of knowing Lester Pearson for two decades, and who has counted him a friend, I shall miss him greatly.

> Canada has lost a great leader.
> We in the United States have lost a firm friend.
> The world has lost a
> great statesman and a wise counsellor.
> — President Richard Nixon

WITH FAITH & GOODWILL

President Gerald R. Ford

On Pierre Trudeau
Interview with Canadian Journalist Arthur Milnes
September 4, 2001

———

I THINK THE CATALYST [OF THEIR FRIENDSHIP] WAS THE INAUGURATION OF THE G7 program where West Germany under [Chancellor Helmut] Schmidt, and French President Valéry Giscard d'Estaing, and [Prime Minister James] Callaghan of Great Britain and I decided who would be a part of the "7." I was very insistent that we needed another Western hemisphere participant; over very strong objections from some of our European friends, I finally got Canada a membership and Pierre was forever grateful for that leadership on my part. Pierre was so grateful that I, frankly, stood up to the French and said, "Damn it, we're going to have one more country from the Western hemisphere …" No doubt about it. It was important to have somebody other than the United States representing the Western hemisphere and Trudeau was a first-class member of that elite group.

[OPPOSITE]
Before heading to Dorado, Puerto Rico, to attend the second G7 Summit between June 27 and 28, 1976, President Gerald Ford and Prime Minister Pierre Trudeau enjoyed a Potomac River cruise aboard the presidential yacht USS *Sequoia* on June 16. The G7 Summit was the first to include Canada.

It was important to have somebody other than the United States representing the Western hemisphere and Trudeau was a first-class member of that elite group.

— PRESIDENT GERALD R. FORD

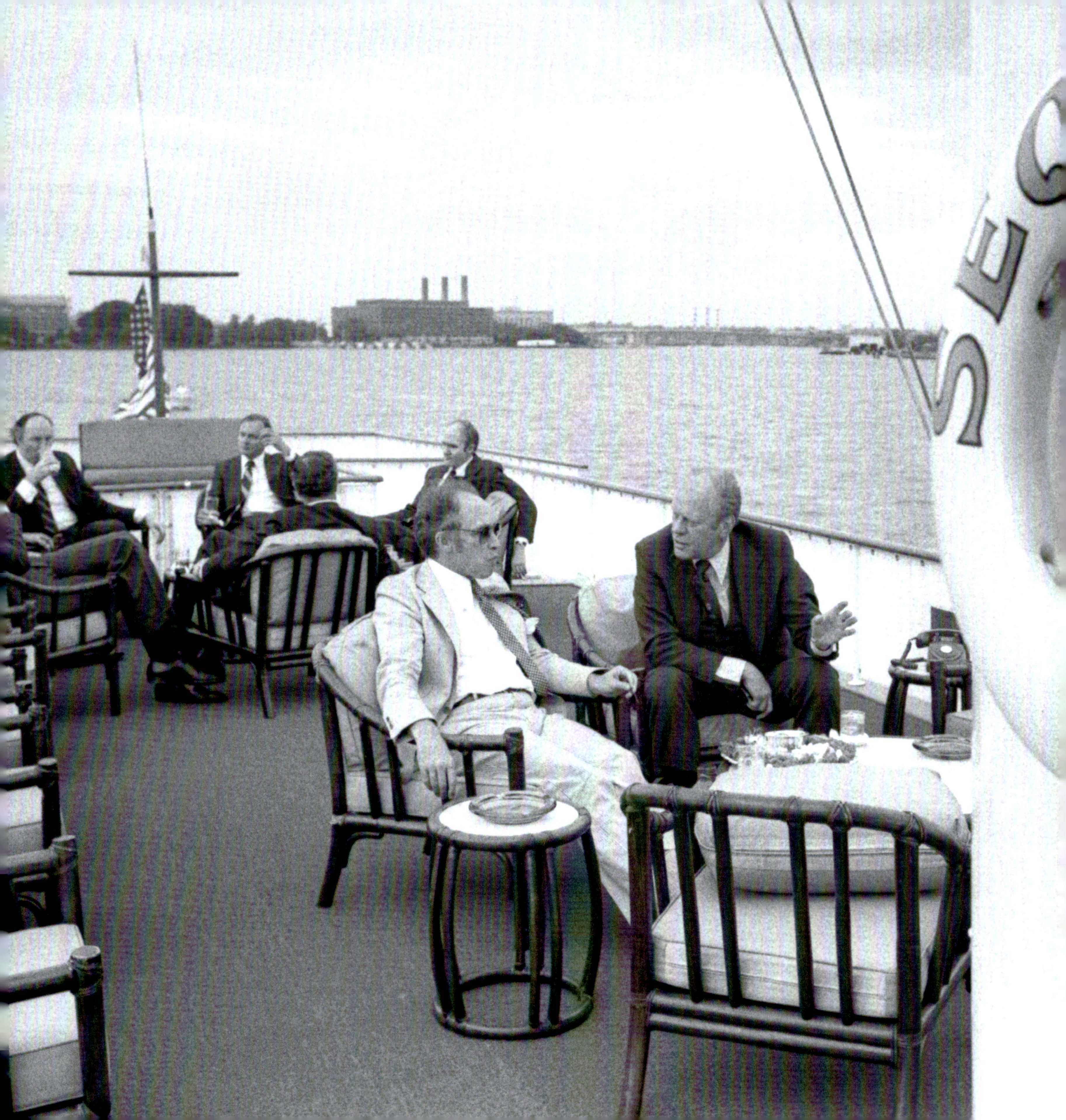

MEMORIES AND REFLECTIONS

Brian Mulroney

On Ronald Reagan, George H.W. Bush, and Bill Clinton
Excerpt from Memoirs, *McClelland & Stewart, 2007*

MY EXPERIENCE HAS BEEN THAT WHEN PRESIDENTS LISTEN CAREFULLY TO CANADIAN prime ministers, they become more thoughtful and more respectful of the sensitivities and needs of the international community and of multilateral institutions.

As I reflect on my association with American presidents, I am struck by just how fortunate I was in the quality of the men whose term in office coincided with my period as prime minister.

Irish eyes smiling. Prime Minister Brian Mulroney and Mila Mulroney entertain President Ronald Reagan and First Lady Nancy Reagan at the famous "Shamrock Summit," March 18, 1985.

TOASTS AND TRIBUTES

My experience has been that **when presidents listen carefully to Canadian prime ministers,** *they become more thoughtful and more respectful of the sensitivities and needs of the international community and of multilateral institutions.*

— Prime Minister Brian Mulroney

Ronald Reagan emerged as a global icon whose impact on American and world history will no doubt lead to his being considered one of the truly great presidents of our time.

George H.W. Bush's sophisticated appreciation of the nuances of foreign policy ensured that the world under U.S. leadership emerged stronger from the convulsive changes he helped to bring about, including the collapse of the U.S.S.R., the implosion of the Warsaw Pact, the reunification of Germany, and the Gulf War victory. His place in history will be a large one.

Bill Clinton, with whom I served for only a matter of months, is clearly the most gifted politician, by far, of his generation. We developed an excellent personal relationship, and I was not surprised to see him evolve into a highly effective world leader.

If in the business world today, cash is king, in the world of the Canada-U.S. relationship, access is worth its weight in gold. It is a privilege that Canada should never squander or surrender.

First Lady Barbara Bush and Mila Mulroney at Kennebunkport, Maine, in 1991.

President Bill Clinton

Toast Delivered at the Canadian Museum of Civilization
Hull, Quebec
February 23, 1995

———

PRIME MINISTER AND MRS. CHRÉTIEN, AMBASSADOR AND MRS. CHRÉTIEN, AMBASSADOR and Mrs. Blanchard, ladies and gentlemen: Let me begin by thanking the prime minister for his generous words and by thanking Prime Minister and Mrs. Chrétien and all of our Canadian hosts for making Hillary and me feel so at home here today in our first day of this wonderful visit.

We all have so much in common, so many roots in common. I couldn't help thinking, when we shared so many jokes in the Parliament today and so many good laughs, of all the things I might have said. One of the things that is most fascinating to Americans about Canada is the way you blend your cultures. I understand, now that we've come across the river from Ottawa to Hull, everything is first in French and then in English. And I'm trying to accommodate to all this. And I thought about a true story that I would share with you.

President Bill Clinton rises to give his remarks before a breakfast meeting of business leaders in the Great Hall at the National Gallery of Canada, February 24, 1995.

One of the members of our official party today came all the way from Georgia, Mr. Gordon Giffin, who's sitting out here, but he was born in Canada. And you should know that Georgia, in the heart of the American South, has a lieutenant governor named Pierre Howard. He was very self-conscious about running with a name like Pierre in the South. And in desperation one day, he said, "Well, you have to understand, Pierre is French for Bubba." *[Laughter.]* And you all know that I come from Arkansas. I can say to you with absolute confidence that if any person from my state were here tonight, he or she would say, "*Je me sens chez moi au Canada* [I feel at home in Canada]." The prime minister and I have a lot in common. We have small town roots and modest backgrounds, his in Shawinigan in Quebec. Did I say that right? Shawinigan? Shawinigan. Better? And mine in Hope — I have a hometown that's easier to pronounce. We began early in political life. He entered the Parliament, I think, when he was twenty-nine. I tried to enter the Congress when I was twenty-eight. I failed, and I have been grateful for it ever since. *[Laughter.]*

Our political persuasions and our programs are so similar that one magazine called me a closet Canadian. I think that is a compliment, and I take it as such. We talk a lot about our humble roots. At home when our friends wish to make fun of me, they say that if I talk long enough

We have a common passion for democracy that has united us
in trying to protect freedom and peace and democracy and enterprise far from our own lands.

— President Bill Clinton

I will convince people that I was born in a log cabin I built myself. And that's what I thought the first time I met Prime Minister Chrétien. *[Laughter.]*

We've had a few agonizing political defeats, and we've managed a comeback. As I think about it, I can only think of one thing that separates me from the prime minister: about fifteen points in the public opinion polls. *[Laughter.]* I resent it, but I'm doing what I can to overcome it.

Mr. Prime Minister, one of the glories of Ottawa is the wonderful old canal that winds through this community. It's protected by sweeping and weeping willows in the summertime, and it's, as I saw today, animated by skaters in the winter. As I understand it, the canal was constructed about 150 years ago by a British engineer to help defend Canada from the United States. Thankfully, I'm

WITH FAITH & GOODWILL

told that if you ask most Canadians today why the canal was built, they can't say. The fact that the canal's origin is unremembered speaks volumes about the unique relationship between our two countries: neighbours, allies, friends. Each of us is blessed to share with the other the bounty of this magnificent continent.

Over the years the partnership we have forged has produced many tangible benefits for our people, as you pointed out. We have a joint defence program that protects our skies and makes us more secure. We have a shared commitment to our environment that improves the quality of the air we breathe and the water we drink. We have economies that are so complementary we enjoy the world's largest trading relationship in ways that create jobs and raise incomes on both sides of our border. We have a common passion for democracy that has united us in trying to protect freedom and peace and democracy and enterprise far from our own lands.

President Bill Clinton, Prime Minister Jean Chrétien, and First Lady Hillary Clinton shake hands in a receiving line at an official state dinner during Prime Minister Chrétien's April 1997 visit.

TOASTS AND TRIBUTES

Canada has shown the world how to build a gentler society
with a deeply felt concern for the health and well-being of all its citizens....
There is much in your country from which Americans
can and do draw inspiration.
— President Bill Clinton

The interests and values we share have allowed us to recognize and respect our differences as well. Canada has shown the world how to build a gentler society with a deeply felt concern for the health and well-being of all its citizens. It has shown the world that strength and compassion are not incompatible. There is much in your country from which Americans can and do draw inspiration.

And so tonight, in celebrating all that unites us, let us also remember that which is unique in our countries. Hillary and I enjoyed very much our all-too-brief tour of this magnificent tribute to your unique culture. Let us resolve to work together to bring out the best in each other as we move forward together as partners and as friends. Long live this great nation.

Mr. Prime Minister, one of your most illustrious predecessors, Lester Pearson, put it well when he said, "I now accept with equanimity the question so constantly addressed to me, 'Are you an American?' and merely return the accurate answer, 'Yes, I am a Canadian.'"

And so tonight, in celebrating our countries and what unites us, let us work together and let us say: Long live Canada! *Vive le Canada!*

First Lady Hillary Rodham Clinton

Remarks at the Ninth Conference of the Spouses of Heads of State
and Government of the Americas
Ottawa, Ontario
September 30, 1999

I am very pleased to be back in Ottawa, a place that my husband and I have very fond memories of from our last visit here nearly five years ago.

I particularly remember ice skating with Aline on the Rideau Canal. And my piece of advice is: do not ice skate with Aline, who is a graceful, beautiful ice skater. But she does everything that way, and over the years I have come to admire and respect and have great affection for her and the way she discharges her duties. I appreciate very much the support and leadership that she has given to this endeavour and the excellent job that she has done in putting together this conference....

Five years ago, at the Summit of the Americas in Miami, our nations pledged to work together to meet our common challenges and to look towards the future as one hemisphere. As the leaders met, we convened a parallel conference to examine how the Summit agenda could address the challenges facing the women and children of our regions. Before we left Miami, we pledged to make the concerns of children and families a priority in our home countries and a focus for co-operation throughout the Americas.

We have continued our work at meetings in Paraguay and Bolivia, Panama, and last year in Chile.... Today we need to renew our pledge to continue our work and co-operation. Over the past five years we have made steady progress on the goals that we set, including the three that were set in Miami. Today, because we pledged to reduce maternal mortalities, health ministries throughout the hemisphere are extending prenatal care to more women, upgrading delivery rooms, and fighting centuries-old ignorance about pregnancy.

Because we set a goal of eliminating measles by the year 2000, measles cases have fallen 76 percent in our regions, and all across the Americas children in the most remote villages are getting their first immunization against that deadly disease.

Because we called attention to education reform, the Partnership for Educational Revitalization in the Americas was formed, and finance ministers, who once only looked at GDP numbers, are now looking at school graduation rates and searching for new ways to give all children chances to learn.

We have made a lot of progress, but with the twenty-first century just weeks away, I know that all of us hope to do more. Every two seconds another child is born somewhere in the Americas.

[OPPOSITE]
Hillary Clinton with Aline Chrétien during the 1996 G7 Summit in Lyon, France.

TOASTS AND TRIBUTES

Each of these precious children is a child of tremendous potential, potential that can be unlocked in the first years of life or locked away for a lifetime. How we empower these children and their parents, how we provide for their education and health care will not only shape their lives, but also shape the lives of our nations and our regions.

The theme today, "A Healthy Start: Investing in Children Ages 0 to 6," is one of the most important themes we could choose. Now there are some who might argue that other meetings where the headlines are trade or security or other matters that finance ministers and presidents and prime ministers discuss are more important. But I think if we take a look at what will really matter in the twenty-first century — preparing our children, investing in and educating our children, making sure they have the health care they need — will determine every other issue we could possibly discuss.

So, therefore, raising awareness about early childhood development is a critical matter. It is one that many of us have worked on for many years. For more than twenty-five years as an attorney and advocate for children, I have tried to make clear that what we do for a young child today matters far more than what happens later. Because we can prevent problems and save money if we invest early instead of waiting for problems or crisis to occur.

U.S. First Lady Hillary Clinton stands with Aline Chrétien after ice skating on Ottawa's Rideau Canal, February 24, 1995.

TOASTS AND TRIBUTES

President George W. Bush

On Prime Minister Stephen Harper
Lima, Peru
November 22, 2008

———

I'M PLEASED TO BE WITH A GOOD FRIEND AND A STRONG LEADER, PRIME MINISTER Stephen Harper. It's been a joy to work with him, and we've accomplished a lot together. Relations between the United States and Canada are strong, sometimes complicated, but nevertheless based on common values. I appreciate your candour, your strength of character, and your consistent philosophy.

President George W. Bush meets with Canadian Prime Minister Stephen Harper during the North American Leaders' Summit, August 20, 2007, in Montebello, New Brunswick.

Prime Minister Stephen J. Harper

Joint Press Conference
Ottawa, Ontario
February 19, 2009

———

It is a great pleasure to welcome President Obama to Canada. We are deeply honoured that he has chosen Canada for his first foreign visit since taking office. His election to the presidency launches a new chapter in the rich history of Canada-U.S. relations. It is a relationship between allies, partners, neighbours, and the closest of friends, a relationship built on our shared values: freedom, democracy, and equality of opportunity, epitomized by the president himself.

Our discussions today focused on three main priorities. First, President Obama and I agree that Canada and the United States must work closely to counter the global economic recession by implementing mutually beneficial stimulus measures, and by supporting efforts to strengthen the international financial system.... Second, President Obama and I agreed to a new initiative that will further cross-border co-operation on environmental protection and energy security.... Third, the President and I had a productive discussion about our shared priorities for international peace and security, in particular, our commitment to stability and progress in Afghanistan.

[OPPOSITE]

Prime Minister Stephen J. Harper and President Barack Obama held a joint press conference on Parliament Hill during the president's first-ever foreign visit in February 2009.

TOASTS AND TRIBUTES

President Barack Obama

Joint Press Conference
Ottawa, Ontario
February 19, 2009

I CAME TO CANADA ON MY FIRST TRIP AS PRESIDENT TO UNDERSCORE THE CLOSENESS and importance of the relationship between our two nations, and to reaffirm the commitment of the United States to work with friends and partners to meet the common challenges of our time. As neighbours, we are so closely linked that sometimes we may have a tendency to take our relationship for granted, but the very success of our friendship throughout history demands that we renew and deepen our co-operation here in the twenty-first century. We're joined together

> As neighbours, we are so closely linked that sometimes **we may have a tendency to take our relationship for granted,** but the very success of our friendship throughout history demands that we renew and deepen our co-operation here in the twenty-first century.
> — PRESIDENT BARACK OBAMA

by the world's largest trading relationship and countless daily interactions that keep our borders open and secure. We share core democratic values and a commitment to work on behalf of peace, prosperity, and human rights around the world. But we also know that our economy and our security are being tested in new ways. And the Prime Minister and I focused on several of those challenges today.

[OPPOSITE]
Prime Minister Harper and President Obama walk down the Hall of Honour in Ottawa during President Obama's first foreign trip since assuming the presidency, February 19, 2009.

TOASTS AND TRIBUTES

President Donald J. Trump

Joint Press Conference
Washington, D.C.
February 13, 2017

On February 13, 2017, the atmosphere surrounding the first face-to-face meeting between Donald Trump and Justin Trudeau was crackling with electric potential for problems. The "America First" Republican and his guest, the open-borders, multiculturalist Liberal, could hardly be less alike. Trudeau was a believer in strength through diversity; Trump preached the virtues of extreme vetting. Citizens on either side of the border wondered if the price to be paid for the vast differences between the two men might be strained relations, fewer jobs, and diminished trade.

Nevertheless, Trump helped set a constructive tone in this first meeting, keeping it short and formal while peppering his remarks with talk of building bridges to the north. Trump emphasized co-operation and collaboration with his neighbour and stuck to a script that sounded for all the world as if it might have been delivered by any president who had come before.

Conventionality from such an unconventional chief executive was greeted with happy relief by his Canadian counterpart — even as tougher, tenser days were set to come for U.S.-Canada relations during Trump's time in the Oval Office.

. . .

Prime Minister Trudeau, on behalf of all Americans, I thank you for being with us today. It is my honour to host such a great friend, neighbour, and ally at the White House, a very special place. This year, Canada celebrates the 150th year of Confederation. For Americans, this is one of the many milestones in our friendship, and we look forward — very much forward, I must say — to many more to come.

Our two nations share much more than a border. We share the same values. We share the love, and a truly great love, of freedom. And we share a collective defence. American and Canadian troops have gone to battle together, fought wars together, and forged the special bonds that come when two nations have shed their blood together — which we have.

In these dangerous times, it is more important than ever that we continue to strengthen our vital alliance. The United States is deeply grateful for Canada's contribution to the counter-ISIS effort. Thank you. And we continue to work in common, and in common cause, against terrorism, and work in common co-operation toward reciprocal trade and shared growth.

We understand that both of our countries are stronger when we join forces in matters of

[OPPOSITE]

A good start. In early 2017 Prime Minister Justin Trudeau and President Donald J. Trump met for the first time.

TOASTS AND TRIBUTES

international commerce. Having more jobs and trade right here in North America is better for the United States and is also much better for Canada. We should coordinate closely — and we will coordinate closely — to protect jobs in our hemisphere and keep wealth on our continent, and to keep everyone safe.

Prime Minister, I pledge to work with you in pursuit of our many shared interests. This includes a stronger trading relationship between the United States and Canada. It includes safe, efficient, and responsible cross-border travel and migration. And it includes close partnership on domestic and international security.

America is deeply fortunate to have a neighbour like Canada.
We have before us the opportunity to build even more bridges.
— President Donald J. Trump

America is deeply fortunate to have a neighbour like Canada. We have before us the opportunity to build even more bridges, and bridges of co-operation and bridges of commerce. Both of us are committed to bringing greater prosperity and opportunity to our people.

We just had a very productive meeting with women business leaders from the United States and Canada, where we discussed how to secure everything that we know the full power of women can do better than anybody else. We know that. I just want to say, Mr. Prime Minister, that I'm focused and you're focused on the important role women play in our economies. We must work to address the barriers faced by women and women entrepreneurs, including access to capital, access to markets, and, very importantly, access to networks.

In our discussion today we will focus on improving the ways our government and our governments together can benefit citizens of both the United States and Canada, and, in so doing, advance the greater peace and stability of the world.

Mr. Prime Minister, I look forward to working closely with you to build upon our very historic friendship. There are incredible possibilities for us to pursue, Canada and the United States together.

Again, thank you for joining us, and I know our discussions will be very, very productive for the future of both countries.

A NEW OLD FRIEND

ON JANUARY 20, 2021, FORMER VICE PRESIDENT JOE BIDEN SUCCEEDED Donald Trump as the United States' commander-in-chief, moving into the White House after one of the most troubled transitions in American history. The new president, well acquainted with Prime Minister Justin Trudeau and exceptionally familiar with Canada, quickly set about repairing strained relations between the two countries.

Restoring a long-standing tradition, Biden made Canada's prime minister his first call to a foreign leader two days following his inauguration. Pipelines were a point of early contention as Biden made good on his campaign promise to cancel the Keystone XL permit, but the two leaders committed to working together on a diverse agenda, including trade, defence, energy, and climate change. Above all else, Biden and Trudeau directed their joint energies toward combatting Covid-19 and finding strategies to relieve the impact of the pandemic.

President Joe Biden and Prime Minister Justin Trudeau met face-to-face at the G7 summit in Carbis Bay, Cornwall, England, in mid-June 2021.

President Joe Biden and Prime Minister Justin Trudeau

*White House Press Release of the President's Telephone
Call to the Prime Minister
Washington, D.C.
January 22, 2021*

President Biden spoke with Canadian Prime Minister Justin Trudeau in his first call to a foreign leader as president of the United States, highlighting the strategic importance of the U.S.-Canada relationship and reinvigorating our bilateral co-operation on an ambitious and wide-ranging agenda, including combatting the Covid-19 pandemic, strengthening economic ties, defence, and global leadership to address the pressing challenge of climate change. The president acknowledged Prime Minister Trudeau's disappointment regarding the decision to rescind the permit for the Keystone XL pipeline, and reaffirmed his commitment to maintain an active bilateral dialogue and to further deepen co-operation with Canada. The president and the prime minister discussed their shared vision to promote a sustainable economic recovery and to work together to achieve a net-zero-emissions future, including advancements in the automotive sector. The two leaders agreed to speak again in a month to continue to build out our bilateral co-operation.

In the face of Covid-19, of climate change, of rising inequality, this is our moment to act.

— Prime Minister Justin Trudeau

President Joe Biden and Prime Minister Justin Trudeau

Joint Statement on a Roadmap for a Renewed U.S.-Canada Partnership

February 23, 2021

It is in the shared interest of the United States and Canada to revitalize and expand our historic alliance and steadfast friendship to overcome the daunting challenges of today and realize the full potential of the relationship into the future. The Roadmap for a Renewed U.S.-Canada Partnership announced today establishes a blueprint for an ambitious and whole-of-government effort against the Covid-19 pandemic and in support of our mutual prosperity. It creates a partnership on climate change, advances global health security, bolsters cooperation on defense and security, and it reaffirms a shared commitment to diversity, equity, and justice. Bound by history and geography, the partnership between the United States and Canada endures because we invest in each other's success.

Prime Minister Justin Trudeau

Press Conference After Online Meeting with President Joe Biden

Ottawa, Ontario

February 23, 2021

Back in 2016, I had the pleasure of hosting you here in Ottawa as Vice President. Over dinner, I remember talking about how the extraordinary friendship between Canada and the United States has not just weathered changing seasons; it has grown ever deeper and stronger.

Well, today, we're taking our next step forward. The President and I discussed the ambitious new partnership roadmap, based on shared values and priorities, that will guide our countries' work together over the coming years.

In the face of Covid-19, of climate change, of rising inequality, this is our moment to act.

So we're not wasting any time in getting down to work. Job one remains keeping people safe and ending this pandemic.

This afternoon, the President and I discussed collaboration to beat Covid-19 — from keeping key supplies moving and supporting science and research, to joint efforts through international institutions. We're standing united in this fight.

I know the President and I are on the same page when it comes to standing up for the middle class and people working hard to join it.

And with millions of families relying on the Canada-U.S partnership, this is work we must do together. Just take the energy industry. Canadian energy workers power homes on both sides of the border. It goes to show that we're all better off for this partnership.

Today, the President and I discussed leveraging supply chains and support for businesses to create well-paying jobs and help people who've been hardest hit get back on their feet.

We're facing tough times, there's no doubt, but we're not facing them alone. Canada and the United States are each other's closest allies, most important trading partners, and oldest friends.

And we stand united to beat this pandemic and build a better tomorrow. And I know our bond will grow even stronger.

Thank you, Mr. President. Thank you, Joe, for your leadership, for your engagement. And thank you in advance for all the great work we're going to be doing together. *Merci beaucoup*.

Prime Minister Justin Trudeau and Finance Minister and Deputy PM Chrystia Freeland meet virtually for the first time with newly inaugurated President Joe Biden and Vice President Kamala Harris on February 23, 2021.

ENTRE NOUS

When Kamala Harris was sworn into office as the forty-ninth vice president of the United States, history was being made in many ways. Immediately, she laid claim to an impressive string of firsts. First female vice president. First Black vice president. First vice president of Indian heritage. And, perhaps less well known, first vice president to have lived her teen years in Canada. A recognition of the responsibilities and the opportunities that come alongside all those firsts featured prominently in her victory speech.

From 1978 to 1981, Harris attended the multicultural, English-speaking Westmount High School after her mother secured a teaching post in Montreal. It was a time of political upheaval, with the separatist Parti Québécois holding power provincially and spearheading a campaign to lead Quebec out of Confederation. Harris returned to the United States to attend Howard University after graduation, but living in Canada during those formative years created a personal connection to Canada that surpasses that of any of her predecessors.

Vice President Kamala Harris

Election Victory Speech
Wilmington, Delaware
November 7, 2020

We are so grateful to Joe and Jill for welcoming our family into theirs on this incredible journey. And to the woman most responsible for my presence here today — my mother, Shyamala Gopalan Harris, who is always in our hearts.

When she came here from India at the age of nineteen, she maybe didn't quite imagine this moment. But she believed so deeply in an America where a moment like this is possible. So, I'm

WITH FAITH & GOODWILL

Newly elected Kamala Harris is sworn in as vice president on January 20, 2021, at the U.S. Capitol.

thinking about her and about the generations of women — Black women, Asian, white, Latina, and Native American women throughout our nation's history who have paved the way for this moment tonight.

Women who fought and sacrificed so much for equality, liberty, and justice for all, including the Black women, who are often — too often — overlooked, but so often prove that they are the backbone of our democracy.

All the women who worked to secure and protect the right to vote for over a century: one hundred years ago with the Nineteenth Amendment, fifty-five years ago with the Voting Rights Act, and now, in 2020, with a new generation of women in our country who cast their ballots and continue the fight for their fundamental right to vote and be heard.

Tonight, I reflect on their struggle, their determination, and the strength of their vision — to see what can be unburdened by what has been — I stand on their shoulders.

And what a testament it is to Joe's character that he had the audacity to break one of the most substantial barriers that exists in our country and select a woman as his vice president.

But while I may be the first woman in this office, I won't be the last, because every little girl watching tonight sees that this is a country of possibilities. And to the children of our country, regardless of your gender, our country has sent you a clear message: Dream with ambition, lead with conviction, and see yourself in a way that others might not see you, simply because they've never seen it before. But know that we will applaud you every step of the way....

Vice President Kamala Harris and Prime Minister Justin Trudeau

*White House Press Release of the Vice President's
Telephone Call to the Prime Minister
Washington, D.C.
February 1, 2021*

———

Earlier today, Vice President Kamala Harris spoke with Canadian Prime Minister Justin Trudeau in her first call to a foreign leader as vice president. The vice president underscored Canada's deep importance to the United States as an economic and strategic partner, and she expressed the United States' desire to work closely with Canada on a wide range of issues, including combatting the Covid-19 pandemic, addressing climate change, and expanding our economic partnership in ways that advance the recovery and create jobs in both countries.

The vice president also expressed strong solidarity with Canada regarding the issue of two Canadian citizens unjustly detained by China, and she made clear that the United States would continue to do everything it can to secure their release.

The vice president and the prime minister agreed to remain in close touch, and to support all efforts to expand bilateral co-operation.

ALIGNED AND ALLIED: THE TWO MICHAELS

In December 2018, Canadians Michael Spavor and Michael Kovrig were arbitrarily jailed in China following the Vancouver arrest of Huawei CFO Meng Wanzhou at the request of U.S. officials who sought her extradition on charges of fraud. Their imprisonment launched a 1,020-day geopolitical ordeal that tested and demonstrated the strength of the Canada-U.S. alliance.

Upon taking office, President Joe Biden made his position clear: the White House would regard the so-called Two Michaels as American citizens, insisting that no resolution of the Meng case could be had without a corresponding return of the imprisoned Canadians. And he kept his word. On September 25, 2021, the Two Michaels touched down on Canadian soil, just as Meng returned to China following a settlement with the U.S. Department of Justice. A steadfast partnership between Canada and the United States had led to a spectacular bit of statecraft — and the safe return of two Canadian sons.

Prime Minister Justin Trudeau greets Michael Kovrig (first at far right) and Michael Spavor (second at far right) in Calgary after their release from imprisonment in China.

TIMELINE OF PRIME MINISTERS

Prime Ministers of Canada	Presidents of the United States of America	Prime Ministers of Canada	Presidents of the United States of America
	Andrew Johnson 1865–1869	Sir Robert Borden 1911–1920	William Howard Taft 1909–1913
Sir John A. Macdonald 1867–1873	Ulysses S. Grant 1869–1877		Woodrow Wilson 1913–1921
Alexander Mackenzie 1873–1878			
Sir John A. Macdonald 1878–1891	Rutherford B. Hayes 1877–1881	Arthur Meighen 1920–1921	
		William Lyon Mackenzie King 1921–1926	Warren G. Harding 1921–1923
	James Garfield 1881		Calvin Coolidge 1923–1929
	Chester A. Arthur 1881–1885	Arthur Meighen 1926	
	Grover Cleveland 1885–1889	William Lyon Mackenzie King 1926–1930	
		R.B. Bennett 1930–1935	Herbert Hoover 1929–1933
Sir John Abbott 1891–1892	Benjamin Harrison 1889–1893		Franklin D. Roosevelt 1933–1945
Sir John Thompson 1892–1894	Grover Cleveland 1893–1897	William Lyon Mackenzie King 1935–1948	
Sir Mackenzie Bowell 1894–1896			
Sir Charles Tupper 1896	William McKinley 1897–1901		
Sir Wilfrid Laurier 1896–1911			
	Theodore Roosevelt 1901–1909		Harry S. Truman 1945–1953

AND PRESIDENTS, 1865–2022

Prime Ministers of Canada	Presidents of the United States of America
Louis St. Laurent 1948–1957	
	Dwight D. Eisenhower 1953–1961
John Diefenbaker 1957–1963	
	John F. Kennedy 1961–1963
Lester B. Pearson 1963–1968	Lyndon Johnson 1963–1969
Pierre Trudeau 1968–1979	Richard Nixon 1969–1974
	Gerald R. Ford 1974–1977
Joe Clark 1979–1980	Jimmy Carter 1977–1981
Pierre Trudeau 1980–1984	Ronald Reagan 1981–1989
John Turner 1984	

Prime Ministers of Canada	Presidents of the United States of America
Brian Mulroney 1984–1993	
	George H.W. Bush 1989–1993
Kim Campbell 1993	Bill Clinton 1993–2001
Jean Chrétien 1993–2003	
	George W. Bush 2001–2009
Paul Martin 2003–2006	
Stephen Harper 2006–2015	
	Barack Obama 2009–2017
Justin Trudeau 2015–	
	Donald J. Trump 2017–2021
	Joe Biden 2021–

CONCLUSION

O**N THE DAY OF MY THIRTY-SIXTH BIRTHDAY, I WAS STANDING IN THE** Oval Office staring at the president of the United States of America. The most powerful man in the world looked agitated. Worse, I was the source of his irritation.

George W. Bush and my boss, Prime Minister Paul Martin, were minutes away from moving to the Rose Garden to take questions from the media. I was briefing them on what to expect.

"What will your guys ask me?" President Bush wondered.

"Well, sir," I replied steadily, entirely blocking from my mind the fact that I was standing where Abraham Lincoln once walked and Richard Nixon once taped. "A range of topics are likely. Softwood lumber will certainly come up. Ballistic missile defence. BSE and cattle. You might get climate change."

Then PMO Director of Communications Scott Reid (second from left) in the Oval Office, April 30, 2004, with (from left to right) PMO Chief of Staff Tim Murphy, White House Press Secretary Scott McClellan, President George W. Bush, and Prime Minister Paul Martin.

I stopped, catching that look of irritation from the president.

"I thought I was taking just two questions from your guys."

"That's correct."

"Then what will those two questions be?"

I paused for a moment before the disconnect occurred to me. You see, when taking questions from the White House press corps, the president's staff would identify in advance which reporters to call upon and what topics they would pursue. But in Canada, we left that to the press gallery. After explaining this nuance in approach and why it meant I could not be certain of exactly what the president would be asked, he slapped my shoulder and laughed about giving me a hard time.

"I guess we do things a bit different," he cracked.

I think about that exchange whenever asked about the relationship between our two countries. We share so much history. And geography. We have so very many things in common. But, as President Bush put it, we still sometimes do things "a bit different." That surely goes a long way to explain how we've made the relationship work so well for so long.

Collecting and cataloguing these stories of prime ministers and presidents serves as a reminder of how personal and persistent that relationship has been. Read their words. Listen to their anecdotes. Reflect on their accomplishments. You cannot help but feel how these personal stories have contributed to shaping our national stories — encompassing all that brings us together, and at times, the things we do "a bit different."

Working as a political staffer, I was privileged to see some of those stories unfold in front of me. Working on this book and its second edition, I was fortunate to find so many more stories from the pages of history.

SCOTT REID

AFTERWORD

In 1939, Winston Churchill was in London addressing the Canada Club. He spoke with admiration about Canada's relationship with its southern neighbour, saying: "She clasps the American hand with her faith and goodwill. That long frontier from the Atlantic to the Pacific Oceans, guarded only by neighbourly respect and honourable obligations, is an example to every country and a pattern for the future of the world." Churchill was right about the bilateral relationship, and his admonition is now more important than ever about how countries must treat each other.

From my vantage point, first as U.S. ambassador to Canada and then as my country's ambassador to the United Nations, I learned first-hand the importance of notions like faith and goodwill to guide foreign relations.

Canada and the United States have shared in the adventures of the world. The beaches of Europe are the highest memorial of our continuous effort to maintain our fountainhead — democracy.

U.S. Ambassador to Canada Kelly Craft addresses the Canadian American Business Council's twenty-third annual State of the Relationship Dinner in Ottawa in November 2017.

We have joined in a multitude of other endeavours over the years, from relief efforts, to most recently, the historic United States-Mexico-Canada Agreement (USMCA). The example of goodwill, co-operation, and mutual respect between our countries that has existed almost from the beginnings of both is a beacon for a troubled world.

I cannot think of a country more linked to my own by fundamental values — democracy, respect for culture, a common inheritance from great traditions — than Canada. Nor does any other nation have the bounty of resources, and those greatest resources of all — goodwill and simple decency — that Canada possesses. I came to appreciate how much those non-economic elements are as fundamental as the economic ones, that those things that speak to the spirit of a country are a light toward which we should always aim.

The highest praise for a book is to share it with friends. The first edition of *With Faith & Goodwill* was widely shared, as I expect, this second edition will be. The occasion of this book only sharpens the consciousness of my respect and admiration for Canada and its people.

Faith and Goodwill.

May Canada and the United States continue to embrace those truths.

THE HON. KELLY CRAFT
U.S. Ambassador to United Nations (2019–21)
U.S. Ambassador to Canada (2017–19)

ACKNOWLEDGEMENTS

from Arthur Milnes

ANY WRITER BUILDS UPON THE SCHOLARSHIP OF THOSE WHO HAVE written before him or her, and it is therefore important to acknowledge the seminal work of Canadian journalist Lawrence Martin, whose book *The Presidents and the Prime Ministers* remains a foundational study of the relations between Canadian and American leaders. Grateful recognition is also made to the University of Toronto Press through Lisa Jemison for permission to quote sections from the memoirs of Lester B. Pearson, *Mike*, and Sir Robert Borden's *Letters to Limbo*. The Queen's University School of Policy Studies, joined by *The New Yorker*, McClelland & Stewart, and Northern News Services, also assisted in this area. Library and Archives Canada, joined by past prime ministers Brian Mulroney and Stephen J. Harper, helped with photographs, as did my colleague from the Harper PMO, Deb Ransom. Special thanks are extended to John Keller of the William J. Clinton Presidential Library and Michael Pickney of the Ronald Reagan Presidential Library.

My greatest debt is owed to Maryscott Greenwood and her team, including Ronnie Di Iorio, Desiree Godin, Zach Jones, and Kyle MacDonald. Scott Reid was a special joy to work with once again. Finally, the impressive team at Dundurn, especially Associate Publisher Kathryn Lane and freelance editor Michael Carroll, deserve recognition and thanks for the hard work, dedication, and skill that brought this volume together.

Arthur Milnes in his garden with former President Jimmy Carter and former First Lady Rosalynn Carter.

ACKNOWLEDGEMENTS

from Maryscott Greenwood, CABC

THE INSPIRATION FOR THIS BOOK CAME FROM THE 1976 VOLUME *Between Friends/Entre Amis*, which the Government of Canada produced on the occasion of the bicentennial of the United States of America. That kind of grand gesture of friendship is one that makes an impact on people for many years to come, as is evidenced by this project. While *With Faith & Goodwill* features presidents and prime ministers who led their two countries for more than 150 years, the staff and officials who support the leaders are the ones who underpin the strength and vibrancy of Canada-U.S. relations. In recognition of this, I first thank everyone who has ever worked in the White House or in the Prime Minister's Office, regardless of era, regardless of party, for your service to your country and to our great bilateral friendship. In particular, I am honoured that the first women to be appointed ambassadors to the United States and Canada, Kelly Craft with an afterword and Kirsten Hillman with a foreword. respectively, have penned additions for this volume. Both Kelly and Kirsten are phenomenal exemplars of all that is good in bilateral relations.

I would be remiss if I didn't mention another great ambassador to Canada, Gordon D. Giffin, who managed to talk his friends in the White House into having me appointed by President Bill Clinton to serve in the U.S. Foreign Service as chief of staff at the U.S. Embassy in Ottawa. I can never thank Ambassador Giffin and President Clinton properly for the opportunities that assignment opened up. I am also forever grateful to the endlessly generous James H. Greenwood, who quit his law practice in Atlanta on a moment's notice so that we could move our young family to Canada and begin a new adventure together. The adventure continues today. Thanks as well to Grace, Olivia, and James O. Greenwood for putting up with the Canadian stories, the travel, and the constant reference to all things maple- or Nanaimo bar–related.

The editorial curation and keen commentary for this book come from two Canadians who know more about American politics than most Americans, not to mention their encyclopedic knowledge of the politics of Canada. They are the long-suffering public historian Art Milnes, and

Acknowledgements

the hilariously brilliant Scott Reid. We also appreciate the team at Dundurn Press in Toronto who guided us through the project with patience and professionalism.

The team of the Canadian American Business Council (and Crestview Strategy, which houses the organization) deserves credit for helping this project all along the way, including my colleagues Desiree Godin, Ronnie Di Iorio, Munro Watters, Beth Burke, and Allison Archer.

Finally, I want to express my gratitude to the former presidents and prime ministers and their respective libraries and teams that participated in the first edition book launch: Presidents Jimmy Carter, George W. Bush, and William J. Clinton; and Prime Ministers Joe Clark, Stephen J. Harper, Jean Chrétien, and Paul Martin.

A deep and sincere thank-you to the Board of Directors of the Canadian American Business Council, who believe so strongly in the importance of this unique bilateral relationship. They enthusiastically celebrate it every chance they have, including in the publication of this book. Space prevents us from listing all the board members who have served throughout CABC's thirty-plus-year history, but I am pleased to list the current members, in appreciation of their contributions.

CABC Board of Directors

Brianna Ames	Coca-Cola Canada
Lesia Babiak	Johnson & Johnson
Gabe Batstone	Contextere
Dina Brachman	Pfizer
Kevin Chan	Facebook
Gary Clement	TD Bank Group
Giselle Commissiong	Hatch
Blair Dickerson	Vale Base Metals
Rebekah Dopp	Google
Christina Erling	Barrick Gold Corporation
Sean Finn	CN
Marlene Floyd	Microsoft Canada
Hélène V. Gagnon	CAE Inc.
Joshua Greene	A.O. Smith Corporation
Peter Jost	Blank Rome LLP
Robert Klager	Shell Canada Ltd.
Kevin Kolevar	Dow
Andrew Lundquist	ConocoPhillips
Aylin Lusi	UPS

Toby Mack	Energy Equipment and Infrastructure Alliance
James Maunder	Amazon Canada
Arielle Meloul-Wechsler	Air Canada
João Augusto de Castro Neves	ExxonMobil
Wendy Noss	Motion Picture Association — Canada
Clint Odom	T-Mobile
David Paterson	General Motors Canada
Pierre Pyun	Bombardier Inc.
Jean Quenneville	Rio Tinto
Alexander Russ	Association of Equipment Manufacturers
Nancy Ziuzin Schlegel	Lockheed Martin
Pete Sheffield	Enbridge Inc.
Jennifer Sloan	MasterCard Canada
Mary Catherine Toker	General Mills
Lena Trudeau	CABC Member
Herb Tyson	Scarlet Oak Strategies
Cathy Worden	Cisco Canada
Alexandra Zanella	Beauty Revolution Consulting

CABC Advisory Board

The Hon. Rona Ambrose	Leader of the Conservative Party of Canada (2015–17)
The Hon. John Baird	Minister of Foreign Affairs (2011–15)
The Hon. James J. Blanchard	United States Ambassador to Canada (1993–96)
The Hon. Scott Brison	President of the Treasury Board (2015–19)
Derek Burney	Canadian Ambassador to the United States (1989–93)
John de Chastelain	Canadian Ambassador to the United States (1993–94)
Raymond Chrétien	Canadian Ambassador to the United States (1994–2000)
The Hon. Christy Clark	Premier of British Columbia (2011–17)
The Hon. Kelly Craft	United States Ambassador to Canada (2017–19)
The Hon. Kenneth M. Curtis	United States Ambassador to Canada (1979–81)
The Hon. Howard B. Dean	Governor of Vermont (1991–2003), Presidential Candidate (2004)
The Hon. Gary Doer	Canadian Ambassador to the United States (2009–16)
The Hon. Gordon D. Giffin	United States Ambassador to Canada (1997–2001)
Pamela Goldsmith-Jones	Parliamentary Secretary to the Minister of International Trade (2017–19)
The Hon. Heidi Heitkamp	United States Senator for North Dakota (2013–19)

ACKNOWLEDGEMENTS

The Hon. David Jacobson	United States Ambassador to Canada (2009–13)
Michael Kergin	Canadian Ambassador to the United States (2000–05)
The Hon. Ronald Kirk	United States Trade Representative (2009–13)
The Hon. John LaFalce	Member of the U.S. House of Representatives (1975–2003)
Chief Wilton Littlechild	Grand Chief of the Confederacy of Treaty Six Nations (2016-18)
The Hon. John Manley	Deputy Prime Minister (2002–03)
The Hon. Sergio Marchi	Canadian Ambassador to the WTO and U.N. Agencies (1999–2004)
The Hon. Barbara McDougall	Secretary of State for External Affairs (1991–93)
The Hon. Frank McKenna	Canadian Ambassador to the United States (2005–06)
The Hon. James Moore	Minister of Industry (2013–15)
The Hon. Thomas M.T. Niles	United States Ambassador to Canada (1985–89)
The Hon. William L. Owens	Member of the U.S. House of Representatives (2009–15)
The Hon. Lisa Raitt	Minister of Transport (2013–15)
The Hon. Edward G. Rendell	Governor of Pennsylvania (2003–11), Mayor of Philadelphia (1992–2000)
The Hon. Paul H. Robinson	United States Ambassador to Canada (1981–85)
The Hon. Peter Teeley	United States Ambassador to Canada (1992–93)
The Hon. Brad Wall	Premier of Saskatchewan (2007–18)
The Hon. David Wilkins	United States Ambassador to Canada (2005–09)

ABOUT THE EDITORS

Maryscott Greenwood is the chief executive officer of the Canadian American Business Council and a partner at Crestview Strategy U.S., a public affairs consultancy. A former U.S. diplomat appointed by President Bill Clinton, Scotty is a champion for the Canada-U.S. relationship and serves on corporate and philanthropic boards. She lives in Arlington, Virginia.

Arthur Milnes is a journalist and public historian and served as a speechwriter for Prime Minister Stephen Harper. He has edited volumes about the presidencies of George H.W. Bush and Jimmy Carter, and the leadership of Prime Ministers Sir John A. Macdonald and Sir Wilfrid Laurier, as well as other Canadian leaders. He also served as research assistant to former prime minister Brian Mulroney on his bestselling memoir. Arthur lives in Kingston, Ontario.

Scott Reid served as director of communications and senior adviser to Prime Minister Paul Martin from 2003 to 2006. He is the co-owner and principal of Feschuk.Reid, providing strategic and executive communications to leaders in the private, public, and not-for-profit sectors. He also serves as an on-air analyst for CTV News, Newstalk 1010AM, and Bell Media, while writing for a variety of leading media publications. Scott lives in Toronto.

IMAGE CREDITS

AP: 165, 181, 231; Jacques Boissinot: 49; Charles Dharapak: 43; Michel Euler: 223; Benjamin E. "Gene" Forte/picture-alliance/dpa: 72; Andrew Hamik: 56, 57; Pablo Martinez Monsivais: 83; Denis Paquin: 224

Arthur Milnes: 249

Bjorn Bjornson, Courtesy Harry S. Truman Library: 104, 106

Brian Stanton, Courtesy Economic Club of New York: 77

Canadian American Business Council: xv, xvii, xviii, 48, 79, 247

Canadian Press: Peter Bregg, 175

City of Vancouver Archives: 69, 70 (top and bottom), 41, 189

Dave Chan: 245

Dwight D. Eisenhower Presidential Library and Museum/National Park Service: 114, 115

Franklin D. Roosevelt Presidential Library and Museum: 92, 97, 196, 197

Gerald R. Ford Presidential Library and Museum: 215

Government of Canada: 240

Hessler Studio of Washington D. C., Leo Hessler, Courtesy of Harry S. Truman Library: 100

Hon. Peter Milliken, Office of the Speaker: 130

Indiana Historical Society: 24

Jean-Marc Carisse: 159 (top and bottom), 161, 218

Jerry M. Malloy, *Buffalo History Gazette*: 133, 134, 135, 137

Jimmy Carter Presidential Library and Museum: 9, 14, 50, 176, 182–83

Library and Archives Canada: xxv, 19, 29, 31, 111; Duncan Cameron: 140, 147; Department of National Defence: 88–89; Yousuf Karsh, Yousuf Karsh Fonds: 33; Chris Lund/National Film Board of Canada, Phototheque: 109; Bill and Jean Newton: 102; Rt. Hon. Brian Mulroney,

Mulroney Collection: xxviii, 46, 93, 126–27, 152, 154, 157, 201, 217; U.S. Army: 94

Library of Congress: 190, 191, 207; New York Historical Society: 24; Prints & Photographs Division, photograph by Harris & Ewing: 187

National Park Service: 193

Picture Alliance/Newscom/German Federal Government: 86

Prime Minister's Office: xx, 82, 85, 177, 225, 227, 229; Jason Ransom, 122, 123, 125; Adam Scotti, 53, 54, 131, 233, 236

Queen's University Archives: 96, 206

Richard Nixon Presidential Library and Museum (National Archives and Records Administration): 8, 68, 71

Ronald Reagan Presidential Library and Museum: 44, 62 (bottom), 149, 216

TR Birthplace National Historic Site and the Theodore Roosevelt Digital Library, Dickinson State University: 186

U.S. Department of Defense: U.S. Air Force Senior Airman Kevin Tanenbaum, 238

White House Photo Office: Official White House Photo by Shealah Craighead, 177; Official White House Photo by Chuck Kennedy: 202–03; Official White House Photo by Pete Souza: xxx–1, 7, 11

White House Photo Office Collection, Courtesy LBJ Presidential Library: xxvi, 65 (top and bottom)

White House Photographs, John F. Kennedy Presidential Library and Museum, Boston: Robert Knudson: 58–59, 62 (top), 211; Abbie Rowe: 209; Cecil Stoughton (Harold Sellers): 166–67, 170, 172

William J. Clinton Presidential Library: 4, 5, 52, 220

INDEX

Page numbers in italics indicate the presence of photos.

9/11, 6, 93, 118, 121, 124

Abbott, Sir John, 242
acid rain, 146–47, 153, *154*, 155
Address to a Joint Session of Parliament
    Barack Obama's, 4
    Bill Clinton's, 3–4, *5*
    Dwight Eisenhower's, 3, 108, *109*, 110, 112–14, 116
    Franklin Roosevelt's, 4, 95–96, 98–99
    Harry Truman's, 101, 103–07
    history of, 3–5
    John F. Kennedy's, 164, *165–67*, 168
    Richard Nixon's, 3, 67, 69–70, *71*, 73–75
    Ronald Reagan's, 3, 143–47
Address to the U.S. Congress
    Brian Mulroney's, *126–27*, 129, 148, 150–51
    history of, 4–5
    Pierre Elliott Trudeau's, 4–5, 174–75, *176*
    Vincent Massey's, 5
Afghanistan, 6, 93, 118, 121, *122–23*, 124, 226
Aherne, Brian, 194
Air Quality Agreement (1991), 153, *154*, 155
Alaska boundary dispute, 18, 24

Alberta, 80, 175
Aleutian Islands, 96
Ambrose, Rona, 252
Ames, Brianna, 251
Archer, Allison, 251
Arctic, 147, 168, 199
Arctic char, 185
Arctic Circle, 145
Arctic National Wildlife Refuge (ANWR), 80
Argo, 15
Arkansas, 3, 219
Arthur, Chester A., 61, 63, 185, 242
Ashburton, Lord, 169
Asia-Pacific Economic Cooperation (APEC), 42, 116, *117*
Atherton, Ray, *104*, 105
Atlanta (Georgia), xvii, *48*, 250
Atlantic Alliance, 73
Atlantic Charter, 99
Atlantic City (New Jersey), 194
Attu, 96

Babiak, Lesia, 251
Baie-Comeau (Quebec), 131
Baird, John, 252
Baker, James, *93*
Baldwin, Stanley, 133, 138
Batstone, Gabe, 251
Battle of Queenston Heights, *xxii*
Belgian Constitution (1893), 171

Bennett, R.B., 139, 242
Berlin Wall, 56, 93, 118
Between Friends/Entre Amis, xviii, 250
Bevington, Rickey, *48*
Biden, Jill, 237
Biden, Joe, xviii, *xx*, xxi, *53–54*, *131*, *233*, 234–35, *236*, 237, 240, 243
bilateral co-operation, 131, 230, 234, 239, 248
bilateral meetings, xviii, xix, 42
bilateral relationship, xvii–xviii, xxv, 3, 67, 247, 250–51
"birtherism," 63
Blanchard, James, 3, *4*, *52*, 252
Blanchard, Mrs., 218
Bolivia, 222
Book-Lover's Holiday in the Open, A (Theodore Roosevelt), 188, 190–91
Borden, Sir Robert, 28, *29*, 130, 194, 242
    Letters to Limbo, 194, 249
Bowell, Sir Mackenzie, 242
Brachman, Dina, 251
Brison, Scott, 252
Britain, xxi, xxv, *62*, 101, 105–06
    See also England, Great Britain, United Kingdom
British colonialism, xxi, 160–61
British Commonwealth, 91, 108, 143
British North America, xxi–xxii, xxv
Brock, Sir Isaac, *xxii*
Brussels (Belgium), 44–45, 55–56
Bryce, James, 39
bull moose incident, xxix, 185, 188, *189*, 190–91
Bull Moose Party, xxix, 185–86
Burke, Beth, 251
Burney, Derek H., 153, *154*, 252
Busan (South Korea), 116, *117*

Bush, Barbara, xvii, *217*
Bush, George H.W., xvii, xxv, *xxvii*, *xxviii*, 4, 42, *46*, 55, *56–57*, 93, 153, *154*, 155–56, *157*, 185–86, 199–200, *201*, 216–17, 243
Bush, George W., xvii, *xviii*, 4, 79, 116, *117*, 120, 205, *225*, 243, *245*, 251
Bush, Laura, xvii, *xviii*

Calder, John, 196
Calgary (Alberta), *240*
Call It a Day, 194
Callaghan, James, 214
Camp David, xxvi, *xxviii*, 64
Camp David Peace Accord, 61
Campbell, Kim, *xxix*, 243
Campobello Island (New Brunswick), xxviii–xxix, 186, 195, *196–97*, 198
Canada-U.S. Free Trade Agreement, *62*, 131, 142, 144–45, 150–51, 156
    See also free trade, North American Free Trade Agreement (NAFTA), reciprocity, United States-Mexico-Canada Agreement (USMCA)
Canadian American Business Council (CABC), *xv*, *xvii–xviii*, 247, 251–52
Canadian Caper, *14*, 15, 17, 51
Carbis Bay (United Kingdom), *233*
Carter, Jimmy, xvii–xviii, 4, *9*, *14*, 15–17, 47, *48–50*, 51, 56, 61, *176*, *182–83*, 185, 243, *249*, 251
Carter, Rosalynn, 17, *50*, 51, *176*, 249
Carter Presidential Center, xvii–xviii
Castro, Fidel, *49*
Cellucci, Paul, 118–19
Chalk River Reactor, 51
Chan, Kevin, 251
Charlevoix (Quebec), *86*
Chastelain, John de, 252

INDEX

Chicago, xxvi–xxvii, 9, 18, 20, 47
Chicago Council on Foreign Relations, 47
Chile, 222
China, 50, 79, 84, 105, 177, 239, *240*
    See also People's Republic of China
China Seas, 96
Chrétien, Aline, 218, 222, *223–24*
Chrétien, Jean, *xviii*, 3, *4*, *52*, 118–19, *159*, 160, *161*, 218–19, *220*, 243, 251
Chrétien, Raymond, *4*, *52*, *159*, 252
Churchill, Sir Winston, v, *92*, 93, 94, 143, 151–52, 208, 247
Clark, Christy, 252
Clark, Joe, xvii–xviii, *14*, 15–17, 47, *48*, 49–51, 243, 251
Clean Air Act (1990), 57, 153
Clement, Gary, 251
Cleveland, Grover, 242
climate change, xv, 84–85, 131, 180, 233–35, 239, 245
Clinton, Bill, *xvii*, xviii, *xxix*, 3, *4–5*, *38*, *52*, 56, 158, *159*, 160, *161*, 162, 174, 206, 216–17, *218*, 219, *220*, 221, 243, 250, 251
Clinton, Hillary Rodham, *56*, 218, *220*, 221–22, *223–24*
Cold War, 64, 91, 93, 100–17
Columbia, 23
Commissiong, Giselle, 251
Confederation (1867), xix, xxiii, xxv, 43, 174, 230, 237
Connally, John, *65*, 210
Connecticut, 173
Cooke, Alistair, 173
    One Man's America, 173
Coolidge, Calvin, 242
Cooper, Gladys, 194
Cornell, Katharine, 194
Covid-19, xviii, 129, 131, 177, 233–36, 239

Cowl, Jane, 194
Craft, Kelly, *247*, 248, 250, 252
Crestview Strategy, 251
Cuba, *49*, 50
Curtis, Kenneth M., 252

Dallas (Texas), xvii, *xviii*
Dante, Jeanne, 194
Davenport, Colonel, 173
Davis, Bill, 147
Davis, Jefferson, xxv
Davis, Norman, 196
Dawes, Charles G., *133–34*, 137–38
    Notes as Vice President, 137–38
Dawes, Mrs., 137
Dean, Howard B., 252
Deh Cho Drum (newspaper), 199–200
Di Iorio, Ronnie, 249, 251
Dickerson, Blair, 251
Diefenbaker, John, xxv, *58–59*, 61, *62*, 64, 114–15, 164, *166–67*, 168, 243
Diefenbaker, Olive, 114, *115*
diversity, xvi, 13, 69, 75, 162, 175, 230, 235
Doer, Gary, 252
Dopp, Rebekah, 251
Dorado Beach Resort (Puerto Rico), 214, *215*
Douglas, Tommy, 212
draft dodgers, 64, 91, 93
Dulles, John Foster, 110, *111*
Durham, John George Lambton, Earl of, xxiii

East Timor, 160
Economic Club of New York, 76, *77*, 78, *79*, 80
Edward VIII, King, *133–35*
Eisenhower, Dwight D., 3, 108, *109*, 110, *111*, 112–13, 114, *115*, 116, 139, *140–41*, 243

Eisenhower, Mamie, 114, *115*, *141*
Elizabeth II, Queen, 75, *140–41*
Emerson, Ralph Waldo, 151
England, 20, 22, 23
    See also Britain, Great Britain, United Kingdom
Erling, Christina, 251
exports
    American, 70, 76, 150, 156
    Canadian, 150, 156

Fairbanks, Charles, *24–25*, 26–27
Fala (dog), 96, *97*
family theme, xix, xxi, 10
Finn, Sean, 251
First Gulf War, 57, 217
First Lady, 194
First Ministers' Meeting, *xx*, xxi, 53
fishing, 163, *182–83*, 185–86, *187*, 196, 199–200, *201*
Fishing for Fun, and to Wash Your Soul (Hoover), 186
Floyd, Marlene, 251
Ford, Gerald R., 4, 186, 214, *215*, 243
Forum of Federations Conference, 158, *159*, 160, *161*, 162
Foster, Sir George, 75
Four Freedoms, 99
Fowler, R.M., 168
France, xxi, 12, 34, 101, 105, 150, 222, *223*
Fredericton (New Brunswick), 163
free trade, 28–29, 57, 78, 105, 129–31, 142, 144–45, 153, 156–57
    See also Canada-U.S. Free Trade agreement, North American Free Trade Agreement (NAFTA), reciprocity, United States-Mexico-Canada Agreement (USMCA)

Free Trade Area of the Americas, 160
Freeland, Chrystia, *236*
Frost, Robert, 169

G7, *xxix*, 42, *44*, 86, 214, *215*, 222, *223*, *233*
G20, 42
Gagnon, Hélène V., 251
Galbraith, John Kenneth, xxviii
Gander (Newfoundland and Labrador), 118
Garfield, James, 242
Gatineau (Quebec), 120
General Agreement on Tariffs and Trade (GATT), 144, 151, 156
Geneva Naval Disarmament Conference, 138
George, Prince, 132, 134, *135*
Germany, 56, 94, 98, 171, 217
    See also West Germany
Giffin, Gordon, *xvii*, xviii, 63, *159*, 219, 250, 252
Giscard d'Estaing, Valéry, 214
Godin, Desiree, 249, 251
Goldilocks conundrum, 63
Goldsmith-Jones, Pamela, 252
golf, *38*, *52*, 192, 198
Gorbachev, Mikhail, *43*
Grant, Ulysses S., xxiii, 242
Great Britain, 20, 22, 27, 29, 98, 100, 105, 132, 164
    See also Britain, England, United Kingdom
Greene, Joshua, 251
Greenwood, James H., 250
Greenwood, James O., 250
Greenwood, Maryscott (Scotty), xvii, *xviii*, 249, 250–53
Grégoire-Trudeau, Sophie, 6, *7*, *202–03*, 205
G'witchin people, 80

Habitat for Humanity, 47, 49
Halifax (Nova Scotia), xxi, 205
Hall of Honour, 228, *229*
Harding, Florence, 34, *35*
Harding, Warren G., 34, *35*, 36, *37*, *38*, 39–40, *41*, 242
Harper, Stephen, xvii, *xviii*, 82, *83*, *85*, 121, *122–23*, 124, *125*, 225, 226, *227*, 228, 243, 249, 251
Harris, Kamala, *236*, 237, *238*, 239
Harris, Shyamala Gopalan, 238
Harrison, Benjamin, 242
Hayes, Helen, 194
Hayes, Rutherford B., 242
Heitkamp, Heidi, 252
Hillman, Kirsten, *xv*, xvi, 250
Hills, Carla, *157*
Holmes, Sr., Oliver Wendell, 164
Hong Kong, 143
Hoover, Herbert, 139, 185, 186, *187*, 194, 242
    Fishing for Fun, and to Wash Your Soul, 186, *187*
Howard, Pierre, 219
Howard University, 237
Hull (Quebec), 218
Hussein, Saddam, 93
Hyde Park Agreement (1941), 103

ice skating, 222, *224*
immigration, 36
Indigenous people, xvi, xxi, xxii, 54
Indonesia, 160
infrastructure, 83, 122, 132, 180
Inter-American Development Bank, 73
International Joint Commission, 134, 136
International Monetary Fund, 144
International Trade Organization, 106
Iran Hostage Crisis, xviii, *14*, 15–17, 51

Iraq, 6, 93, 118, 120
Italy, 98, 150

Jacobson, David, xxii, 253
Japan, 55, 70, 79, 96, 98, 144, 150
Jefferson, Thomas, xxi, 171
Jemison, Lisa, 249
Johnson, Andrew, xxv, 242
Johnson, Claudia Alta ("Lady Bird"), *65*
Johnson, Lyndon, *xxvi*, 64, *65*, 243
Jones, Zach, 249
Jost, Peter, 251

Kabul (Afghanistan), 93, 123
Kandahar (Afghanistan), 93, 121
Keller, John, 249
Kelley, Richard, *52*
Kellogg, Frank B., 138
Kennebunkport (Maine), xvii, *46*, 186, 200, *201*, *217*
Kennedy, Jacqueline, *166–67*, 168, 208, *209*, 210, *211*
Kennedy, John F., xxv, *58–59*, 61, *62*, 64, 163–64, *165–67*, 168–69, *170*, 171, *172*, 173, 208, *209*, 210, *211*, 212, 243
Kergin, Michael, 253
Keystone XL pipeline, 81, *82–83*, 84–85, 233–34
King, Jr., Martin Luther, 119
King, William Lyon Mackenzie, xxv, *xxvii*, xxviii, 18, 30, *31*, 32, *33*, *92*, 93, *94*, *96–97*, 98, *102*, 103, 132–34, 136, 138, 142, *206*, 242–43
Kingston (Ontario), xxi–xxii, *96*, *206*
Kirk, Ronald, 253
Kiska, 96
Klager, Robert, 251
Kolevar, Kevin, 251

Korean War, 100, 108
Kovrig, Michael, *240*

La Malbaie (Quebec), xxviii
    See also Murray Bay (Quebec)
LaFalce, John, 253
Lagos, Ricardo, 116, *117*
Landon, Alf, 194
Lank, Ed, 196
Laurier, Sir Wilfrid, xxiii, *xxiv*, xxv–xxvi, 18, *19*, 20, 22–23, 28, 69, 129–31, 142, *186*, 207, 242
Laurier, Zoé, 186
Lee, Robert E., xxiii
Lennoxville (Quebec), xxv
Letters to Limbo (Borden), 194, 249
Lévesque, René, 174, *175*
Lewis, Drew, 147
Libel (Wooll), 194
Lincoln, Abraham, *xxiii*, xxiv–xxv, *207*, 245
Lirette, Arthur, 188, 190–91
Littlechild, Wilton, 253
Lively, Blake, 53
London (United Kingdom), xxi
Lothian, Lord, *93*
Lower Canada
    rebellion in, xxiii
    See also Quebec
Lundquist, Andrew, 251
Lusi, Aylin, 251

MacDonald, Flora, 51
Macdonald, Sir John A., xxiii, *xxv*, 63, 129, *130*, 142, 186, 242
MacDonald, Kyle, 249
Mack, Toby, 252
Mackenzie, Alexander, 242
Macmillan, Harold, *58–59*, 61, *62*

MacNaughton, David, 86–87
mad cow disease, 79
Manila (Philippines), 143
Manitoba, 175
Manley, John, 253
Manulife Centre (Toronto), xviii
Marchi, Sergio, 253
Marion (Massachusetts), 198
Martin, Lawrence, 63, 249
    Presidents and the Prime Ministers, The, 63, 249
Martin, Paul, xviii, 76, *77*, 78, *79*, 80, 116, *117*, 243, *245*, 251
Maryland, xix, 44
Massachusetts, 163–64, 169
Massey, Vincent, 5, 69
Maunder, James, 252
McClellan, Scott, *245*
McDougall, Barbara, 253
McGee, Thomas D'Arcy, xxiii, 43
McKenna, Frank, 253
McKinley, William, 20, *21*, 243
Meighen, Arthur, 242
Meloul-Wechsler, Arielle, 252
Meng Wanzhou, 240
Merchant, Livingston T., *172*
Merivale, Philip, 194
Merkel, Angela, *86*
Mexico, xviii, 50, 81, 131, 142, 156, *157*, *177*, 179–81
Mike (Pearson), xxvi, 249
Miller, Paul, 198
Milnes, Arthur, xix–xxix, 52, 214, *249*, 250
Mitchell, Captain, 196
Mitterrand, François, 44–45
Mondale, Walter, *176*
Montebello (New Brunswick), *225*
Montebello (Quebec), *104*

INDEX

Montreal, *xviii*, xxiii–xxv, xxviii, 9, 44, 46, *49*, 168, 237
Moore, James, 253
Mulroney, Brian, xxv, *xxvii*, *xxviii*, 42, *43–44*, 45, *46*, 55, *56–57*, *62*, *93*, *126–127*, 129, 131, 142, 144–45, 148, *149*, 150–51, *152*, 153, *154*, 155–56, *157*, 186, 200, *201*, *216*, 217, 243, 249
Mulroney, Mila, *216–217*
Murphy, Tim, *245*
Murray Bay (Quebec), xxviii, 192, *193*
    See also La Malbaie (Quebec)

Nassau (Bahamas), *58–59*, 61
National Cathedral (Washington, D.C.), *43*
National Gallery of Canada, *218*
National Planning Association, 168
National Policy (Canada), 129
National Press Club (Washington, D.C.), xix
National Public Radio, *48*
National Security Council, 112
Neal, Richard, *181*
Neves, João Augusto de Castro, 252
New Brunswick, xxv, 163–64, *165*, 186, 195
New Yorker, The, 192, 249
Niagara River, 134
Niles, Thomas M.T., 253
Nineteenth Amendment (1920), 238
Nixon, Pat, 6, *8*
Nixon, Richard, xix, 3, 6, *8*, 64, 67, *68*, 69–70, *71–72*, 73–75, 198, 213, 243, 245
Nixon Doctrine, 69
North American Aerospace Defense Command (NORAD), 100, 120, 146
North American Conservation Conference, *186*
North American Free Trade Agreement (NAFTA), xv, 57, 76, 78, 80, 87, 142, 156, *157*, 179, 181
    See also Canada-U.S. Free Trade Agreement, free trade, reciprocity, United States-Mexico-Canada Agreement (USMCA)
North American Leaders' Summit, *83*, 225
North Atlantic Treaty Organization (NATO), 12, 44, 55–56, 100, 108, 113, 121, 145, 177
Northern News Services, 249
Noss, Wendy, 252
Notes as Vice President (Dawes), 137–38
Nova Scotia, xxv
nuclear age, 51
nuclear arms, 146
nuclear war, 110

Obama, Barack, *xxx–1*, 3, 4, 6, *7*, 10, *11*, 42, 53, *56*, 63, 81, *82–83*, 84, *85*, 124, *125*, *202–03*, 205, 226, *227*, 228, *229*, 243
Obama, Malia, 8
Obama, Michelle, 6, *7*, *56*
Obama, Sasha, 8
Odilon, 188, 191
Odom, Clint, 252
Ogdensburg Agreement (1940), 103
oil, 80–81, 84, 108, 150
"Old Flag" election poster, 129
One Man's America (Cooke), 173
Ontario, xxv, 51, 91
    See also Upper Canada
    industry protection and, 129
    trade and, 144
Operation Yellow Ribbon, 118
Organization of American States, 73
Owens, William L., 253

Palais des congrès (Montreal), *xvii*, xviii
Panama, 222
Paraguay, 222
Paris Accord, 180–81
Parliament Hill, xxvi, 4, 69, *88–89*, 91, *94*, 118, 226, *227*
Parti Québécois (PQ), 174, 237
Partnership for Educational Revitalization in the Americas, 222
Paterson, David, 252
peace, xxi, xxiii, 23, 26–27, 29, 31–32, 34, 39, 52, 74–75, 91, 95–96, 99, 100, 104, 106–08, 114, 116, 122–23, 134, 136, 138, 139, 141, 144–47, 163, 169, 196, 208, 210, 213, 219–20, 226, 228, 232
Peace Bridge, 132, *133*, 137
Pearl Harbor, 94–95, 103, 143
Pearson, Lester B., *xxvi*, 64, *65*, 66, 110, *111*, 208, 210, *211*, 213, 221, 243, 249
    Mike, xxvi, 249
Pearson, Maryon, *65*
Pelosi, Nancy, *178*, 179–80, *181*
Peña, Enrique Nieto, *177*
People's Republic of China, 74
    See also China
Permanent Joint Board on Defence, 103, 113
Perot, Ross, *157*
Philip, Prince, *141*
Pickney, Michael, 249
Picton (Ontario), 198
Presidents and the Prime Ministers, The (Martin), 63, 249
Prime Minister's Office (PMO), xix, 61, *79*, 86–87, *152*, 153, *245*, 249, 250
Pyun, Pierre, 252

Quebec, 55, 98–99, 101, 146, 188, 191, 208
    See also Lower Canada
    Canadian Museum of Civilization in, 218
    Charles Fairbanks's speech and, 24, *25*, 26–27
    Confederation and, xxv
    Jefferson Davis and, xxv
    Kamala Harris and, 237
    nationalists and, 130
    protection of industry in, 129
    separatism question and, 158, 160, 162, 174, *175*, *176*
Quebec City, xxi, 42
Quebec Conference, *92*, 93, 96, *97*, 98
Quenneville, Jean, 252
Queen's University, 95, *96*
Queen's University School of Policy Studies, 249

Raitt, Lisa, 253
Ransom, Deb, 249
Reagan, Nancy, 42, 45, *216*
Reagan, Ronald, 3, 42, *43*, *44*, 45, *62*, 93, 131, 142, 143–47, 148, *149*, *216*, 217, 243
Reciprocal Trade Agreements (1936 and 1939), 105
reciprocity, 28–29, 130–31, 142
    See also Canada-U.S. Free Trade Agreement, free trade, North American Free Trade Agreement (NAFTA), United States-Mexico-Canada Agreement (USMCA)
Reid, Scott, xviii, *79*, *245*, 246, 249, 251
Reisman, Heather, xviii, *79*
Rendell, Edward G., 253
revolution, and the origins of the United States, xviii, 10, 91
Reynolds, Ryan, 53
Rideau Canal (Ottawa), 222, *224*

INDEX

Roadmap for a Renewed U.S.-Canada Partnership, 131, 235
Robinson, Paul H., 253
Rogers, William, 198
Roh Moo-hyun, 116, *117*
Roosevelt, Eleanor, 96, *97*
Roosevelt, Franklin Delano, xxv, *xxvii*, xxviii–xxix, 4, 32, *33*, *88–89*, 91, *92*, 93, *94*, 95, *96*, 98–99, 150, 186, 194, 195, *196–97*, 198, *199*, 208, 242
Roosevelt, James, *32*
Roosevelt, Sara Delano, 195, *196*
Roosevelt, Theodore, xxvi, *24*, 26, 185, *186*, *187*, 188, *189–91*, 242
    Book-Lover's Holiday in the Open, A, 188, 190–91
    moose incident and, xxix, 185, 188, 190–91
Roosevelt Campobello International Park, 186
Royal Canadian Mounted Police (RCMP), 36, *37*
Rush-Bagot Agreement (1817), 101, 103, 134
Rusk, Dean, *65*
Russ, Alexander, 252
Russell, John, 171
Russia, 50, 56, 105, 160
    See also Soviet Union, U.S.S.R.

Saint Joan, 194
Salinas de Gortari, Carlos, 156, *157*
San Antonio (Texas), 156
Saskatchewan, 175
Schlegel, Nancy Ziuzin, 252
Schmidt, Helmut, 214
Scowcroft, Brent, *152*, 153
Sea Island (Georgia), 194
Seigniory Club (Quebec), *106*
Serra Puche, Jaime, *157*
Shamrock, 23
Shamrock Summit, *216*
Shawinigan (Quebec), 3, 219
Sheffield, Pete, 252
Sicily (Italy), 96
Sifton, Clifford, *186*
slavery
    Lincoln on, xxiii–xxiv
Sloan, Jennifer, 252
Smith, Al, 138
softwood lumber dispute, 76, *77*, 78, 80, 245
Soviet Union, 56–57, 74, 100
    See also Russia, U.S.S.R.
Spain, 180–81
Spavor, Michael, *240*
speeches
    on freedom, 100, 107–08, 110, 119, 139, 143–48, 150
    on the future, 8–9, 12–13, 98–99
    importance of, 3
    on partnership, 69
    on peace, 30–32, 34, 36, 39–40, 74, 106–07, 114
    on progress, 110, 112
St. Laurent, Louis, 110, *111*, *114*, 243
St. Lawrence–Great Lakes System, 105, 112
St. Lawrence Power Project, 113
St. Lawrence River, 26, 192
St. Lawrence Seaway, 75, 100, 139, *140–41*, 164, 168
Stanfield, Robert, 74
Stanley Park (Vancouver), *38*, 40, *41*
state dinners, xxvi, 18, 53
    in 1960, 114, *115*
    in 1977, *9*
    in 1997, *220*
    in 2016, 6, 8–10, 12–13, *202–03*, 205

State of the Relationship Dinner, *247*
Stonewall (Texas), *65*
Stuart, R. Douglas, 168
Summit of the Americas, 222

Taft, William Howard, xxviii, 28, 130–31, 192, *193*, 242
Taliban, 121, 124
Taylor, Ken, 15–16, 51
Taylor, L.D., 188, *189*
Taylor, Pat, 51
Teeley, Peter, 253
Temple University (Philadelphia), 64
terrorism, 52, 119, 121, 124, *125*, 230
Texas, 50, 64, 156, 210
Thatcher, Margaret, *43*, 150
Thompson, Sir John, 63, 242
toasts
    Barack Obama's, 9
    George W. Bush's, 120, 205
    Justin Trudeau's, 13, 53–54, 235
    Richard Nixon's, 6
Toker, Mary Catherine, 252
Tokyo Economic Summit (1979), *48*, 49
Toluca (Mexico), *83*
trade balances, 70, 76, 78, 104–06, 144–45
trade barriers, 110, 112, 144, 156
Tran Duc Luong, 116, *117*
Tree River pools, 199–200
Trudeau, Justin, xv, xviii–xix, *xx*, xxi, *xxx–1*, 3, 6, *7–9*, 10, *11*, 12–13, 42, *53–54*, 81, 86, *87*, *131*, *177*, *202–03*, 205, 230, *231*, *233*, 234–35, *236*, 239, *240*, 243
Trudeau, Lena, 252
Trudeau, Margaret, *8*, *50*, *176*
Trudeau, Pierre, xix–xx, xxviii, 4–5, 6, *9*, *49–50*, 51, 54, 64, 67, *68*, 69, *72*, 73, 174, *175–76*, 186, 214, *215*, 243

Truman, Harry S., 10, *100*, 101, *102*, 103, *104*, 105, *106*, 107, 243
Trump, Donald J., xviii, 56, *86–87*, 131, *177*, 179–80, *181*, 230, *231*, 232, 233, 243
    tweets of, 86, *87*
Trump, Melania, *56*
Tupper, Sir Charles, 242
Turner, John, *62*, 243
Tweedsmuir, John Buchan, Lord, 32, *33*
Tyson, Herb, 252

United Empire Loyalists, xxi, 91
United Kingdom, *58–59*, 61, 105, 150
    See also Britain, England, Great Britain
United Nations (U.N.), 57, 95, 99, 100, 103, 114, 121, 158, 208, 247
United States-Mexico-Canada Agreement (USMCA), xviii, 87, 131, *177–78*, 179, 180, *181*, 248
    See also Canada-U.S. Free Trade Agreement, free trade, North American Trade Agreement (NAFTA), reciprocity
University of Massachusetts, 171
University of New Brunswick, 163–64, *165*, 170–71, 173
Upham, Charles Wentworth, 164
Upper Canada, 91
    See also Ontario
    rebellion in, xxiii
U.S. Articles of Confederation, xix
U.S. Capitol, 208, *238*
U.S. Civil War, xxiii–xxv, 20
U.S. Declaration of Independence, 99
U.S. House of Representatives, 164, *178*, 179, 180, *181*
USS *Henderson*, 34, *35*
USS *Sequoia*, 214, *215*

U.S.S.R., 113, 217
    See also Russia, Soviet Union

Vancouver, 34, *35*, 36, *37*, 162, 188, *189*, 240
Venice (Italy), *44*, 145, 151
Victoria, Queen, 171
Vietnam War, 64, *65*, 66, 91, 100
Virginia House of Burgess, 171
Voting Rights Act (1965), 238

Wake Island, 143
Wall, Brad, 253
Wall Street Journal, 78–79
War of 1812, xix, xxi, *xxii*, 101
Warsaw Pact, 56–57, 217
Watergate, 47, 64, 67
Watergate Tapes, 67, *72*, 73
Watters, Munro, 251
Webster, Daniel, 169
Webster-Ashburton Treaty (1842), 169
West Germany, 150, 214
    See also Germany

"When Irish Eyes Are Smiling," 42
White House, xix, xxi, xxvi, 3, 6, *7*, *9*, 17, *50*, 63, 76, 86, 124, *125*, 148, *149*, 177, 181, *202–03*, 205, 208, *209*, 230, 233, 240, *245*, 246, 250
    Oval Office, xviii, 3, 10, *11*, 55, *72*, 73, 131, 230, *245*
    Rose Garden, *xxx–1*, 3, 245
Whittier, John Greenleaf, 20
Wilkins, David, 253
William and Mary College, 171
Wilson, Michael, *157*
Wilson, Woodrow, 34, 160, 171, 242
Wooll, Edward, 194
    Libel, 194
Worden, Cathy, 252
World War I, 34, 70, 74, 160, 162
World War II, 51, 74, 94–95, 98, 100, 104, 116

Zanella, Alexandra, 252